David Grummitt is Lecturer in British History at the University of Kent. He is the author of *The Calais Garrison: War and Military Service in England, 1436–1558* (2008).

I.B.TAURIS SHORT HISTORIES

I.B.Tauris Short Histories is an authoritative and elegantly written new series which puts a fresh perspective on the way history is taught and understood in the twenty-first century. Designed to have strong appeal to university students and their teachers, as well as to general readers and history enthusiasts, *I.B.Tauris Short Histories* comprises a novel attempt to bring informed interpretation, as well as factual reportage, to historical debate. Addressing key subjects and topics in the fields of history, the history of ideas, religion, classical studies, politics, philosophy and Middle East studies, the series seeks intentionally to move beyond the bland, neutral 'introduction' that so often serves as the primary undergraduate teaching tool. While always providing students and generalists with the core facts that they need to get to grips with the essentials of any particular subject, *I.B.Tauris Short Histories* goes further. It offers new insights into how a topic has been understood in the past, and what different social and cultural factors might have been at work. It brings original perspectives to bear on manner of its current interpretation. It raises questions and – in its extensive further reading lists – points to further study, even as it suggests answers. Addressing a variety of subjects in a greater degree of depth than is often found in comparable series, yet at the same time in concise and compact handbook form, *I.B.Tauris Short Histories* aims to be 'introductions with an edge'. In combining questioning and searching analysis with informed history writing, it brings history up-to-date for an increasingly complex and globalised digital age.

A Short History of . . .

'You get two for the price of one with David Grummitt's *Short History of the Wars of the Roses*. You get an accessible narrative of the Wars, seen by him to have originated in the Lancastrian usurpation of 1399 that skilfully steers the reader through the complexities and controversies of the story. Grummitt knows his subject well and writes with considerable insight. But you also get, in the book's concluding chapters, a revaluation of these civil wars. The author gives renewed emphasis to their scale and the involvement of the whole population in them. He also highlights significant changes in the corresponding political culture. His reassessment in these pages of the pivotal importance of the later fifteenth century in English history will put a cat amongst some Tudor pigeons.'

A J Pollard,
Emeritus Professor of History, Teesside University

'David Grummitt has succeeded triumphantly in writing a refreshing and multi-layered book. It will engage the general reader (and the writer of fiction and non-fiction too!), the student who needs a clear, up-to-date and informative guide, as well as those already acquainted with the Wars of the Roses – including Dr Grummitt's fellow historians. In comparing the campaigns of 1459–64, 1469–71 and 1483–7 between Lancaster and York, David Grummitt offers vivid and often fresh judgments on the characters and failings of kings, most notably Henry VI, Edward IV and Richard III, and those nobles – Richard of York, Warwick the Kingmaker and the Duke of Buckingham – whose intrigues promoted the struggles. He deftly weaves the results of recent research (some of it his own) into the discussion. In a particularly elegant chapter, he takes the story beyond 'high politics' to locate the commons of shire and town within the 'political nation' and with a shared responsibility for the 'commonweal'. As a notable historian of fifteenth- and early sixteenth-century England, Dr Grummitt writes with mature confidence and a pellucid style. He is robust and challenging without being opinionated: he values the opinions of other historians and likes a controversy, thereby helping his readers to come to their own conclusions. To this end, the book is thoughtfully structured: its substantial Dramatis Personae, three royal and noble Family Trees and an authoritative Bibliography linked to each chapter make this book a valuable work of reference as well as a compelling and stimulating read.'

Ralph A Griffiths,
OBE, Emeritus Professor of Medieval History, Swansea University

A SHORT HISTORY OF

THE WARS OF THE ROSES

David Grummitt

I.B. TAURIS

LONDON · NEW YORK

Published in 2013 by I.B.Tauris & Co Ltd
6 Salem Road, London W2 4BU
175 Fifth Avenue, New York NY 10010
www.ibtauris.com

Distributed in the United States and Canada Exclusively by Palgrave
Macmillan, 175 Fifth Avenue, New York NY 10010

ISBN: 978 1 84885 874 9 (hb)
ISBN: 978 1 84885 875 6 (pb)

A full CIP record for this book is available from the British Library
A full CIP record is available from the Library of Congress

Library of Congress Catalog Card Number: available

Typeset in Sabon by Ellipsis Digital Limited, Glasgow
Printed and bound by TJ International Ltd, Padstow, Cornwall

Contents

Part 3: Consequences

Preface

The Wars of the Roses, once an integral part of 'Our Island Story', now occupy a rather curious position in the British historical memory.[1] Despite a recent plethora of popular and academic titles on the subject, the Wars, their causes, course and consequences, remain more contested than ever. For a generation of youngsters they are a bit of a mystery, sandwiched between the mud and disease of the 'Measly Middle Ages' and the blood and fire of the 'Terrible Tudors'. Although the last fifty years has seen an explosion in detailed academic research into the fifteenth century, it remains, to some extent, the 'Dark Century' of English medieval history, too complex to be incorporated into the new, integrated history of the British Isles. In part this is the inevitable consequence of the efforts of generations of professional historians who have played down the impact of the Wars and obscured the historical wood by their very detailed description of the trees. The trend to diminish the Wars' importance has only intensified in recent years and the most authoritative recent survey sees English society and government as essentially unchanged between the Black Death and the Reformation.[2]

But it is only part of the historian's task to identify continuities; he or she must also account for change. English society underwent a significant transformation in the fifteenth century, not least because of the series of violent, political confrontations we know as the Wars of the Roses. The English had to cope with disease, defeat in foreign war, the deposition and murder of their kings, as well as a deep crisis in the domestic and international economy. This encouraged the development of new ways to think about politics, the relationship between princes and their subjects, and the structure of government and society. England was also transformed because of the impact of broader cultural, economic and social changes. It happened at a time when the Renaissance and the spread of Humanism heralded a new era of introspection and the challenging of old orthodoxies, and further opened new possibilities in what was considered politic and moral behaviour. Towards the end of the fifteenth century the printing press meant a proliferation of texts and a widening engagement with new ideas, but it also offered the possibility of new means of wielding power and proscribing debate.

This short history of the Wars of the Roses attempts three things. First, it provides an accessible introduction to both the Wars themselves and historical writing about them. Second, it sets the Wars in the context of individual experiences and responses and to assess their impact both individually and communally. Finally, it considers the ways in which the experience of civil war shaped English culture, politics and society in the years after 1450. It is divided into three parts: the causes of war from 1399 until 1459; the course of events during the three periods of open conflict from 1459–64, 1469–71, and 1483–87; and, finally, their consequences.

Such a broad synthesis must inevitably rely heavily on the work of others. First and foremost is the debt owed to my former colleagues at the History of Parliament Trust: Linda Clark, Hannes Kleineke, Charles Moreton and Simon Payling. Their combined knowledge and understanding of the fifteenth century is unsurpassed and I feel extremely privileged to have shared it with them for more than a decade now. Thanks are also due to the Trustees of the History of Parliament Trust for permission to draw on research ahead of its publication. I am also indebted to the work of John Watts and his support and encouragement have meant a great deal. Similarly, I have benefitted immensely from the friendship of Michael K. Jones, who understands the fifteenth century as well as anyone. Thanks are also due to Caroline Barron, Jim Bolton, Christine Carpenter, Paul Cavill, Sean Cunningham, Peter Fleming, Ralph Griffiths, Steven Gunn, Michael Hicks, Malcolm Mercer, Cath Nall, Tony Pollard, James Ross, David Starkey and Anne Sutton whose published work, seminar papers and conversation has informed my own understanding of the period. My Special Subject students at Kent discussed my ideas and corrected my more outlandish claims. Finally, thanks are due to my family: my mother-in-law who cast the expert gaze of an A-level history teacher (who had herself been taught the Wars of the Roses by none other than Ralph Griffiths) over the entire manuscript; my daughter, Emma, whose inquiring mind has, I hope, enjoyed journeying through the Wars; and, finally, my wife Hil, a fellow historian, who continues to provide love and support in everything I do.

Introduction

THE WARS IN HISTORY

WHY THE 'WARS OF THE ROSES'?

The phrase 'the Wars of the Roses' is what the philosopher of history, W.H. Walsh, dubbed a 'colligatory term'. That is to say, like the 'Industrial Revolution', 'the Scientific Revolution' or even 'the Cold War', it is a term invented by historians to make sense of and order an otherwise confused and chaotic series of events. 'The Wars of the Roses' therefore provides a context for episodes such as Cade's Rebellion in 1450 or the usurpation of Richard III in 1483. It gives both historians and students a framework within which they can order their narratives, write their essays, and seek to understand the past.[1] In an age of professional historical scepticism, the term and its 'usefulness' can be dissected, the beginning and end of the Wars endlessly debated, new examples found to challenge academic ortho-doxies, and even the very existence of the Wars themselves called into question. The Wars of the Roses, we are told, was a concept 'invented' by Sir Walter Scott in his 1829 novel *Anne of Geierstein* and was a phrase unknown to fifteenth-century minds. Indeed, such was the limited nature of conflict in the mid-fifteenth century that most Englishmen and women were not even aware that they were living through a civil war.[2]

Nevertheless, we should not despair of the 'Wars of the Roses'. As Margaret Aston pointed out over forty years ago, the term does have a near contemporary relevance. In simple terms, the White Rose was one of the many badges or devices adopted by the House of York (from the Mortimer earls of March). Equally, the Red Rose was one of an even larger collection of badges used by the dukes and later by the royal House of Lancaster. Elizabeth of York, daughter of Edward IV, appears to have adopted the White Rose as her personal badge before 1485 and Henry Tudor seized upon the opportunities presented by the Red Rose immediately following his victory at Bosworth. Contemporaries were certainly aware of this imagery and the symbolism of the roses as badges of ancient royal lines. The chronicler of the Lincolnshire abbey of Crowland, one of the most astute commentators of the time, wrote shortly after the Battle of Bosworth that in Tudor's victory 'the tusks of the boar (Richard III) were blunted and the red rose (Tudor), the avenger of the white (the murdered sons of Edward IV), shines upon us'.[3] Within a year Henry had adopted the familiar Tudor Rose, the White Rose of York superimposed upon the red one of Lancaster, and this badge was to adorn royal palaces, greet the king on progress, and decorate the houses of his servants and courtiers. Thus, by the end of the fifteenth century the recent civil wars were being portrayed as a long struggle between the two warring factions of the same royal line, represented by the two roses, and the happy reunion symbolised by the marriage of Henry and Elizabeth and the intermixing of the two. The image of the warring roses, an unnatural struggle between two branches of the same family and a bloody century of civil war ended by the accession of Henry VII and confirmed in the person of Henry VIII, the physical embodiment of the union of the two houses of Lancaster and York, was a compelling one. It remained the dominant narrative of the fifteenth century for some five hundred years.

EARLY HISTORIANS OF THE WARS OF THE ROSES

Already by the third quarter of the fifteenth century there were efforts to analyse and explain the bloody conflicts that had dominated English politics in recent years. A number of chronicle accounts, mainly but not solely arising from a London vernacular tradition, presented a broadly similar version of events. They identified various low-born counsellors of Henry VI whose ambition and greed had led to the loss of the crown's French possessions, the murder of the king's uncle, Humphrey, Duke of Gloucester, and the outbreak of popular rebellion. This had led to a noble revolt, led by the Duke of York, against the king and his 'evil councillors'. The deposition of Henry VI in 1461 was followed by an uneasy decade of Yorkist rule. In 1471 the death of both Henry and his son, Edward, Prince of Wales, had offered the prospect of lasting peace but civil war had ensued again with Richard of Gloucester's usurpation in 1483 only to be ended at Bosworth Field two years later. Both Yorkist partisans, such as the author of *An English Chronicle*, and those with Lancastrian sympathies, such as the author of the short chronicle of the years 1431 to 1471 found in John Vale's commonplace book, could agree on the fundamentals of this narrative (at least up to 1471). Whether they regarded Henry VI as a hopeless case who, in the words of one Yorkist writer, had 'helde ne householde nor meynteyned ne werres'[4] or as a king unlawfully deposed by an ambitious usurper, they could agree that the tensions inherent in English political society had come to a head with defeat in the Hundred Years War and the events of 1450 and that they had been largely healed by the symbolic union between Henry Tudor and Elizabeth of York in 1485.

This narrative formed the basis of the most influential of the late-fifteenth century chronicles, that written by the London draper, Robert Fabyan. His chronicle, covering the period from 1223 until 1485 (with a continuation to 1509) was printed by the king's printer, William Pynson, in 1516. The London chronicles also formed the basis of Polydore Vergil's history, written at the behest of Henry VII but first published in 1534. Vergil combined elements of both the Lancastrian version (the saintly Henry VI and the ambitious Duke of York) and Yorkist account (the evil Duke of Suffolk and 'Good Duke Humphrey' of Gloucester) accounts into a new Tudor narrative which portrayed the fifteenth century as an extended crisis, created by the deposition of Richard II in 1399 and ended by the restoration of legitimate kingship in 1485. Much has been made of the fact that Vergil, along with his contemporary Sir Thomas More whose *History of King Richard III* was written around 1513 but only published in 1543, represented a new kind of analytical history inspired by the Humanist learning and the Italian Renaissance. They stressed the long term causes of the civil wars and exaggerated their destructive effects, moralising and developing the notion that the wars were somehow a divine punishment for the sin of 1399. This analysis, however, did not rely on the genius of Vergil and More for its novelty. It was in fact the argument made in Edward IV's first parliament in 1461, repeated by Richard III in 1483 and explicit in the papal bull of 1486 permitting the marriage of Henry Tudor and Elizabeth of York.

The Tudor narrative of the Wars of the Roses developed further in 1548 with the publication of Edward Hall's *The Union of the Two Noble and Illustre Families of Lancaster and York*. Hall also begun his narrative in 1399, but his analysis of the fifteenth century was more nuanced and critical than that of either Vergil or More. Hall agreed that the usurpation of 1399 had led to nearly a century of civil war, but it was not a divine punishment. Richard II's deposition had been both lawful and justified and Hall stressed the parliamentary approbation of Henry IV's title. The problems arose from ambitious and self-serving noblemen: Edmund Mortimer, Earl of March, and Richard, Earl of Cambridge (uncle and father respectively of Richard, Duke of York) because these men 'were with these doynges neither pleased nor contente'.[5] Later Tudor commentators, such as Sir Thomas Smith writing in 1561, saw dynastic uncertainty as the chief malaise of the fifteenth century. This encouraged the ambition of noblemen and undermined law and order: 'No man sure of his Prince, no man of his goods, no man of his life'. In a wonderful piece of Tudor hyperbole Smith claimed that 'almost half England by civil war slain, and they which remained not sure, but in moats and castles, or lying in routs and heaps together'.[6]

William Shakespeare, in his two historical tetralogies, is often considered to have fixed the 'Tudor Myth' of the Wars of the Roses in the national consciousness. The narrative of a century of civil war and discord stemming from the unlawful deposition of Richard II in 1399, halted only by the triumph of Henry VII and the union of the Houses of Lancaster and York represented in the marriage between

Henry and Elizabeth of York, is the thread that runs through *1, 2 and 3 Henry VI* and *Richard III*, and *Richard II, 1* and *2 Henry IV* and *Henry V*. Shakespeare's histories, like Hall's chronicle, presented a much more subtle and complex version of the Wars. Shakespeare certainly saw Henry VI as a pious, if lethargic, king whose inability to offer effective rule fatally compromised the Lancastrian regime, but he also drew attention to the ambition and cunning of leading noblemen, most notably Richard, Duke of Gloucester (later Richard III), but also Gloucester's father, Richard, Duke of York. The ideal king emerges only at the end of the first tetralogy in the person of Henry Tudor. The second tetralogy is more complex still, presenting a developing notion of kingship. Richard II is certainly a flawed individual and king and the political nation is faced with a dilemma whether to depose or endure a tyrannical ruler for the sake of the commonwealth. This analysis probably owed more to the contested politics of later Elizabethan England than to the historical reality of 1399. Bolingbroke, later Henry IV, emerges, like Richard III, as a rather Machiavellian figure, as indeed does Henry V who, once crowned king, unceremoniously dumps his old drinking companion and mentor, Falstaff. Other later Tudor commentators, such as Samuel Daniel whose epic poem *The Civil Wars* appeared in several editions between 1595 and 1609, revealed equally ambiguous accounts of the Wars of Roses, even referencing opposing views of the same events and allowing readers to determine the truth for themselves. Far from presenting a homogenous 'Tudor Myth' these sixteenth-century historians recognised the complexity of the Wars of the Roses and offered a variety of explanations for the traumatic fifteenth century.

THE WARS OF THE ROSES AND PROFESSIONAL HISTORY

A profound change in the way in which history was written and taught occurred in the mid-nineteenth century. From the 1820s the German historian, Leopold von Ranke, popularised a new 'professional' style of history, located in the universities and based upon the critical interpretation of archival, usually governmental, records. This new history was discussed in seminars and its practitioners, publishing in multivolume works or in the newly emerging professional historical journals, sought to establish powerful grand narratives of national development. The most influential admirer of von Ranke's methods in England was William Stubbs, Bishop of Oxford (1825–1901), appointed Regius Professor of Modern History at the University of Oxford in 1866. Stubbs made two important contributions to our understanding of medieval history in general and the Wars of the Roses in particular. First, as a champion of the publication of original records he began the tradition that led to the scholarly editing of vast numbers of manuscript sources relating to the fifteenth century. Second, his monumental three-volume work, *The Constitutional History of England in its Origins and Development*, offered a comprehensive framework for understanding English history in its broadest terms and stressed the importance of the fifteenth century within this sweeping narrative.

Stubbs and his disciples offered what Shakespeare and the Tudor historians had failed to do: a simple and all-encompassing explanation of the causes, course and consequences of the Wars of the Roses. Derided in the twentieth century as 'the Whig interpretation of history', their account was brilliant in its simplicity and audacious in its scope. Stubbs placed the fifteenth century within a continuum of English constitutional development which had begun with the forest-dwelling Germanic tribes of Roman times and crystallised in the mature, constitutional monarchy of mid-Victorian Britain. Like Von Ranke, Stubbs believed in a national destiny, ordained by some divine order, in which individuals and events were subsumed in a grander narrative: medieval history, he wrote, was 'not then the collection of a multitude of facts and views, but the piecing of the links of a perfect chain.'[7] Stubbs argued that the successful late-medieval kings were those who, like Edward I, recognised that their power lay in gaining the approbation of the political nation embodied in parliament. He saw the origins of the Wars of the Roses in the compromises and mistakes made by Edward III. Edward, in his need for money to fight the Hundred Years War, had sacrificed the power of the crown in large part to the ambitions of his nobility by allowing them to raise armies by contract. He had weakened the crown further by having too many sons and dividing the royal patrimony between them. In itself this was not fatal and kings who ruled with their parliaments, as Henry IV did with his 'Lancastrian Constitutional Experiment', could mitigate these inherent weaknesses in royal government. Nevertheless, weak kings, most notably Henry VI, could not control the destructive forces at the heart of the polity and civil war became inevitable. Equally, the Yorkist kings attempted to arrest this decline not by resorting to the constitution (and parliament) but by Machiavellian politics and violence. It needed, Stubbs argued, the despotism of the Tudors to rescue England from its late-medieval nadir and to create the preconditions for parliamentary liberty to again flourish in the seventeenth century: 'the nation needed rest and renewal, discipline and reformation, before it could enter into the enjoyment of its birthright.'[8]

This abject picture of the fifteenth century as an interlude in the nation's progress, a period beset by weak, irresolute monarchs and violent, ambitious nobles, proved an enduring one. It found its fullest expression in the work of another Oxford historian, Charles Plummer, whose 1885 edition of Sir John Fortescue's *Governance of England*, refined the analysis of royal collapse under Henry VI. In his assessment the Wars of the Roses were due to the poverty of the crown, the presence of 'overmighty subjects' financially and politically more powerful than the king, and the general lawlessness caused by bands of armed retainers. Plummer coined the phrase 'Bastard Feudalism' to characterise the impermanent relationships between the lords and their followers which were based upon cash payments rather than, as in feudalism proper, the tenure of land. Plummer, a student of the Rankean school of historical scholarship, used contemporary sources, such as the Paston Letters, to illustrate the parlous state of fifteenth-century England. William Denton, a Church of England clergymen and another Oxford graduate, published a widely read history of the fifteenth century, which almost caricatured this view, blending it with the more hysterical accounts of Tudor writers like Sir Thomas Smith. For Denton the troubles began with the deposition of Richard II but then spiralled out of control due to the violent designs of a morally degenerate nobility (a degeneracy caused, not least, by their practice of indulging in sexual relations by the age of fourteen!) By the turn of the twentieth century the general view of the Wars of the Roses and the fifteenth century, established by Stubbs but dramatised by Plummer and Denton, was a negative one, summed up in the 1911 edition of the *Encyclopedia Britannica* as a 'name given to a series of civil wars in England during the reign of Henry VI, Edward IV and Richard III . . . matched by a ferocity and brutality which are practically unknown in the history of English wars before and since'.[9]

The Stubbsian (or Whig) view of the fifteenth century continued to dominate historical interpretations until well into the twentieth century. There were a few dissenters, but they did not seriously undermine the dominant narrative. Another clergyman, John Richard Green (1837–83), a contemporary of Stubbs and a political radical, published his enormously popular *Short History of the English People* in 1874. Green's account of the fifteenth century introduced two important new concepts. The first was that of the 'New Monarchy' of Edward IV and Henry VII in which the crown's fortunes and the nation's stability was restored by administrative innovation and fiscal retrenchment. The second was that Green questioned the destructiveness of the wars. Green's political sympathies persuaded him to look at the experience of ordinary men and women, rather than kings and nobles, and in so doing he questioned the gloomy view of the fifteenth century advanced by Denton and Plummer. While the aristocracy murdered each other on the battlefields of Towton, Tewkesbury and Bosworth 'for the most part the trading and agricultural classes', Green argued, 'stood wholly apart'.[10] Green, who disdained archival research and wrote for a popular audience, never made much impact upon his more academic contemporaries in England (although his picture of Henry VII particularly was important for American historians, in particular Frederick Dietz and Walter Richardson), but his arguments in some ways prefigured those of one of the most influential early twentieth-century historians of the Wars, Charles Lethbridge Kingsford (1852–1926). Kingsford also largely ignored governmental records and pointed to the richness of literary sources, particularly the vernacular chronicles and private letters for the mid-fifteenth century. For Kingsford (whose 1923 Oxford Ford lectures were published two years later as *Prejudice and Promise in Fifteenth Century England*) Tudor historians had 'prejudiced' their successors against the fifteenth century. Instead he highlighted the cultural and intellectual spirit of an age in which Lollardy flourished as a forerunner of later Protestantism, vernacular writing fore-shadowed Elizabethan literature, and the lawlessness of much of the West Country presaged the spirit of adventure that found its fullest expression in Tudor explorers like Drake and Raleigh.[11]

K.B. MCFARLANE AND THE WARS OF THE ROSES

In the mid-twentieth century another Oxford academic established a new orthodoxy for researching and writing on the fifteenth century. K.B. McFarlane (1903–66), through his teaching if not through the bulk of his published work, influenced generations of historians and transformed the way in which we understand the Wars of the Roses.[12] McFarlane questioned both Stubbs's teleological approach to the fifteenth century, seen in terms of the development of the English constitution, and the administrative and institutional approach that had grown out of the Manchester school of historians led by T.F. Tout. Instead, McFarlane concentrated on the public careers and private networks of the nobility and land-owning classes. His teaching and writing had three important consequences for the way in which historians approach the Wars of the Roses. First, and most importantly, he challenged Plummer's notion of 'Bastard Feudalism' and the characterisation of the late-medieval nobility as degenerate, ill-educated and innately violent. Rather than sweeping generalisa-tions McFarlane offered detailed portraits of individual noblemen. This was based on research in their private archives (estate papers and, in a few cases, letters) as well as governmental records and chron-icle accounts. Related to this he gave a new awareness of the homogeneity on the one hand, yet individualism on the other, of the landowning classes. As a whole, the nobility (defined as the parlia-mentary peerage) and the gentry formed a landowning aristocracy whose cultural values were broadly similar, based on notions of chivalry and gentility, a respect for the king and the principle of lordship, and a belief in the sanctity of landownership. Within this framework, however, individual landowners enjoyed relative freedom to choose whether or not to support their lord in times of political crisis, while their individual fortunes were constrained by their ability, by illness or some other incapacity, by their economic circumstances, or, most commonly, simply by their inability to produce male offspring.

This emphasis on individual agency led McFarlane to develop the second of his basic assumptions about the mid-fifteenth century. Fundamentally, he argued, there was nothing structurally wrong with the English polity. Its structures and institutions were robust and survived virtually unscathed throughout the fifteenth century and, indeed, for most of the sixteenth too. These included not only its administrative, fiscal and judicial institutions but also, crucially, its social institutions. Thus McFarlane removed the pejorative overtones of 'Bastard Feudalism'. Rather than being a system which undermined social stability and lordship, the system of cash payments and the distribution of livery compensated for the multiplication of tenures and the weakening of traditional ties based on homage and knight service. He later drew attention to the fact that indentures were not only a means of recruiting armies and defining military service but that they also regulated service in peacetime in the lord's household, on his estates and in his legal council. The social and political system based upon reciprocal notions of good lordship that lay at the heart of English political society was not a corruption of 'pure' feudalism but a necessary adaptation to the changing circumstances of the later middle ages. The problem that lay at the heart of the Wars of the Roses, therefore, was not structural but revolved around the effectiveness of kingship and, in particular, the inadequacies of Henry VI. McFarlane thus dismissed the notion that Edward III's provisions for his offspring had fundamentally weakened the fiscal, political and military base of the crown, leaving it defenceless at the mercy of its greater subjects who were wealthier and more powerful than it. He scorned the very idea of the 'Overmighty Subject' (and thus a powerful Whiggish narrative that saw the Tudor subjection of the nobility as an essential precursor to modern forms of government). McFarlane brilliantly summed up this position in his 1964 lecture to the British Academy: 'But in fact only an undermighty ruler had anything to fear from overmighty subjects, and if he was undermighty his personal lack of fitness was the cause, not the weakness of his office and its resources'.[13] In a nutshell, then, the origins of the Wars of the Roses should be sought in the personal inadequacies of Henry VI, while the renewal of the wars in 1469–71 and 1483–87 were to be found in the ill-judged decisions of Edward IV (in marrying Elizabeth Woodville) and Richard, Duke of Gloucester (in usurping the throne from his nephew, Edward V).

Finally, McFarlane revised the abject picture of the fifteenth century that had first emerged from the pens of the Tudor writers and had been dramatised by Plummer, Denton and others. Instead, while he recognised the bloody nature of some battles and the relatively high casualty rate among the nobility and their servants, McFarlane stressed that involvement in the wars and the suffering this caused was patchy, both in terms of chronology and geographically. The slide to war was not inevitable; the political nation was on the whole slow and reluctant to take up arms. Again, McFarlane's research stressed the individuality of experience and the freedom that even those at the top of the social hierarchy had to determine their own fate. Sir Henry Vernon, a retainer of the Earl of Warwick, felt able to ignore his master's summons before the Battle of Barnet in 1471, and he cited many other examples of men who refused to commit themselves unequivocally to one lord. If anything this trend intensified during the second half of the fifteenth century testifying to a growing reluctance among the landowning class to become embroiled in the struggles of those who would be king.

Despite a relatively limited output in terms of published work, McFarlane's legacy and his impact on fifteenth-century history is huge. His students at Oxford (and eventually their students and their students' students) dominated the resurgence of research and writing on the Wars of the Roses from the 1970s. His successor at Magdalen College, Oxford, Gerald Harriss, supervised an influential group of historians who have come to dominate writing on the period into the present day. The concerns of these historians were very much driven by the McFarlane agenda. Indeed, many of his arguments about the nature of fifteenth-century society (such as the relationship between the king and his greater subjects and the location of dynamic forces within the English polity) are axiomatic in their published work. The most enduring part of McFarlane's legacy must be the now almost universal acceptance of the notion that the late-medieval English polity was a robust one that adapted itself successfully to both social and economic crises (such as the Black Death or the Great Bullion Famine of the mid-fifteenth century), internal political conflict, and the demands of foreign war. This was made possible through the nature of its established institutions (above all the Common Law courts and, from the mid-fourteenth century, parliament) and an essentially common outlook shared by the king, his nobles and the majority of the political nation. England rode out successive crises, and its essential structure as a 'mixed monarchy' remained unchanged from the beginning of the fourteenth century until the Personal Rule of Charles I began in 1629. It achieved this through a mutually supportive partnership of crown and landowners in the government of the realm and the broad acceptance of a 'continuum of wealth, status, and authority which incorporated as twin concepts both hierarchy and common good.'[14] The Wars of the Roses were therefore something of an anomaly caused primarily by the 'grisly reality' of the absolute failure of Henry VI to provide effective royal leadership in three key areas: first, his failure to provide leadership in war; second, his failure to rise above the affairs of his nobility and to act as the ultimate, independent arbiter in their quarrels; and, finally, his failure to respond properly, and to be seen to respond properly, to the advice of his counsellors. It was not until 1471 that Edward IV restored stability by eliminating Henry VI and other potential rivals to his throne, working properly with his nobility, and fulfilling contemporary expectations of what constituted effective kingship. Nevertheless, the long crisis of kingship that had characterised Henry VI's reign returned to haunt the polity on the accession of the young Edward V in 1483. If the wars of the 1450s and 1460s had any real significance it was to weaken the bonds of obedience that made possible, even probable, renewed conflict in the mid-1480s.

One slightly paradoxical aspect of McFarlane's thinking on the Wars was his conviction, influenced by Marxist historiography, that the actions of the political elite were driven, above all, by their material condition. Thus politicians sought not to change the system but to maximise the power and rewards they gained from it. Equally, the interest of the English aristocracy in the Hundred Years War was directly proportional to the profit they made out of it. Therefore patronage, the ability of the king to reward the nobility and they in turn to return their gentry servants and so on, was the 'essential lubricant of government' and the thing that kept the polity functioning. When this system failed, when the crown or the nobility was too poor or patronage began to be dispensed according to favouritism and partiality, then political crisis ensued. Equally, the outbreak and course of the Wars were directly related to wider economic conditions. The middle decades of the fifteenth century saw an acute economic crisis in Europe. This was manifested in a serious shortage in the amount of available bullion affecting both royal revenue and private incomes, and intensifying the struggle for patronage. This reading of the fifteenth century, of course, presupposes that men were driven, consciously or unconsciously, by essentially selfish ends and as such owes as much to sixteenth-century writers, like Vergil, as it does to McFarlane. Nevertheless, it remains an influential argument. The most recent scholarly synthesis of the Wars ties the chronology of conflict directly into the ebbs and flows of the European economy, arguing that the slow return to stability after 1487 owed much to the 'feel-good factor' that accompanied economic recovery.[15]

AFTER MCFARLANE

So where do we stand now in our understanding of the Wars of the Roses and the broader panorama of fifteenth-century English history? Most current thinking continues to take place within what we might term a 'McFarlanite Paradigm', but it differs in one fundamental way: recent scholarship has stressed the important of political ideas, principles and the 'constitution'. In recent years, two related intellectual movements, with profound consequences for the writing of history in general, have made their impact felt on studies of the Wars of the Roses. The first of these is a move away from the study of politics towards the study of political culture. This, at first, might seem a change in semantics and little else, but it is an immensely important distinction. The difference between politics and political culture has been defined as 'the difference between political action and the codes of conduct, formal and informal, governing those actions. A history of the former treats the players of the game, a history of the latter, what the players assume the nature and limits of their game to be. If the reconstruction of lost political 'realities' comprehends the recovery of political cultures, the challenge for the historian lies in discovering the relevant cultural context'.[16] It is precisely this, the identification of the proper context for explaining what people did during the Wars of the Roses, that has driven the best research in the past twenty years or so.

The second intellectual shift that has had an impact on the historiography of the Wars of the Roses is the so-called 'linguistic turn'. This has its roots in the philosophy of language but, as far as the historian is concerned, can usefully be summarised as a notion that language does not merely reflect social reality, but is in itself constitutive of it. Thus historical documents are texts, intrinsically no different to any other text (say a poem, a chronicle or a romance) and written in language that both represented and shaped the cultural practices of that age. Language and the precise meaning of words and concepts at particular times (and the ways in which those meanings shift, are contested and are rewritten) have emerged as the dominant concern of historians and other scholars working on the fifteenth century.

Initially at least this interest in language and concepts was not couched in overtly theoretical terms. Maurice Keen, Michael K. Jones and Simon Walker examined the importance of chivalry as an ordering concept that determined political allegiances and actions. Christine Carpenter and Ted Powell considered the 'unspoken assumptions' that conditioned landowners and their involvement with and attitude towards the Common Law, while John Watts explored the expectations of kingship and the notions of hierarchy and authority that were at the heart of the English polity.[17] More recently, however, scholars have begun to theorise more explicitly. In part this has been due to the fact that academics based in university English departments have increasingly turned their attention to the mid-fifteenth century. Texts like Sir Thomas Malory's *Morte D'Arthur* or William Worcester's *Boke of Noblesse* have emerged as key texts for understanding the political culture of fifteenth-century England. Equally, we have been reminded of the importance of Humanism, of new ways of reading and understanding texts in the fifteenth century, and of the importance of the printing press by scholars coming to the Wars of the Roses from outside the discipline of history. Key terms that defined the limits of political debate, such as the 'Commonweal', the 'Commons' and 'Policie', have attracted the attention of historians and literary scholars alike.

Nevertheless, this interest in language and political culture has not yet translated into a new and sophisticated understanding of the causes, course and consequences of the Wars of the Roses. The reason for this is simple: few scholars have yet attempted to marry the detailed, archival research into individual experiences and actions (the central pillar of the McFarlane legacy) with a theoretically sophisticated understanding of language and political culture. This short history of the Wars of the Roses cannot hope to achieve this in isolation, but in the pages that follow I will attempt to relate the broad cultural currents of fifteenth-century England with the personal experience and choices of men and women in what was, I will argue, a transformative period in English history.

Dramatis Personae

Beaufort, Henry (d. 1447), Cardinal of England and Bishop of Winchester. The second of four illegitimate children of John of Gaunt and Katherine Swynford, he entered the church, becoming Bishop of Winchester in 1404 and a cardinal in 1417. He also served as Chancellor of England (1403–05, 1413–17, 1424–26). His great wealth bankrolled the Lancastrian regime, although his policies consistently advanced the status and claims of his family.

Beaufort, John (d. 1444), Duke of Somerset. The son of John Beaufort (d.1410), Duke of Somerset and Marquess of Dorset and the illegitimate grandson of John of Gaunt (d. 1399), he was one of the leading English captains in the French wars but died in ignominy after the failure of his expedition to Maine. He was succeeded by his brother, **Edmund (d. 1455)**, also an experienced soldier whose reputation was tarnished by the loss of Normandy in 1450. This led to a deadly feud with the Duke of York resulting in his death at the Battle of St Albans. He was succeeded by his eldest son, **Henry (d. 1464)**, who was an implacable opponent of the Duke of York. He was briefly reconciled with Edward IV but he rebelled and was killed at the Battle of Hexham. His brother, **Edmund (d. 1471)** escaped from the battle and fled into exile in Burgundy. He returned to England in 1471 with Queen Margaret but was defeated at the Battle of Tewkesbury and subsequently executed.

Beaufort, Margaret (d. 1509), Countess of Richmond. The daughter and heir of John, Duke of Somerset (d. 1444), she married Edmund Tudor, half-brother to Henry VI, in 1455. Her efforts were instrumental in establishing their son, Henry Tudor, as a viable claimant to the English throne in 1483.

Bonville, William (d. 1461), Lord Bonville. A major landowner in the south-west, his career was dominated by his dispute with the Courtenays, arising from the disputed office of Steward of the Duchy of Cornwall. He backed the Yorkists in 1460 and both his son and grandson were killed alongside the Duke of York at Wakefield, while William himself was captured at the second Battle of St Albans and subsequently executed.

Bourchier, Henry (d. 1483), 1st Earl of Essex. One of the most experienced commanders of the French wars, by the mid-1450s he had emerged as a supporter of the Duke of York. Throughout the 1460s and 1470s he was a mainstay of Yorkist government alongside his brother, **Thomas (d. 1486)**, who served as Chancellor of England (1455–56) and Archbishop of Canterbury (1455–86).

Cade, Jack (d. 1450). The leader of the rebellion against Henry VI's allegedly corrupt councillors in 1450, his real identity is unknown. His claim to kinship with the Duke of York, and adoption of the name Mortimer, was almost certainly fabricated. He was captured by the Sheriff of Kent and died of his wounds.

Courtenay, Thomas (d. 1458), Earl of Devon. Embroiled in a local struggle with Lord Bonville in the south-west, Earl Thomas committed himself to the Duke of York in 1452. His son, also **Thomas (d. 1461)**, was, however, a supporter of Queen Margaret, and was captured at the Battle of Towton and subsequently executed.

de la Pole, William (d. 1450), 1st Duke of Suffolk. Distinguishing himself in France after the premature death of his father and elder brother as a result of the wars in 1415, he emerged as the principal councillor of Henry VI in the 1430s. Blamed for the 'peace policy' of the mid-1440s and the loss of Normandy in 1450, he was murdered while leaving England to exile. His son, **John (d. 1492)**, the 2nd duke, married Elizabeth, daughter of the Duke of York, in

1458, and fought for the Yorkists in the wars of 1459–61 and 1469–71. His son, **John (d. 1487)**, **Earl of Lincoln**, supported Richard, Duke of Gloucester's usurpation in 1483 and following the death of Richard's son in 1484 was regarded as his heir apparent. He rebelled against Henry VII in 1487 and was killed at the Battle of Stoke.

De Vere, John (d. 1513), 13th Earl of Oxford. His father, the 12th earl, had been executed for treason by Edward IV in 1462. He fled to join Margaret of Anjou in 1470 and was present alongside the Earl of Warwick at the Battle of Barnet. He was subsequently imprisoned in Hammes Castle but escaped in 1484 to join Henry Tudor. He emerged as one of the leading magnates in early Tudor England.

Dynham, Sir John (d. 1501), Lord Dynham. A supporter of the Yorkist lords in 1459–61, he was ennobled by Edward IV in 1467. In command at Calais in 1483, he acquiesced in Richard III's usurpation and also remained aloof from events in 1485. He was appointed Treasurer of England by Henry VII in 1486. He died peacefully.

Edward IV (d. 1483), King of England. Eldest son of Richard, duke of York. He was catapulted into prominence by the premature death of his father in 1460. He proved himself a capable general but as king he was at times lazy. His own premature death left the throne in the hands of his twelve-year-old son, **Edward V (d. 1483)**, and resulted in the usurpation of his brother, **Richard III (d. 1485)**. Richard was defeated and killed at the Battle of Bosworth by Henry VII.

Fiennes, Sir James (d. 1450), Lord Saye and Sele. A veteran of Agincourt, he rose to prominence in the household of Henry VI during the 1430s. Associated with the hated Duke of Suffolk, he was murdered by Cade's rebels in 1450. His son, **William (d. 1471)**, succeeded to the title, supported the Yorkist lords in 1460–61 and accompanied Edward IV into exile in 1470. He was killed at the Battle of Barnet the following year.

Fortescue, Sir John (d. 1479). Chief Justice of the King's Bench (1442–61), he fled with Queen Margaret into exile where he wrote several political tracts. Pardoned by Edward IV in 1471, he was restored as a royal councillor and is regarded the most important English political writer of the fifteenth century.

Grey, Thomas (d. 1501), Lord Groby and Marquess of Dorset. The elder son of Queen Elizabeth Woodville by her first marriage to Sir John Grey (d. 1461), he owed his title and position to his mother's influence. He joined Buckingham's Rebellion and fled into exile in 1483. He was never fully trusted by Henry VII but died peacefully.

Hastings, Sir William (d. 1483), Lord Hastings. A long-standing servant of the House of York, he was elevated to the peerage by Edward IV. As Chamberlain of the Household and Lieutenant of Calais during the 1470s he was among the most powerful men in the kingdom. He supported the Duke of Gloucester's coup against the Woodvilles in 1483 but was subsequently executed by Richard.

Henry IV (d. 1413), King of England. Henry Bolingbroke, Earl of Derby, was the eldest son of John of Gaunt, the third son of Edward III. Exiled by Richard II in 1398 for his part in the noble opposition to him earlier in the reign, he returned to England the following year, ostensibly to recover his Duchy of Lancaster but in reality to usurp the throne. His eldest son, **Henry V (d. 1422)**, distinguished himself against the Welsh rebels, but in the latter years of his father's reign relations with the king were difficult. As King Henry conquered Normandy and secured the Lancastrian succession to the throne of France, but his premature death had disastrous consequences for the dynasty. His only son, **Henry VI (d. 1471)**, ascended the throne aged just nine months. He attained his formal majority in 1437, but his adult reign was compromised by his obvious shortcomings. He was deposed by Edward IV in 1461, only to be briefly restored in 1470–71 by the Earl of Warwick. After being deposed for a second time he was almost certainly murdered in the Tower of London.

Henry VII (d. 1509), King of England. Son of Edmund Tudor and Margaret Beaufort, he spent much of his adult life in exile before returning in 1485 to take the throne from Richard III. His dynastic claim was weak and he spent much of the first half of his reign resisting Yorkist plots. He died peacefully, leaving the throne to his second son, **Henry VIII (d. 1547)**.

Herbert, Sir William (d. 1469), Lord Herbert and Earl of Pembroke. A long-standing servant of the House of York, he was elevated to the peerage by Edward IV. He was created Earl of Pembroke in 1468, but was defeated at the Battle of Losecote Field and subsequently executed by the Yorkshire rebels the following year.

Holland, Henry (d. 1475), 2nd Duke of Exeter. Driven to reckless and violent actions by his dire financial situation, Exeter sided with the Percys in the 1450s in their dispute with the Nevilles. On the losing side at the Battle of Towton, he fled into exile to France. He was imprisoned in the Tower in 1471, but joined Edward IV's French campaign of 1475. He drowned in mysterious circumstances on the return journey.

Howard, Sir John (d. 1485), Lord Howard and 1st Duke of Norfolk. The cousin of John Mowbray, Duke of Norfolk, he followed him in supporting the Yorkist lords in 1460–61. He was one of the leading figures in the Yorkist regime and supported Richard, Duke of Gloucester's usurpation in 1483, being rewarded with the Duchy of Norfolk. He was killed fighting for Richard at Bosworth. His son, **Thomas (d. 1524), Earl of Surrey and 2nd Duke of Norfolk,** was subsequently pardoned by Henry VII and emerged as one of the leading figures in early Tudor England, serving as Treasurer of England (1501–22) and defeating James IV of Scotland at the Battle of Flodden in 1513.

Humphrey (d. 1447), Duke of Gloucester. The fourth son of Henry IV, he fought alongside Henry V at Agincourt, but on his brother's death was denied the governance of England on behalf of the young Henry VI by his fellow peers. An outspoken opponent of the 'peace policy' of the mid-1440s, he died in mysterious circumstances at the parliament of 1447.

John (d. 1435), Duke of Bedford. The third son of Henry IV, he distinguished himself in the French wars and in 1422, on Henry V's death, was appointed Regent of France for his nephew. His regency was marked by disagreements with his brother, the duke of Gloucester, over the conduct of the war.

Kemp, John (d. 1454), Archbishop of Canterbury. A long-standing servant of the Lancastrian kings, he served as Chancellor of England (1426–32, 1450–54), Archbishop of York (1425–52) and was chosen as cardinal in 1439. His was a conciliatory voice in the politics of the early 1450s.

Margaret of Anjou (d. 1482), Queen of England. Daughter of René, Duke of Anjou, she married Henry VI in 1445. She emerged during the 1450s as the leader of the Lancastrian party, championing the rights of her son, **Edward (d. 1471), Prince of Wales.** She left for exile in France in 1463, returning to England in 1471. She was released from Yorkist captivity in 1475 and returned to France, where she died seven years later. Her son was killed after the Battle of Tewkesbury.

Mowbray, John (d. 1461), 3rd Duke of Norfolk. One of the leading magnates in England and in the early 1450s an implacable enemy of Edmund, Duke of Somerset, Mowbray kept a low profile in the second half of the decade, but was among those lords who acclaimed Edward IV as king in 1461 and he fought at Towton. He died peacefully in November that year.

Neville, George (d. 1476), Archbishop of York. The fourth son of Richard, Earl of Salisbury, he entered the church becoming Bishop of Exeter (1456–65) and Archbishop of York (1465–76). He was also Chancellor of England (1460–67, 1470–71).

Neville, Richard (d. 1460), 5th Earl of Salisbury. The eldest son of Ralph Neville (d. 1425), 1st Earl of Westmorland, by his second wife, Joan Beaufort (d. 1440). he played a prominent role in the defence of the northern borders and in the French wars. By 1455 he was associated with the Duke of York. He was one of the Yorkist lords who fled into exile in 1459 and was captured at the Battle of Wakefield in 1460 and subsequently executed.

Neville, Richard (d. 1471), 16th Earl of Warwick and 6th Earl of Salisbury, 'The Kingmaker'. Eldest son of Richard, Earl of Salisbury, his support of the Duke of York in 1455–60 was crucial and he emerged as one of the leading military commanders of the Wars. He rebelled against Edward IV in 1469–70, making an alliance with Margaret of Anjou and restoring Henry VI. He was killed at the Battle of Barnet on Good Friday, 1471.

Neville, Sir John (d. 1471), Marquess Montagu and Earl of Northumberland. The third son of Richard, Earl of Salisbury, he distinguished himself fighting alongside his brother, the Earl of Warwick, in the north in 1461–64 and was rewarded with the earldom of Northumberland. Created Marquess Montagu in 1470, he died fighting with Warwick at Barnet in 1471.

Oldhall, Sir William (d. 1460). Another veteran of the French wars, Oldhall was Richard, Duke of York's chamberlain by 1443. He served as speaker in the parliament of 1450 and was subsequently accused of treasonable plotting on York's behalf.

Percy, Henry (d. 1455), 2nd Earl of Northumberland. Restored in 1416 to the earldom forfeited by his grandfather, Percy's career was defined by his struggle for local influence in the north of England with the Neville family. It was this that led to his death at the Battle of St Albans in 1455. His son, **Henry (d. 1461)**, the 3rd earl, was a committed Lancastrian and was killed at the Battle of Towton. His son, also **Henry (d. 1489)**, the 4th earl, was a minor and initially he was made a ward of Sir William Herbert. He was restored to the title and lands of Northumberland in 1470 and supported Edward IV during the Readeption. He was close to Richard, Duke of Gloucester, and acquiesced in his usurpation but crucially did not fight for him at Bosworth. Eventually appointed as Lieutenant of the North by Henry VII he was murdered by a mob hostile to royal taxation in 1489.

Percy, Sir Thomas (d. 1460), Lord Egremont. The younger brother of the 2nd Earl of Northumberland was the instigator of the conflict between the Neville and Percy families in the 1450s. A notoriously unstable character, he was captured by the Yorkists at the Battle of Northampton in July 1460 and subsequently executed.

Richard (d. 1460), Duke of York. Descended through his mother, Anne Mortimer, from Edward III's second son, Lionel (d. 1368), Duke of Clarence, and through his father, Richard (d. 1415), Earl of Cambridge, from Edward's fourth son, Edmund (d. 1402), Duke of York, he was a loyal Lancastrian servant before 1450. Thereafter he emerged as the leading opponent of royal policy before claiming the throne himself in 1460. He was killed at the Battle of Wakefield that year.

Richard II (d. 1399), King of England. The son of Edward, the Black Prince (d. 1376), eldest son of Edward III (d. 1377), he ascended to the throne as a minor. His adult reign was plagued by squabbles with his nobles and he was deposed by Henry Bolingbroke in 1399.

Stafford, Humphrey (d. 1460), 1st Duke of Buckingham. Great-grandson of Edward III (through his youngest son, Thomas of Woodstock), he supported the king and Duke of Somerset during the early 1450s. Emerged as a stalwart supporter of Queen Margaret and was killed at the Battle of Northampton in July 1460. His son **Henry (d. 1483)**, the 2nd duke, was a minor when his father died and was largely excluded from government during the 1470s. He supported Richard III's usurpation in 1483, but soon afterwards rebelled and was captured and executed.

Stafford, Sir Humphrey (d. 1469), Lord Stafford of Southwick and Earl of Devon. A former Lancastrian captured by Yorkist forces at Calais in 1460, he fought alongside Edward IV at Towton and was rewarded with a peerage. He emerged as one of the most unpopular figures in Edward's household. Shortly after his creation as Earl of Devon he was lynched by a mob in Bridgwater.

Stanley, Thomas (d. 1504), Lord Stanley and 1st Earl of Derby. Stanley played ambiguous role in the civil war of 1459–61, but was accepted into Edward IV's grace in 1461. He emerged a leading councillor in the 1470s and in 1472 married Margaret Beaufort. He failed to actively support Richard III in 1485 and was created Earl of Derby by Henry VII. His brother, **Sir William (d. 1495)**, played a pivotal role at Bosworth, intervening in favour of Henry Tudor, and was made chamberlain of his household. He was executed for treason in 1495.

Talbot, John (d. 1453), 1st Earl of Shrewsbury. Talbot was one of the most experienced English soldiers of the fifteenth century, carving out a distinguished career in Ireland and, from 1420, in France. He led the last English expedition to Gascony, being killed at the Battle of Castillon in 1453.

Tudor, Edmund (d. 1456), 1st Earl of Richmond. The eldest son of Owen Tudor (d. 1461) and Catherine of Valois, and half-brother to Henry VI. His control of royal government in south Wales was resisted by the Duke of York's supporters in 1456 who imprisoned him. He died shortly afterwards of plague before the birth of his only son, the future Henry VII. His younger brother, **Jasper (d. 1495), Earl of Pembroke and Duke of Bedford,** supported Henry VI in the civil war of 1459–61. He spent most of the 1460s and 1470s in exile before returning to England with his nephew in 1485.

Wenlock, Sir John (d. 1471), Lord Wenlock. A long-standing Lancastrian servant, by the early 1450s he was a supporter of the Duke of York. Elevated to the peerage by Edward IV, he was one of the Earl of Warwick's closest supporters during the 1460s and died fighting for the restored Lancastrian regime at the Battle of Tewkesbury in May 1471.

Woodville, Sir Richard (d. 1469), 1st Earl Rivers. A long-standing servant of the House of Lancaster who married Jaquetta of Luxembourg (d. 1472), the widow of John, Duke of Bedford, his fortunes were transformed by the marriage of his daughter, **Elizabeth (d. 1497), Queen of England,** to Edward IV in 1464. He was despised by the Earl of Warwick and captured and executed in 1469. His son, **Anthony (d. 1483), Lord Scales and 2nd Earl Rivers,** succeeded his father but was captured by Richard, Duke of Gloucester, prior to his usurpation in 1483 and subsequently executed.

Timeline

1399	Usurpation of Henry Bolingbroke and deposition of Richard II.
1415	Renewal of the Hundred Years War and Henry V's victory at the Battle of Agincourt.
1420	Treaty of Troyes: Charles VI of France recognises Henry V of England as heir to the French throne.
1422	Death of Henry V and Charles VI and accession of Henry's nine-month old son, Henry VI, as king of England and France.
1449	French reconquest of Normandy after five years of truce.
1450	English defeat in Normandy, murder of the Henry VI's leading councillor, the Duke of Suffolk, and Cade's Rebellion against the king's 'evil counsellors'. Return to political prominence of Richard, Duke of York.
1455	22 May: first Battle of St Albans. Death of the Duke of Somerset, the Earl of Northumberland and Lord Clifford at the hands of the Duke of York and his allies.
1458	25 March: 'The Loveday' at St Pauls. Henry VI and the moderate lords attempt to reconcile the factions led by the Duke of York and Queen Margaret of Anjou.

The First War, 1459–1464

1459	23 September: Yorkist uprising and defeat of Lancastrian forces at the Battle of Blore Heath.

13 October: defeat of the Yorkist lords at the Battle of Ludford Bridge. York flees to Ireland, the Earls of Warwick, Salisbury and March to Calais.

20 November: the 'Parliament of Devils' at Coventry and the attainder of the Yorkist Lords.

1460   26 June: Warwick, Salisbury and March land at Sandwich and march to London.

10 July: Yorkist victory at the Battle of Northampton, Henry VI is taken prisoner.

October: at the Westminster parliament Richard, Duke of York, makes his formal claim to the throne. He is recognised as Henry VI's heir.

30 December: York, Salisbury and York's son, the Earl of Rutland, killed by Lancastrians at the Battle of Wakefield.

1461   2–3 February: victory of Edward, Earl of March, over Lancastrian forces at the Battle of Mortimer's Cross.

17 February: the Earl of Warwick defeated by Margaret of Anjou's army at the second Battle of St Albans. Margaret refused entry into London.

4 March: the Earl of March is acclaimed King Edward IV in London.

31 March: Yorkist victory at the Battle of Towton.

1464   15 May: final defeat of Lancastrian forces at the Battle of Hexham, followed by the capture of the fugitive Henry VI in July 1465.

The Second War, 1469–71

1469   July: Robin of Redesdale's revolt in Yorkshire against perceived misgovernment by Edward IV and the influence of the relatives of his queen, Elizabeth Woodville.

26 July: royal forces defeated by rebels at the Battle of Edgecote; deaths of the Yorkist Earls of Devon and Pembroke and of the queen's father, Earl Rivers. Edward IV taken into captivity by the Earl of Warwick.

1470 12 March: Lincolnshire rebels, supported by the Earl of Warwick and Edward IV's brother, the Duke of Clarence, defeated by royal forces at Losecote Field.
9 April: Warwick and Clarence flee to France where Warwick is reconciled with Margaret of Anjou and agrees to restore Henry VI to the throne.
13 September: Warwick invades England, Edward flees to the Low Countries, and Henry VI's Readeption begins on 6 October.

1471 14 March: Edward IV returns to England.
14 April: Warwick defeated and killed by Edward IV at the Battle of Barnet.
4 May: Lancastrian forces defeated at the Battle of Tewkesbury. Death of Henry of Lancaster, Henry VI's son, and of Henry VI himself on 21 May.

The Third War, 1483–1487

1483 9 April: death of Edward IV and accession of his young son as Edward V.
30 April: Edward IV's brother, Richard, Duke of Gloucester, launches a *coup d'etat* against his Woodville relations and on 4 May is named Lord Protector.
13 June: Gloucester murders William, Lord Hastings, his erstwhile ally, and begins plans to seize the throne himself.
22 June: Gloucester's claim to the throne, probably on the grounds of Edward IV's illegitimacy, is proclaimed and on 26 June he is acclaimed as King Richard III.
October: rebellion of Richard's ally, the Duke of Buckingham, with an alliance of Woodville supporters and former members of Edward IV's household in favour of Henry Tudor amidst rumours of the demise of Edward's sons.

1484 25 December: at Rennes cathedral in Brittany Henry Tudor promises to marry Edward IV's daughter, Elizabeth of York.

1485	7 August: Henry Tudor lands at Milford Haven at the head of a small force of English exiles and French mercenaries.
	22 August: Richard III is killed and defeated at the Battle of Bosworth; accession of Henry VII.
1486	18 January: marriage of Henry VII to Elizabeth of York. April: pro-Ricardian rebellions in the midlands and the north.
1487	4 June: landing at Furness, Lancs., of Lambert Simnel who claims to be Edward, Earl of Warwick, son of the Duke of Clarence. He is backed by the Irish Earl of Kildare and Richard's heir apparent, John, Earl of Lincoln.
	16 June: defeat of Simnel and the death of the Earl of Lincoln at the Battle of Stoke.
	25 November: coronation of Elizabeth of York at Westminster brings a symbolic conclusion to the Wars of the Roses.

1. LANCASTER AND YORK

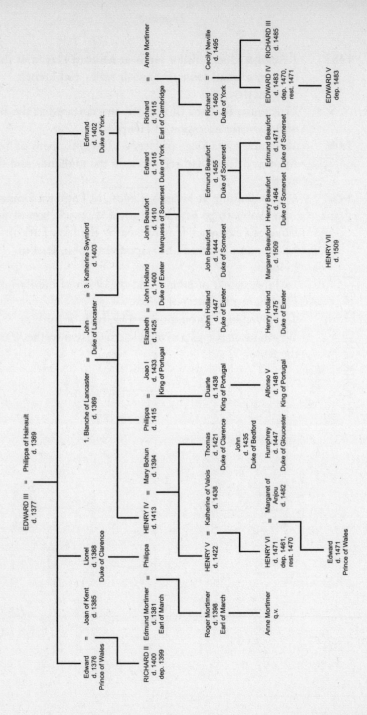

2. YORK AND NEVILLE

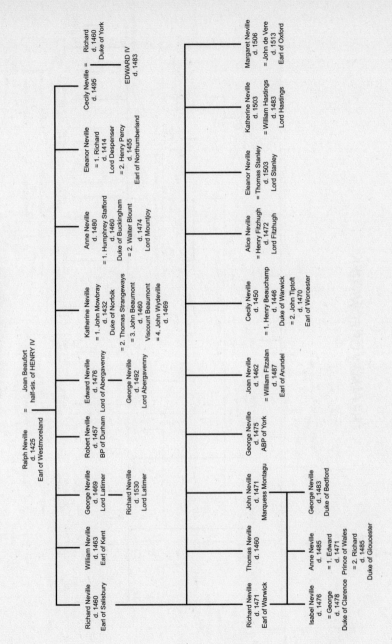

Ralph Neville = Joan Beaufort
d. 1425   half-sis. of HENRY IV
Earl of Westmoreland

Richard Neville
d. 1460
Earl of Salisbury

William Neville
d. 1463
Earl of Kent

George Neville
d. 1469
Lord Latimer

Richard Neville
d. 1530
Lord Latimer

Robert Neville
d. 1457
BP of Durham

Edward Neville
d. 1476
Lord of Abergavenny

George Neville
d. 1492
Lord Abergavenny

Katherine Neville
= 1. John Mowbray
d. 1432
Duke of Norfolk
= 2. Thomas Strangeways
= 3. John Beaumont
d. 1460
Viscount Beaumont
= 4. John Wydeville
d. 1469

Anne Neville
d. 1480
= 1. Humphrey Stafford
d. 1460
Duke of Buckingham
= 2. Walter Blount
d. 1474
Lord Mountjoy

Eleanor Neville
= 1. Richard
d. 1414
Lord Despenser
= 2. Henry Percy
d. 1455
Earl of Northumberland

Cecily Neville = Richard
d. 1495   d. 1460
              Duke of York

EDWARD IV
d. 1483

Richard Neville
d. 1471
Earl of Warwick

Thomas Neville
d. 1460

John Neville
d. 1471
Marquess Montagu

George Neville
d. 1483
Duke of Bedford

George Neville
d. 1475
ABP of York

Joan Neville
d. 1462
= William Fitzalan
d. 1487
Earl of Arundel

Cecily Neville
d. 1450
= 1. Henry Beauchamp
d. 1446
Duke of Warwick
= 2. John Tiptoft
d. 1470
Earl of Worcester

Alice Neville
= Henry Fitzhugh
d. 1472
Lord Fitzhugh

Eleanor Neville
= Thomas Stanley
d. 1503
Lord Stanley

Katherine Neville
d. 1503
= William Hastings
d. 1483
Lord Hastings

Margaret Neville
d. 1506
= John de Vere
d. 1513
Earl of Oxford

Isabel Neville
d. 1476
= George
d. 1478
Duke of Clarence

Anne Neville
d. 1485
= 1. Edward
d. 1471
Prince of Wales
= 2. Richard
d. 1485
Duke of Gloucester

3. THE FAMILY OF EDWARD IV

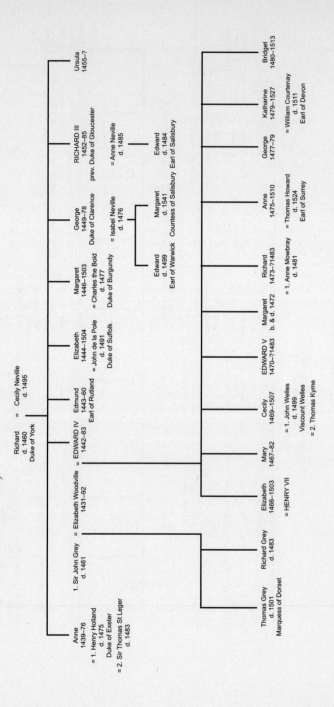

Part 1

CAUSES

1

THE LANCASTRIAN LEGACY: ENGLAND 1399–1449

To understand why the Wars of Roses occurred we must go back to 1399 and the deposition of Richard II by Henry Bolingbroke, Duke of Lancaster. Contemporaries recognised as much. Edward IV's declaration of his title in the parliament of 1461 outlined how Bolingbroke, 'ayenst Godds lawe, mannes liegeaunce, and oth of fidelite,' had usurped the crown and murdered Richard. This had not been forgotten in England 'which therfore hath suffred the charge of intollerable persecucion, punicion and tribulacion, wherof the lyke hath not been seen or herde in any other Cristen reame, by any memorie or recorde.'[1] The importance of 1399 was a central feature in Tudor accounts of the civil wars, yet modern scholarship has, in the main, offered more short-term explanations for the outbreak of open conflict. Nevertheless, we do not have to accept the notion of divine judgement to afford 1399 a critical significance in explaining the Wars. The circumstances in which the House of Lancaster took the throne, the nature of their royal power and the constraints upon it, and the ways in which they sought to confirm their legitimacy dominated the Lancastrian polity in the first half of the fifteenth century and provided the essential preconditions for the outbreak of war in 1455.

King Henry IV by unknown artist oil on panel, 1590–1610
© National Portrait Gallery, London

1399–1413: THE QUESTION OF LEGITIMACY

On 30 September 1399 the Bishop of St Asaph read out loud to the assembled lords and Commons in parliament the 33 articles of deposition of King Richard II. They outlined his tyrannical actions in collecting unjust taxation, unlawfully killing his subjects, being in contempt of the Magna Carta, and oppressing his subjects. The accusations were largely grounded in fact, seem to have been accepted on the whole by Richard himself, and demonstrated beyond doubt that he was unfit to rule. When the articles had been read, Bolingbroke got to his feet and announced his claim to the throne through descent from Henry III and his intention to rescue the realm from 'lack of government and undoing of the laws and customs of the realm'.[2] The Earl of Northumberland and the Treasurer of England then asked if the parliament would accept Henry as their king, to which they unanimously gave their assent.

The events of 1399 were indeed revolutionary. Richard II had a view of kingship which was increasingly at odds with that held by the majority of his subjects. Simply put, Richard believed he was above the law, made in parliament with the assent of the community of the realm. He was, however, an anointed and unquestionably legitimate king and his deposition transformed the political culture of medieval England. More precisely, the justification offered for his deposition and for Lancastrian monarchy more generally was a radical departure from what had gone before. Henry's kingship was based on three principles. First and most importantly, the new Lancastrian polity stressed the king's obligations to uphold his coronation oath and rule for the common good. Richard had been deposed because he had broken his oaths and for the 'lack of government'. Henry IV thus had a renewed obligation to uphold justice, defend the realm, not to tax unjustly and ensure the stability of royal finances. This expectation dominated the political process during the first decade of Lancastrian rule and revolved around issues of taxation and royal accountability to parliament. On his accession Henry, in an action that underlined the relative weakness of his position, had promised to not to overburden his subjects with taxation. He may have hoped that Richard's not inconsiderable treasure and the resources of the Duchy of Lancaster would provide the basis for stable royal finances. Before long, however, he was faced with rebellion at home and war with Scotland and was forced to ask for parliamentary taxation. In 1401 parliament demanded redress of their grievances before granting supply, and three years later the grant of a subsidy was made conditional on the appointment of special treasurers who would oversee its collection and spending. Even worse, in 1406 all royal expenditure was put under the scrutiny of the king's council, appointed by parliament, forcing Henry to complain that 'kings were not wont to render account'.[3]

Second, Lancastrian legitimacy was based on an appeal to popular support. Henry IV was king by acclamation in parliament, but the nature of Lancastrian political culture meant that his kingship was not only judged by the parliamentary Commons. As Michael Bennett has argued, 'it was widely believed that Henry had been raised to the throne on the basis of a covenant with the people'.[4] By 1402 there were complaints that Henry was raising taxation not for the public good but to enrich his household and retainers. Moreover, Henry was increasingly characterised as a man who had gone back on his word, not only in the way he ruled but also in that he had committed perjury in 1399 by usurping the throne when he had initially claimed his only intent was to recover the Duchy of Lancaster. It was this complaint that lay behind Archbishop Scrope of York's rebellion in 1405. As early as May 1402 proclamations had been issued throughout the realm denouncing those who were spreading rumours that the king had broken his promises and reminding people 'that it always had been and will be the king's intention that the common profit and laws and customs of the realm shall be observed and kept'.[5] For much of the first decade of Lancastrian rule the king was on the back foot, so to speak, constantly reacting to challenges to his kingship and authority. According to one chronicler, his was even forced to claim publicly that he did not seize the crown, but was 'properly elected'. If this were true, it was a remarkable admission of the shaky foundations of Lancastrian rule.

Finally, there was his dynastic claim. Henry had initiated searches throughout the realm's monastic archives to establish that Edmund 'Crouchback', Earl of Lancaster, had been in fact the eldest son of Henry III. These had, however, confirmed that Edward I, great-great grandfather to Richard II, had indeed been the rightful heir. Henry IV's claim, as hinted at in parliament, therefore was a feeble one, based on that of his mother, Blanche of Lancaster. Nevertheless, his descent from John of Gaunt, Edward III's third son, gave him a stronger title if we accept that Edward had entailed the crown in the male line in 1376. Yet Henry's implicit acknowledgement of descent through the female line left open the stronger claim of the Mortimer family, descended from Edward III's second son, Lionel of Clarence, and his daughter, Philippa. The weakness of Henry's dynastic claim was evident in the fact that on no fewer than four occasions in the first seven years of his reign he was forced to confirm and strengthen the Lancastrian succession by act of parliament.

The reasons for Henry's weakness are not difficult to see. He had come to the throne as the head of a small faction; in effect, his baronial household was now propelled into being the governing elite of the kingdom. Thus Henry relied on his and his father's trusted servants, men like Sir Thomas Erpingham, Sir Thomas Rempston, Sir Hugh and Sir Robert Waterton, and John Norbury, and a few close companions in exile, such as Thomas, Earl of Arundel. Thomas Arundel, Archbishop of Canterbury, who Richard II had replaced in 1397 for his support of the Appellants in 1386, had also accompanied Bolingbroke on his return to England and emerged as a key pillar of the Lancastrian regime. Henry's reliance on the Lancastrian affinity in government and his appeal to popular sentiment to strengthen his kingship are also explicable by the fact that in 1399 the nobility was depleted in number. Edmund, Duke of York, was aged and impotent and died in 1402, while his son, the Earl of Rutland, was untrustworthy; Thomas Mowbray, heir to the Duchy of Norfolk, was still a minor, as were the Earls of Oxford and March. The earldoms of Kent, Salisbury and Huntingdon were in the king's hands from 1400 by reason of rebellion, while the Earls of Devon, Suffolk and Warwick, for various reasons, played little part in affairs of state. The Earls of Arundel and Stafford were young men and inexperienced. Henry could not rely therefore on a powerful nobility to assist in the governance of the realm. Only the Earls of Northumberland, Worcester and Westmorland and their kinsmen (men such as Sir Henry Percy or Thomas Neville, Lord Furnival) were active and able to play a full role in supporting royal government. The king's illegitimate half-brother, John Beaufort, Earl of Somerset, (a former Ricardian) was also quickly rehabilitated and became another stalwart of Lancastrian rule. The problem with this narrow basis of support was that Henry felt compelled to reward them with grants of land and money in an effort to guarantee their continued support, a support which he should have been able to count upon unquestionably as king. This royal largesse, however, angered the Commons who resented granting taxation while the king apparently squandered his resources with grants of annuities and lands to his supporters.

The early years of Henry's reign were thus beset by criticism in parliament and rebellion. The most serious uprising was that of the Welsh esquire, Owain Glyn Dŵr. This led to war with Scotland in 1402 and in the following year the king's erstwhile Percy allies joined Glyn Dŵr. In 1406, as a response to parliamentary demands, a new royal council was appointed, headed by Archbishop Arundel. However, from 1407 the king's eldest son, Henry, Prince of Wales, already with an established reputation as a military and political leader from his experiences in Wales, began to play a more active role in government. As the king's health deteriorated so the prince assumed the reins of power, backed by Arundel and assisted by his three able brothers and a new generation of young noblemen. During 1410–11 the prince effectively ruled through the council, earning the loyalty of the Lancastrian affinity and consolidating his own military reputation as captain of Calais. He overreached himself, however, and his attempt to intervene in the French civil war on the side of the Burgundians was vetoed by the king and Prince Henry was forced into a humiliating submission to his father. By the end of 1412, however, the prince was again playing a full role

King Henry V by unknown artist oil on panel, late sixteenth or early seventeenth century © National Portrait Gallery, London

in the government of the realm, and his brother, Thomas, Duke of Clarence, had led a successful raid into France regardless of the accommodation between the warring Burgundian and Armagnac factions. On 20 March 1413 Henry IV died, 'worn out by the stress and strain of kingship'.[6] The throne passed, without contention, to his eldest son, who was crowned King Henry V on 9 April that year.

The Lancastrian regime had survived the crisis of legitimacy created by the circumstances of 1399. This was a combination of luck, the skill of men like Arundel, and the loyalty demonstrated by the ever-expanding Lancastrian affinity. Nevertheless, there was a price to be paid. First, the cost of the royal household and the other expenses of government spiralled, placing ever greater strains on the body politic. Second, the king's reliance on the Lancastrian affinity in the localities had led to a re-ordering of local political society in many parts of the realm and a fear that government for the public good was being overtaken by government driven by private interest. Most importantly, Henry IV had compensated for the weakness of his hereditary title by appealing to popular sentiment; the parliamentary Commons, rebellious subjects, and Lancastrian poets all questioned the king's manner of ruling if not his right to rule *per se*. In the final analysis the Lancastrian regime was dependent on the support of the political nation in its broadest sense and this simple fact would have far-reaching consequences for much of the remainder of the fifteenth century.

1413–1437: THE ILLUSION OF STABILITY

Henry V has been called 'the greatest man that ever ruled England' and many modern historians have agreed with K.B. McFarlane that his reign proved that strong and effective kingship could effectively mobilise the resources of government and provide effective justice and financial strength alongside a robust and successful foreign policy.[7] At the beginning of his reign Henry benefitted from the unpopularity of his father. The period 1410–11, when as Prince of Wales he had led the royal council, was remembered as a time of effective government, something which Henry IV, on the whole, had conspicuously failed to deliver. Henry also benefitted from the unflinching loyalty of the Lancastrian affinity, something which he had also cultivated as prince, and a new generation of nobility, untainted by rebellion or Ricardian loyalism. Families such as the Hollands, Mowbrays, Montagues and Percies were partially restored and their full rehabilitation made contingent on their loyal service to the new king. Henry personified contemporary expectations of effective kingship and the upholding of his coronation vows were the touchstone of his reign. On his accession he also set about restoring the crown's credit worthiness. Priority was initially given at the Exchequer to the repayment of royal debts and the defence of the realm, while the crown's regular sources of income (the profits of justice, prerogative rights and the crown lands) were exploited with efficiency. The new king also set about ostentatiously restoring law and justice. Campaigns against public disorder, especially in the midlands and the Welsh marches, were tangible demonstrations of kingly virtue. In the first months of the reign the Earl of Arundel and Lord Furnival fell foul of the king over the violent actions of their feuding servants in Shropshire. Furnival was imprisoned in the Tower and later sent to Ireland, while their servants, Lancastrian loyalists whose misdeeds had been ignored during the previous reign, found themselves before the justices of king's bench and punished. Finally, Henry soon established his credentials as a defender of religious orthodoxy. He took a personal interest in the campaign against Lollardy; even his own servants, such as Sir John Oldcastle, found themselves on the receiving end. In 1414 the Statute of Lollards extended the state's role in the investigation and punishment of heretics, in effect making Lollardy synonymous with treason.

First and foremost, however, Henry V's reputation was built upon war with France. The king prepared well for the first campaign in 1415, mobilising an expeditionary army of some 10,000 men and amassing a war chest of £130,000. The army, drawing heavily on the resources of the Lancastrian affinity, also represented the *familia regis* at war; the lords, knights and esquires were bound personally to the king, their loyalty symbolised by pieces of the crown jewels given to them as security for the future payment of their wages. The Battle of

Agincourt on 25 October was an extraordinary victory, gained against the odds and won by the individual prowess of the king and his servants against the might of French chivalry. The immediate reaction in England was euphoria, resulting in generous grants of taxation (including the wool subsidy for life in the parliament of November 1415) and an increase in the political capital of the House of Lancaster that would sustain it for another generation. Moreover, the capture of the port of Harfleur opened the way to further conquest. In August 1417 Henry set sail for France once more. By January 1419, when its capital Rouen fell after a protracted siege, Henry had conquered the Duchy of Normandy. Later that year the king concluded a new alliance with Philip the Good, the new Duke of Burgundy, and was in a position to demand nothing less than the crown of France itself. In May 1420 the treaty of Troyes realised Lancastrian ambitions. Henry was recognised as heir to the French king, Charles VI, his status confirmed by his marriage to Charles's daughter, Catherine of Valois. Victorious in war, celebrated and loved by his subjects at home, Henry was the exemplar of medieval kingship.

Or so it seems. Henry V's kingship was, however, more ambiguous than many contemporaries or subsequent historians have allowed. In 1413 expectations for the renewal of the English polity were first and foremost expectations of the character and virtue of the new king. Yet, Henry's character and motivations remain problematic. The conquest of Normandy and the treaty of Troyes represented the king's personal and growing ambitions in France. Contemporaries recognised that war grew out of 'coveytise and fals Ambicioun' and Lancastrian poets, such as Thomas Hoccleve and John Lydgate, struggled to square this fact with their portrayal of Henry as a virtuous king. Moreover, in pursuit of his French ambitions and, above all, in the need for money to finance his campaigns Henry undermined the principles of 'bone governance' to which he had committed himself. Henry reneged on his promise to pay his father's debts, exploited the defenceless widows of several noblemen, and arrested his own stepmother, Queen Joan of Navarre, on trumped up charges of witchcraft in order to seize her dower lands. Moreover, his unwillingness to grant away royal resources may explain his failure to create any new nobles or to endow existing Lancastrian supporters with sizeable estates in Normandy. Most importantly, there were signs that the treaty of Troyes was perceived as being a selfish and opportunistic bargain made by the king, acting in his own selfish interests rather than for the common profit. This was behind the Commons' fear in the parliament of December 1420 that the treaty might place Englishmen in 'subjection or obedience' to future kings of France, and the barely disguised expectation that the treaty would mean an end to wartime taxation.[8] By 1421, when the king made his final return to England, the strains on the Lancastrian polity were becoming evident. His new request for loans met with widespread misgivings and open refusals, while there is evidence that the landowning classes were becoming less enthusiastic about the prospect of serving in France. The parliament which met in May discussed the mounting royal debt and may have refused the king's request for taxation (a refusal which would have been made easier by the fact that England and France were officially now at peace). The assembly which met in December did grant a novel peacetime subsidy although this barely made a dent in the growing financial crisis.

Most damning of all Henry failed to provide any means for securing his conquests in France. His early death, on 31 August 1422, left the Lancastrian dream of a dual monarchy in the person of his nine-month old son, Henry VI. Henry's own will reveals a king more concerned with the salvation of his soul than the legacy he had left his son and servants. His provision of 20,000 masses was double the number that Henry VII would make nearly a century later and may hint at a guilty conscience. More tangibly, by placing much of the duchy of Lancaster's estates in the hands of feoffees for the performance of his will, he deprived his son's government of one of its most important sources of revenue. The codicils added to his will just five days before he died reveal a king who had given little thought to the 'bone governance' of his realm. His brother, Humphrey, Duke of Gloucester, was named protector and chief guardian to Henry VI, but they did not define his powers or responsibilities with regard to the government of the realm. Moreover, the impossibility of enforcing the treaty of Troyes was evident even as Henry languished *in extremis.* The English defeat at Baugé the previous year had revealed the scale of the military challenge the English faced in forcing acceptance of the treaty, while Duke Philip of Burgundy had emerged as a fickle ally.

The period from 1422 until Henry VI entered his majority in 1437 reveals one of the fundamental problems of the late-medieval English polity. In the final analysis, the strength and success of royal government was primarily dependant on the abilities and ambitions of the monarch. The treaty of Troyes had committed England to a costly and, in hindsight, virtually unwinnable war because of the personal ambitions of Henry V. In the fifteen years following his death the Lancastrian political establishment struggled to find institutions and methods of government that could protect the common profit of the realm. In other words, how could the body politic be made to work in the absence of its head? Initially at least stability was ensured by the co-operation of the nobility and the willingness of the political nation to act for the common good. In the parliament of 1422 the claims of the Duke of Gloucester to act as regent were defeated by the nobility, and again in 1425 his claims for pre-eminence were rejected in favour of the collective responsibility of the lords to govern until the king came of age. Nevertheless, royal government was to some extent paralysed by the royal minority. The 1420s were marked by a growing disengagement from the war in France, despite the Duke of Bedford's victory at Vernueil in 1424 (a feat which rivalled that of Agincourt). Parliament failed to grant taxation for the war between 1421 and 1429 and it was only galvanised into action by the French resurgence under Joan of Arc and the disasters at Orléans and Patay. The situation was now desperate and it was decided that Henry should cross the Channel in person to be crowned king of France. Before that, however, in December 1429 Henry had been crowned king of England and it was not until two years later that the provisions of the treaty of Troyes were finally realised and Henry was crowned king of France in Notre Dame Cathedral in Paris.

Nevertheless, all this merely papered over the cracks. The noble consensus was showing signs of strain. Local squabbles escalated with the king unable to effectively intervene and arbitrate in disputes between his greatest subjects. In 1432 Gloucester again made an unsuccessful bid for power, accusing his chief rival, the king's great-uncle, Cardinal Beaufort, of illegally importing bullion into the realm. By 1433 the royal finances were in a parlous state: a debt of £160,000 standing against an annual ordinary income of some £60,000. Without the necessary royal authority to overturn the treaty of Troyes the English were also outmanoeuvred in diplomacy. In 1435 the Burgundians concluded the treaty of Arras with the French and in the following year Duke Philip laid siege to the English stronghold of Calais. The perfidy of the Burgundians at least gave the English a renewed sense of purpose in the war in France. The death of the Regent of France, the king's uncle, John, Duke of Bedford, in September 1435 threatened serious consequences and in a remarkable act of national unity armies were assembled under the Duke of York and the Earls of Salisbury, Suffolk and Dorset. The latter was redirected to Calais and lifted the Burgundian siege before a relief army, led by Gloucester, could arrive. Nevertheless, the various expeditionary armies achieved

King Henry VI by unknown artist oil on panel, *c.* 1540
© National Portrait Gallery, London

very little: Paris was lost and the Burgundian alliance, the corner-stone of Henry V's war policy, was no more. The king, moreover, appears to have played little role in the events following the treaty of Arras, despite his well-documented anger at Duke Philip's treachery. Henry VI had begun to authorise grants by the sole authority of his signature in the summer of 1436, as Gloucester's expeditionary army assembled for the relief of Calais, but any plans for him to lead his armies in person seem to have been quickly abandoned. Nevertheless, the need for Henry to take a positive and public role in government was pressing and in November 1437, a month shy of his sixteenth birthday, he assumed the full powers of monarchy, ruling with the assistance of a formally constituted royal council.

1437–1449: THE GROWING CRISIS

The nature of kingship during the adult reign of Henry VI remains one of the most contested issues among historians of the Wars of the Roses. Stubbs regarded him as 'perhaps the most unfortunate king ever to have reigned'. Loyal, pious and committed to ruling England as 'a constitutional kingdom or commonwealth', he failed under the burdens of an ambitious nobility, a costly war in France and a physical and mental frailty unsuited to the rigours of kingship.[9] McFarlane was less charitable. Henry VI's inanity was the root cause of the Wars; he was simply unwilling to, or more likely incapable of, fulfilling his princely obligations and responsibilities. Bertram Wolffe, however, challenged this view of a king-shaped vacuum at the heart of the polity. While admitting that, despite 'a precocious interest in affairs of state from about 1434', Henry did not attend to matters of justice or the dispensation of patronage as carefully as he might, in one key area, the war with France, the king's 'perverse wilfulness' had disastrous consequences. Henry was committed to peace at any price and his 'own wilful efforts had divided, demoralised and hamstrung the English war effort, so that it had dissolved in defeat and recriminations'.[10] This view, in turn, was rejected by John Watts. He carefully delineated the duties of a late-medieval king and the expectations placed upon him and argued that Henry conspicuously failed to play any proper role in government. His adult reign before 1450, there-fore, witnessed an attempt by his counsellors, particularly William de la Pole, Earl and later Duke of Suffolk, to erect a façade of royal authority to mask the king's shortcomings. The polity could not, however, function without an active, adult king and thus, following the defeat in France, the realm collapsed into chaos.

The reality of Henry VI's kingship between 1437 and 1450 prob-ably lies somewhere between the extremes put forward by Watts and Wolffe. First, there is the inescapable conclusion that contemporaries were aware that Henry VI was not as well equipped for kingship as his father, or even his grandfather, had been. There were rumours throughout the 1440s that the king was childlike or somehow lacked the virtues necessary for effective rule. In 1437 he had been given control over the dispensation of patronage, but matters of state, partic-ularly the conduct of the war, were largely left to the council. By 1441 the council's formal influence of the king was waning and three years later an attempt to re-assert conciliar control over the dispensation of patronage failed, revealing an undercurrent of disquiet over the king's profligacy and grants to members of his household. Never-theless, even in regard to patronage and the exercise of royal grace we can discern some consistency in Henry's approach. The king was well served by a group of household servants, personally bound to him and unflinchingly loyal to the House of Lancaster and the memory of Henry V, and he rewarded them generously. Men like Suffolk and James Fiennes (a member of the royal household since 1438 and subse-quently chamberlain to both Queen Margaret and the king) had themselves played active roles in the war in France and had a personal commitment to the maintenance of the Lancastrian position there. These men, by and large, were committed to executing the king's will (particularly, from 1444, in regard to the foundation of his two colleges of King's, Cambridge, and Eton) and maintaining his public author-ity in the localities. Henry rewarded this loyal service consistently.

Most importantly, however, there is compelling evidence that by 1445 the king was committed to peace with France at all costs. Up to that point there was a general consensus that negotiation should take place from a position of military strength. Henry's secret offer to surrender the counties of Anjou and Maine in December that year broke that consensus. Men like Suffolk and the Dukes of York and Somerset were then left with a dilemma: whether or not to support and pursue this new royal policy which flew in the face of what they perceived to be the true Lancastrian legacy of defending Henry V's conquests and the English position in France. The unease that the king's preferred course of action generated can be sensed by Suffolk's extraordinary protestation before the parliament of 1445 that the truce of Tours and any suggestion of surrendering territory or titles had been the king's doing rather than his. Later, in April 1446, the lords as a body declared formally before the estates of your realm in parliament that the desire for peace and a planned meeting between Henry and Charles VII was solely the king's idea, 'Which seid mocions and sterings onely oure lorde hath liked to ster and meve you too, he knoweth, withoute that any of the lordes or other of your suggettes of this youre roialme, in any wise have stered or meved you soo to doo.'[11] Thus, while Henry VI clearly had little interest in the day-to-day business of government and little inclination to exercise the obligations he had recognised at his coronation, he had by his commitment to peace with France launched the Lancastrian polity on a new and ultimately disastrous path.

The consequences of the initial lack of royal direction and then the disastrous intervention of 1445 can be seen in both the war with France and the stability of the domestic polity. From the late 1430s until 1443 the war had been sustained by an alliance of the great lords (with the notable exception of the Duke of Gloucester) and money provided in the form of loans by Cardinal Beaufort. In 1439 peace negotiations, led by Beaufort and Archbishop Kemp, had come to nothing. The parliament of that year saw renewed attacks by Gloucester on Beaufort's policies and influence, but these too came to nothing and in June 1440 it was Richard, Duke of York, rather than Gloucester, who was appointed Lieutenant-General of Normandy. Throughout 1441 and 1442 the English situation in both Normandy and Gascony worsened and it was decided to launch a new expedition, again financed by Beaufort. Beaufort insisted, however, that his incompetent nephew, John, Duke of Somerset, should lead the army and the campaign turned out to be little more than a smash-and-grab raid into Maine in a vain attempt to carve out a French patrimony for Duke John. The expedition was a disaster and the Beauforts were discredited amidst accusations that the war was being pursued for private, covetous ends. The truce of Tours in July 1444 brought a much needed respite, not least because of the parlous state of royal finances, but the king's intervention in the following year turned a bad situation into a potentially catastrophic one. In 1446 Henry also gave his support to his childhood companion, Gilles, the younger brother of Francis, Duke of Brittany, in his claim to the ducal title. This brought the English garrisons in Maine into dangerous confrontation with Duke Francis, a vassal of the French king, Charles VII. In February 1447, perhaps in an attempt to silence his criticism of royal policy, Gloucester was arrested at the Bury parliament, subsequently dying in captivity. Nevertheless, the lords maintained their support of the king, and York, Suffolk and Fiennes (who was created Lord Saye and Sele), were among the beneficiaries of Duke Humphrey's fall. Henry's ill-considered intervention in Breton politics, however, would have far-reaching consequences. In March 1449 the English seized the Breton fortress of Fougères, in flagrant breach of the truce, and by the following July Charles had assembled an army with which to reconquer the Duchy of Normandy.

If the story of the English war effort in France in the 1440s is a dismal one, the record of Henry's government of England during the same decade is surprisingly positive. While it is undoubtedly the case that 'instead of the king ruling through his household, the household ruled through the king', it does not necessarily follow that the decade saw a descent into faction and local disorder.[12] It is still a commonplace among historians that the 'household clique', led by the Duke of Suffolk, exercised a malign influence of the dispensation of royal justice and the granting of patronage, while impoverishing the crown and upsetting local networks of power and influence. The evidence usually cited for this argument is the impressive range of grants and offices amassed by prominent courtiers, the accusations of corruption and misgovernment made in 1450, and the peculiar prominence afforded to the testimony of the Paston Letters. Nevertheless, it is clear that the noble consensus, which had ensured stability during the long minority, continued, at least initially, into Henry's majority. In 1437 leading nobles were granted the stewardship of various parts of the Duchy of Lancaster, an unusual move that may testify to their acceptance of the king's shortcomings. Moreover, during the 1440s the council proved remarkably successful in dealing with outbreaks of disorder and feuds between magnates. The violent dispute in Bedfordshire, for example, between Lord Grey of Ruthin and Lord Fanhope was settled by the council's arbitration in 1439; in 1443 the long-running feud between the senior and junior branches of the Neville family came to end; and in the same year the quarrel between Lord Bonville and the Earl of Devon (both of whom had been granted the stewardship of the Duchy of Cornwall by the king) was temporarily quietened by the council's intervention. These were instances of a generally held commitment among the king's leading subjects, led by Cardinal Beaufort and, increasingly, Suffolk, to uphold royal authority and ensure good governance, even if Henry himself remained largely unwilling, or incapable, to rule effectively.

Nevertheless, from around 1443 things began to change. At first this was due less to the 'malign' influence of the king's household servants than to a simple change of generation. Old Lancastrian stalwarts, like John, Lord Tiptoft, Henry Chichele, Archbishop of Canterbury, Walter, Lord Hungerford, and perhaps most importantly Cardinal Beaufort, gradually disappeared from the political stage, either by death or old age. In 1441 Gloucester's wife, Eleanor Cobham, had been arrested on the spurious charge of sorcery, thus effectively removing Duke Humphrey as a political force. In their place a new group emerged, led by Suffolk, and including courtiers, such as Sir Ralph Butler, Lord Sudeley, John Sutton, Lord Dudley, John, Lord Beaumont and Sir James Fiennes. The interesting thing is that these men were not necessarily younger than the men who had dominated the council during the minority, indeed some like Suffolk, Sudeley and Fiennes, had distinguished themselves in France under Henry V and during 1420s, but that their *locus* of power was the household and their personal relationship to the king. A new generation of ecclesiastical courtiers also emerged, such as William

Aiscough, king's confessor and Bishop of Salisbury, and Adam Moleyns, another household clerk who became keeper of the privy seal early in 1445 and Bishop of Chichester in the following year. These men, with their allegiance firmly committed to the king rather than some wider sense of Lancastrianism, dominated the government and interpreted and implemented the king's will throughout the 1440s. Their influence was felt both at the centre and in the localities and here too the mid-1440s saw a gradual shift in political power to new groups of individuals. In Kent, for example, the connections that had gathered around Cardinal Beaufort and the Duke of Gloucester, dominating the major county offices and based in the east of the county, were gradually eclipsed by a group of men associated with Sir James Fiennes. These men, often lawyers rather than soldiers, were based in the west of the county and exercised something approaching a monopoly of the major county offices from around 1443. Moreover, as the 1440s wore on local tensions increased, and concerns over the conduct of the war, the costs of the household and mounting royal debts intensified. In East Anglia Thomas Daniel, a household esquire but also something of a maverick who abused his proximity to the king, came into conflict from 1447 with both the Duke of Norfolk and his erstwhile patron, Suffolk. Similarly, the ennobling of Sir James Fiennes in February 1447 and the appointment of his young and inexperienced son-in-law, William Cromer, as bailiff of the duke of Gloucester's former lands in Kent in that year may have raised questions over Fiennes's role in Duke Humphrey's demise. In the following year another household squire, the notorious ruffian William Tailboys, sought the help of both Suffolk and Viscount Beaumont to protect him from various investigations into his violent conduct in Lincolnshire. What these incidents suggest is that by the late 1440s it was proving increasingly difficult for those in government to maintain a semblance of order given the king's spectacular failure to offer effective leadership at home and his even more disastrous intervention in the French war.

While the men who carried on the business of government in the king's name throughout the 1430s and early 1440s proved reasonably effective in maintaining local order, it was the collapse of royal finances that demonstrated above all the political bankruptcy of the Lancastrian regime. In the late middle ages effective royal finance relied on the king's political capital to convince the lords, knights and commons assembled in parliament to grant taxation, both direct (in the form of lay subsidies) and indirect (in the form of customs, especially the wool subsidy). Thus Edward I, Edward III and Henry V were able to raise large amounts of taxation and loans in anticipation of future taxation to finance their aggressive foreign policies and extravagance at home. Henry IV, as we have seen, struggled to convince parliament of his legitimacy and fitness to rule and his regime thus struggled to meet its debts and pay for the costs of defence and the household. As an adult Henry VI singularly failed to impress his subjects into granting him the taxes necessary to make government work. In the eight years from 1429 until 1437 parliament had granted direct taxation totalling £207, 821, but in the seventeen years between 1437 and 1453 they granted only £239,950, and most of that too late in the parliaments of 1450 and 1453. The Commons could have little confidence in the king. In 1443 part of the Duchy of Lancaster was again enfeoffed to meet the costs of the king's foundations at Cambridge and Eton; from 1444 the annual cost of the royal household more than trebled from £8,000 to £27,000; by 1449 the wages of the Calais garrison were £20,000 in arrears; and by that year the total royal debt had reached a staggering £372,000. In the 1430s and early 1440s the system had been kept working by private loans to the crown and the employment of merchants in the exchequer who had made their own mercantile credit networks available, but by 1449 the crown's political and fiscal credit was exhausted. With defeat in Normandy seemingly imminent, growing disorder in the localities, and its coffers empty, by September 1449, when writs were despatched summoning a new parliament, the Lancastrian regime was on its knees.

The fifty years from 1399 provided the essential preconditions for the Wars of the Roses. The nature of the change of dynasty in that year had long-lasting consequences. Not least among these was the appeal to 'popular' support made by Henry IV and the recognition of the role played by the wider political nation in conferring legitimacy on kings and their government. Much then depended on the crown's political capital and the king's personal abilities, and while Henry V's conquests in France undoubtedly strengthened Lancastrian kingship in the short term they also committed England to a lengthy and costly war with France. Henry's untimely death and the broad political consensus that ensured stability during his son's long minority partially hid these problems, but Henry VI's shortcomings would eventually exhaust the crown's credit, both in terms of money and political support. Yet Henry VI was no mere puppet of his unscrupulous councillors. If he had been then there is no reason why the system that had persisted from 1422 until 1437 could not continue into the 1440s and beyond. Henry did intervene actively, particularly in first seeking peace with France, then intervening in Breton affairs. His will, ill-considered and erratic as it was (although never, like Richard II, tyrannical), was implemented by his loyal household servants, particularly Suffolk. As we shall see, lacking a political language and culture that allowed them to challenge the king directly over his failures, the political nation looked for scapegoats to explain the deepening political, military and fiscal crisis.

2

THE PRELUDE TO WAR:
1449–55

The parliament that assembled at Westminster on 6 November 1449 did so amidst the news of the fall of Rouen, capital of Lancastrian Normandy, to Charles VII and the ignominious flight of the English Lieutenant-General, Edmund Beaufort, Duke of Somerset. If the fifty years after the Lancastrian usurpation had provided the essential preconditions for the Wars of the Roses, then in the five years following the parliament of November 1449 three crucial developments transformed the political situation into one where civil war was not only possible but likely.

First, the defeat in France led to a popular groundswell of opinion against the Lancastrian regime; the appeal to the commons that had been one of the foundations of Lancastrian rule would, in part, prove its undoing. Second, the personal rivalry between the Dukes of Somerset and York developed into one of national significance, drawing ever more of the political nation into what was, essentially, a private squabble between two great magnates. Finally, Henry VI's sudden mental collapse in the summer of 1453 threw the question of the king's fitness to rule into stark relief and opened up new possibilities for those who might wish to usurp his position.

DEFEAT, RECRIMINATION AND REBELLION

By the summer of 1449 there was evidence of a growing popular backlash against the Lancastrian government, its failures in France and the worsening economic situation. In some respects what was happening in 1448–9 was out the government's control. The 'Great Bullion Crisis' of the mid-fifteenth century was at its height and trade with Normandy, Poitou and Gascony had all but collapsed, while in 1447 Duke Philip the Good of Burgundy had placed an embargo on the import of English cloth into the Low Countries. To the political nation at large, however, the regime was thoroughly implicated in causing these problems. The royal household had misspent taxes, while greedy courtiers had embezzled the crown's money and lands. These sentiments probably lay behind the parliamentary Commons' call for the resumption of royal grants in the assembly of February 1449 and their refusal to grant taxation. Popular poetry and ballads circulated at this time naming those around the king as personally responsible, singling out the Duke of Suffolk, Lord Saye and Bishop Aiscough for particular opprobrium, while numerous indictments for treasonable words reflected a growing national sense of unease. Moreover, the actions of some men closely associated with the regime did little to dissuade this growing tide of popular opinion. Early in 1449 the Dartmouth shipowner, Robert Wennyngton, and two members of the royal affinity from Kent had been commissioned to guard the seas. Ships had been provided by other household men, such as Thomas Daniel, but instead of protecting the coast from French raids they had embarked on a campaign of privateering, notoriously robbing the Hanseatic, Flemish and Dutch ships of the Bay Fleet. The attack on the Bay Fleet caused a diplomatic incident, but for the commons it was evidence of how greed, self-interest and 'covetise' had replaced the common profit as the motivation at the centre of royal government.

On 9 January 1450 Adam Moleyns, the unpopular Bishop of Chichester, was murdered by a mob at Portsmouth. Rumours abounded that he had implicated Suffolk in treasonable dealings with the French. By the time the second session of parliament convened at London's

Dominican Friary by Ludgate on 22 January the Commons were determined to make the duke their scapegoat. They presented detailed, yet scarcely believable, charges that Suffolk had conspired with the French ambassadors and encouraged Charles VII to invade England. The duke had, they claimed, already fortified his castle at Wallingford in preparation. He also had designs on the throne himself, evidenced by his plan to marry his son to Margaret Beaufort, then his ward. On 28 January Suffolk was committed to the Tower. More charges followed, but on 12 February the king intervened preventing the lords from sending the bill of impeachment to the judges. Finally, on 9 March (with yet more charges laid against him detailing his abuses of power at home) Suffolk came to the parliament chamber, refuted the allegations and submitted himself to the king. Henry then made another of his characteristically disastrous interventions. On 17 March, in the king's 'innest chambre' within the palace of Westminster and in the presence of the lords, Henry listened to and dismissed the charges of treason against Suffolk. The duke was to be banished from the realm for five years from 1 May. There is evidence that the king's decision was made against the advice of his lords. Viscount Beaumont 'on the behalf of the seid lordes both spirituelx and temporelx, and by their advis, assent and desire, recited, said and declared to the kynges highnes, that this that so was decreid and doon by his excellence, concernyng the persone of the seid duke, proceded not by their advis and counsell, but was doon by the kynges owne demeanance and rule.'[1] He then asked for this statement to be enrolled on the parliament roll as a formal record of the king's wilfulness and the lords' misgivings. If Henry's decision was reluctantly accepted by the lords, the Commons were even less inclined to be generous. On 30 March parliament was prorogued and the king moved to Leicester. When the new session opened on 29 April the Commons at last received an act of resumption of royal grants, albeit one compromised by no less than fifteen modifying clauses and 186 individual exemptions, in return for a modest tax on incomes.

Suffolk's impeachment and his punishment did not, however, assuage popular opinion. In fact, if anything, it made it worse. The duke was granted a safe conduct to the Low Countries and set sail on 30 March, but his ship was intercepted by the *Nicholas of the Tower* in the Channel. Suffolk was subjected to an impromptu trial and beheaded by the crew with half a dozen strokes of a rusty sword. His body was then thrown ashore on Dover beach. Suffolk's murder was an extraordinary demonstration of popular political engagement. According to their indictment, his murderers had a clear understanding of the constitutional position and the king's obligation to listen to the community of the realm. Rumour and fear quickly reached a crescendo. News of the duke's murder had reached the Leicester parliament by 6 May and in Kent the sheriff, William Cromer, had rashly threatened that the county would as a result be turned into a 'wylde fforest'.[2] Kent was already on the brink of open rebellion. In January a rising in the east of the county, led by one Thomas Cheyne, had called for the death of Suffolk, Saye and others. It had been defeated by the resistance of the citizens of Canterbury and its ringleaders were executed. Suffolk's death changed the mood in the county and elsewhere and emboldened the commons to seek justice on more of the perceived traitors about the king. Moreover, the atmosphere of fear and retribution in its immediate aftermath forced people to take events into their own hands. By the end of May Kent was in uproar. Beginning in the area around Ashford, local communities, using existing institutions of communal organisation such as the commission of array, organised themselves to march upon London under the leadership of Jack Cade. They came, not as rebels, but as 'public petitioners for public justice to be done, and demonstrators of their own grievances and those of the realm'.[3] News quickly spread to the king at Leicester, parliament was dissolved, and Henry and his lords returned to London to meet the crisis.

By 11 June the rebels were encamped on Blackheath, just outside the city. They were met by a delegation led by Archishop Stafford of Canterbury and Cardinal Kemp of York, himself a Kentishman, to whom they presented their grievances. The king and lords were in no mood for compromise, however, and moved in force against the rebels a week later. However, they found the heath deserted. Nevertheless, a group of royal retainers, led by Sir Humphrey Stafford, decided to pursue the rebels into Kent. At Sevenoaks the royal force was ambushed and Stafford killed. This caused something of a panic among the king's party and on 19 June some demanded the arrest of Lord Saye, Bishop Aiscough and others. At this crucial juncture Henry's nerve failed him and he ordered the arrest of several of his household servants, including Lord Saye. On 25 June the king decided to abandon the capital altogether and by 29 June Cade's rebels were back on Blackheath. On 3 July they crossed London Bridge into the city and wrought their vengeance on the 'traitors': Saye and his son-in-law, Cromer, was summarily tried and executed, while proceedings were begun at the Guildhall against Thomas Daniel and other courtiers. The unrest spread had beyond the capital and on the same day Cade entered the capital a mob lynched Bishop Aiscough while he celebrated mass in Wiltshire. Cade's rebels, amidst much looting, had, however, outstayed their welcome in London, and on 5–6 July they were expelled from the city. On 7 July a royal pardon was offered to them, with the exception of their leader, and most seem to have dispersed peacefully. Cade was eventually taken on the Kent/Sussex border on 12 July and died of his wounds. The most serious popular uprising since the Peasants' Revolt of 1381 was over.

Cade's Rebellion was a pivotal event in fifteenth-century history but has received surprisingly little critical analysis from modern historians. Griffiths, Harvey, Wolffe and others have largely accepted the rebels' profession of their grievances at face value. The revolt was a local manifestation of national anger at the misgovernment of Suffolk and his cronies. Cade's rebels claimed to be the 'trewe comyns' representing the commonweal and they lamented the loss of Normandy, the impoverishment of the king and the commons, and the exclusion of 'trewe blode of the Reame' from the king's counsels. In Kent Lord Saye and the 'grete extorcioners' and traitors, Stephen Slegge, William Cromer, William Isle and Robert Est, had presided over a decade of misrule, enriching themselves at the expenses of the wider community.[4] Yet recent research has suggested that Kent in the 1440s was no more misgoverned than most other counties, nor, before 1448, is there much evidence of local animosity against Saye and his circle. In 1450 Suffolk, Saye and the king were ultimately victims of the government's failure to engage with public opinion and recognise that the approbation of the commons was one of the pillars upon which the Lancastrian polity was built. From 1399 politics had been conducted through a discourse with the political nation and its support was an essential bulwark to royal power. The king's reaction to the growing military, financial and political crisis of the late 1440s was to withdraw from Westminster and politics altogether. From 1448 the court became more itinerant, and the personnel involved in government, indeed the very business of government itself, contracted. In this way the actions of the king and those around him fuelled the growing perception that government was being conducted by a self-interested clique of household men. Without direction from the centre it was the commons, and what John Watts has characterised as their 'all-embracing, widely publicised and apparently authoritative critique' of royal government, that dictated the political agenda in 1449–50 and drove events.[5] This critique, of covetous, low-born counsellors subverting the common profit was a commonplace of political discourse in the later middle ages, but in the 1440s the commons were left to their own devices to fit events both in France and at home within this broad interpretative framework. In 1450 parliament reacted to a political process that had been instigated by a popular movement, driven by rumours, ballads and bills copied, posted in public places and read aloud to reach as wide an audience as possible. The language of traitors, evil counsellors and, most crucially, the commonweal that emerged in 1450 provided a framework for thinking, speaking and writing about politics that would endure for next two decades.

SOMERSET, YORK AND THE CRISIS OF COUNSEL

Richard, Duke of York (1411–60), was the greatest magnate of his age. He was descended from Edward III through both paternal and maternal lines, enjoyed the largest baronial income of the mid-fifteenth century (some £5,000 p.a.), and had been a key supporter of the Lancastrian regime, especially in France. Moreover, he was a man acutely aware of his own status and lineage. Yet more importantly perhaps for the politics of the 1450s, others too were aware of York's pedigree. To Cade's rebels he was the 'hye and myghty prince' who along with the other 'trewe lordes' would restore good government.[6] In April 1450 Henry VI had been confronted on his way to the Leicester parliament by John Harries, a Yorkshire shipman. Threshing the air with a flail, Harries had announced that 'the Duke of York then in Yreland shold in lyke manner fight with traytours at Leicester parliament and so thrashe them downe as he had thrashed the clods of erth in that towne'.[7] Harries was hanged, drawn and quartered for his ill-considered outburst, but he revealed an apparently widely held opinion among the commons that York was the champion of reform. In 1450 Duke Richard found himself, at first reluctantly, thrust forward as the saviour of the commonweal and antidote to the disastrous government of Henry VI.

Up to the point at least of his departure as Lieutenant-General of Ireland in June 1449 York had been a loyal and integral part of the Lancastrian regime. His birth had guaranteed him a position close to the throne and he had been elected to the Order of the Garter as early as 1433 in expectation of great things to come. His first taste of responsibility had come in 1436 when he was appointed the king's lieutenant in France. He appears to have relied on his elder brother-in-law, Richard Neville, Earl of Salisbury, and the experienced commander, John, Lord Talbot (from 1442 Earl of Shrewsbury), for both advice and practical assistance, but his first period of office appears to have been reasonably successful. A second period in command (from 1441 until 1445) was less auspicious militarily but the duke proved himself a capable administrator and diplomat. He was fully complicit in the negotiations for the truce of Tours in 1444, and he received the backing of his fellow lords the following year when Bishop Moleyns accused him of embezzlement. From 1446 he was among the leading figures in domestic government and benefitted personally, in terms of land and office, from the demise of Humphrey, Duke of Gloucester. By the late 1440s, however, his position was becoming more difficult. Despite his large income, he was living beyond his means and by 1450 the arrears of wages and debts owed to him by the crown had reached £26,000. Although York had not fared worse than many of the crown's other creditors – indeed, he had fared much better than some – his own financial problems may have confirmed for him the more widely held sense of crisis in 1449–50. There is also evidence that the duke may have left England for Ireland under something of a cloud. It was certainly not the exile that Cade's followers were later to claim, but on his return to England the following year York claimed that certain members of the king's household in north Wales had planned to ambush him both on his departure and when he returned. In Ireland York appears to have been worried about the lack of money to fund his campaign against the rebellious Gaelic chieftains and that the same accusations of incompetence and treason levelled against those in charge of the war in Normandy would be made against him. In June 1450 he wrote to the Earl of Salisbury (and possibly to other lords) complaining that without more money he would be forced to abandon his command. His letter hints at the fear that drove York at this time: 'it shall never be chronicled', he declared, 'that Ireland was lost by my negligence'.[8]

In the summer of 1450 York thus found himself reacting to a series of events over which he had little control and which threatened to destroy him. Cade's rebels and others had identified him as an antidote to the 'traitors' around the king who were subverting the commonweal; the king's household and the other targets of the commons' anger similarly identified the duke as their chief enemy; York himself feared he would be indicted for treason for giving support to Cade (who claimed kinship with the duke and took the alias John Mortimer) and that his position as heir presumptive would be undermined or worse. It was into this atmosphere of suspicion and rumours that York returned to England, probably in the last week of August. One contemporary reported that the king's household were 'aferd right sore' of the duke's return.[9] This fear lay behind the failed attempt by some members of the king's household to way-lay him on his route from North Wales and the duke's protestation of loyalty to the king in September. York's 'first bill', as it has become known, challenged those who had spoke out against the duke to confront him publicly before the king. He protested his loyalty and declared himself 'a true Knighte'. Henry appears to have accepted York's protestations of good faith at face value, the two were reconciled and the king admitted him 'as oure trew faithful subiecte and as oure weel bilovid cosyn'.[10] Shortly afterwards, however, in early October, York moved from being a private petitioner, seeking a confirmation of his own loyalty, into a public spokesman calling for reform of the commonweal. A second bill, addressed to the king but circulated widely and intended to be a public document, took up the call of Cade's rebels and the duke offered his services to ensure 'justice be had a yenst alle suche that [have] ben so endited or openly so noysed' of treason.[11] It was an extraordinary and inflammatory statement of the king's incompetence and an acceptance by the duke that the commons' calls for justice on the traitors were justified. Henry's response was forthright. He did not accept the duke's offer, instead the problems were to be addressed by a 'sad and so substantial council' which York was invited to join but in which he was to have no special importance. York was disappointed but not defeated. A third bill, addressed to the king and the lords, outlined the need for reform but crucially introduced a new angle of attack. For the first time the duke introduced the defeat in France as a result of the greed and evil counsel of those 'broughte up of noughte' and called, in language taken directly from Cade's manifestos, for counsel to be given by 'the trewe lordes and inespeciall the lordes of the mighti roiall blood'.[12] This bill seems to have been met with the same response as his previous complaint. York's campaign was reactive and sought its legitimacy in two contradictory ways: first, by an appeal to his position as chief magnate and (implicitly) as heir presumptive and, second, by an appeal to the commons. It failed because the duke badly misjudged the mood of his fellow peers and the king's steadfast loyalty to those around him. On 6 November 1450 a new parliament assembled at Westminster and the dynamics of politics shifted again.

The period from November 1450 until May 1455 was dominated by the bitter struggle between York and Edmund Beaufort, Duke of Somerset. The origins of their conflict were undoubtedly personal, but this soon merged with public issues and became a crisis of counsel; who was fit and proper to counsel the king in the interests of the commonweal? Edmund was the younger son of John Beaufort, Marquess of Somerset (*c*.1371–1410), John of Gaunt's eldest son by

Katherine Swynford. Like York, he had proved himself a capable soldier and loyal servant to the House of Lancaster. In December 1447 he had been appointed Lieutenant of France and as such had presided over the disastrous defence of the Duchy of Normandy in 1449–50. There is no evidence that York disapproved of his appointment, but Somerset's conduct, especially his surrender of the Castle of Rouen (of which York was still nominally captain) without a fight in October 1449, was considered dishonourable and treasonable by Duke Richard. For York this was a personal affront, and one heightened by Somerset's return from Normandy in August 1450 and his appointment the following month as Constable of England. As far as York was concerned his rival embodied the self-interested and dishonourable men who had undermined government at home and caused defeat in France. His dispute with Somerset was not the reason for his intervention in domestic politics in the summer of 1450, but by the autumn it was giving York's public campaign a much-needed focus. Duke Richard arrived in parliament in great pomp, with a sword carried before him and at the head of a large retinue. One of his leading servants, Sir William Oldhall, was elected speaker. A parliamentary petition called for the banishment of 31 individuals, led by Somerset, from court. The duke was promptly imprisoned in the Tower (albeit briefly), parliament enacted a more effective act of resumption than that passed in 1450, and York seemed in the ascendancy. However, during the following months whatever support Duke Richard could command among his fellow peers appears to have drifted away; the excluded courtiers returned to their posts and the inquiries in Kent failed to satisfy the commons or punish the 'traitors'. In May 1451 one of the MPs for Bristol, Thomas Young, called for York to be formally recognised as heir to the throne. His call appears to have been backed by the Commons but rejected out of hand by the lords and the king, who responded by immediately dissolving parliament. Whether this was a desperate attempt by York to recover his position or an unsolicited intervention by one of his supporters, its effect was to eclipse the duke's political power and return the control of the government to the king, his household and the peers in attendance upon him.

York's interventions in politics had now lost all semblance of legitimacy. His armed involvement on behalf of Thomas Courtenay, Earl of Devon, in his dispute with Lord Bonville in Somerset in September 1451 confirmed the duke's growing reputation among his peers as a disruptive and self-interested individual. York and his new ally, Devon, refused the king's summons to attend a council meeting in the midlands. In London and elsewhere attacks on his servants and proceedings for treason against Sir William Oldhall gathered pace. The king's household doubled the guard around Henry's person in the winter of 1451/2 amidst fears of a rising and an attempt on the king's life by York's supporters. Duke Richard now attempted to repeat the events of 1450. He dispatched open letters to the king protesting his loyalty and called for the removal of Somerset as a danger to the commonweal. In February 1452 he sent calls for his servants and tenants to attend upon him as he marched under arms to demonstrate his loyalty to the king and to remove Somerset. The king reacted promptly, ordering towns to close their gates to the duke, and assembling the lords around him. By 27 February York was encamped at Dartford, supported only by Devon and Lord Cobham. The royal host was three times larger than the duke's and the Earls of Salisbury and Warwick and many other peers accompanied the king. On 3 March Duke Richard submitted himself to the king and presented a set of now familiar articles against Somerset. Henry dismissed them and York was taken, under escort, back to the capital. A few days later at the high altar of St Paul's cathedral the duke solemnly swore that he would in future attend upon the king whenever summoned and never attempt anything by force of arms against the king or his subjects in the future. His humiliation was complete. He had posed as the champion of reform, driven by fear and his own exalted sense of himself; he had hijacked the commons' call for justice on the traitors, using their language to pursue his own personal dispute with Somerset; he had appealed to his fellow peers to support him and they, almost to a man, had failed to back him. In the crisis of 1450 the king's loyalty to his servants and the lords' commitment to uphold inalienable royal authority (whatever the shortcomings of the king himself) had proved stronger and more attractive than York's populist and opportunistic plans for reform. In March 1452 York had tried and failed to assert his claims to be the king's chief counsellor; little could he have imagined that within eighteen months the fates would have intervened again, the king would be reduced to total madness, and Duke Richard would preside over the government as protector and defender of the realm of England.

HENRY VI'S MADNESS, YORK'S FIRST PROTECTORATE AND THE ROAD TO WAR

The parliament that assembled at Reading on 6 March 1453 represented the high watermark of Henry VI's kingship. The king had seen off the challenges to his authority by rebellious subjects and troublesome magnates and he had agreed to an act of resumption in an effort to rescue the royal finances. Expectations were high that he would lead an expedition to recover Normandy in person, following the Earl of Shrewsbury's remarkable success in recapturing much of Gascony during the previous autumn. A grateful Commons made a life grant of the customs of tunnage and poundage (recalling the grant made to Henry V after Agincourt) and devised a generous subsidy to equip 20,000 archers for six months' service overseas, as well as attainting Sir William Oldhall and denouncing Jack Cade as a traitor. The Duke of Somerset was back in the ascendancy, while his rival York was conspicuous by his absence from the first two sessions of parliament (6–28 March and 25 April–2 July 1453). However, on 17 July Shrewsbury was killed leading an ill-advised attack on French gun emplacements laying siege to the Gascon town of Castillon. The English defeat did not lead to an immediate military collapse in the duchy and, although Castillon itself fell two days later, Bordeaux held out until late October. Shrewsbury's death and defeat nevertheless had a catastrophic effect on the king. On hearing the news in early August Henry, then on progress in the Savernake Forest in Wiltshire and attended only by his riding household, collapsed into a stupor, totally unable to speak, act or even at first to eat. He was to remain in this state for over a year.

If Henry had failed to live up to contemporary expectations of kingship for much of his adult reign, he had nonetheless been seen to go through the motions, listening to and responding to counsel and exercising his prerogative powers. On key occasions, such as the decision to release the Duke of Orléans in 1439, to press for peace in 1444–5, or when deciding to banish Suffolk or dismiss York's complaints against Somerset in 1450, Henry's active royal presence is the most convincing explanation of events. The situation in August 1453 was entirely different: when, in March the following year, a delegation of lords visited him to seek the appointment of a new chancellor following the death of Cardinal Kemp they met a king who could not respond to their entreaties in any way. After three attempts to communicate with the king they left 'in a state of hopelessly, unproductive, sorrowful embarrassment'.[13] By the autumn of 1453 a Great Council was effectively in control and in October York was summoned to London to attend its meetings. Immediately York's ally, the Duke of Norfolk, launched a fierce attack against Somerset, who was again accused of responsibility for the loss of Normandy and Gascony. Somerset was committed to the Tower on 23 November and York set about building a new regime. This new regime was, ostensibly at least, built on consensus and compromise. Duke Richard promised to do all 'that sholde or might be to the welfare of the king and his subgettes',[14] and there was to be no repeat of the attempted household purges of 1450. The birth of a son, Henry, to the king and queen in October had raised the spectre of Margaret of Anjou ruling as regent, something which the majority of lords had been keen to dismiss. Thus York's passage to pre-eminence among his fellow councillors was eased by his acceptance on 15 March 1454 of the young Prince Henry as heir to the throne, and on 27 March it was agreed in parliament that the duke should assume the title and duties of 'protector and governor of the realm' during the king's incapacity. York protested that this had arisen not from his own ambitions but from his acceptance of the necessity of the situation and in response to pleas from his fellow peers. As Ralph Griffiths has observed: 'To make him protector in the constitutional uncertainty of 1454 might be deemed by some a dynastic challenge on York's part and the duke may have regarded it in precisely the same light'.[15] In any case it seems certain that the protectorate was something arrived at only reluctantly by the lords, evidenced by the numerous protestations of infirmity, old age or youthfulness which several peers offered as excuses not to serve on the council.

Indeed, the expressions of unity made in parliament and council masked deepening and dangerous divisions among the nobility, some of which had already escalated into violent feuds by the winter of 1453/4. The Bonville/Courtenay dispute in the West Country, in which York had intervened in September 1451, rumbled on, complicated by the involvement of the Earl of Wiltshire, a nobleman close to the court, on the side of Lord Bonville. In 1452 the feckless Henry Holland, Duke of Exeter (who was also York's son-in-law), had seized Ralph, Lord Cromwell's manor of Ampthill in Bedfordshire. Cromwell's attempt to recover the property at law had met a violent response from Exeter who had attacked his rival in Westminster Hall in July 1453. Cromwell now looked for help and allied himself, through marriage, to the powerful Neville family. Maud Stanhope, Cromwell's niece and joint-heiress, was betrothed to the Earl of Salisbury's second son, Sir Thomas Neville. In August, having celebrated their nuptials at Tattershall Castle in Lincolnshire, the couple and their wedding party were attacked on their way north by Thomas Percy, Lord Egremont, the somewhat unstable younger son of the Earl of Northumberland, and his brother, Sir Richard Percy. The Percy/Neville feud, between the two greatest magnate families in the north, had its in origins in the 1440s over the families' respective influence on the Anglo-Scottish marches but it had reached a crisis because Lord Cromwell held some former Percy lands that the current earl now hoped to recover. This hope was now seriously threatened by the alliance between Cromwell and the ambitious Nevilles. The Nevilles' ambitions caused problems elsewhere too. In the midlands Salisbury's eldest son, Richard Neville had married Anne, the sister and principal heiress of Henry Beauchamp, late Duke of Warwick. This worsened his existing dispute with the Duke of Somerset, who was married to one of Anne's half-sisters, Eleanor. Richard, now Earl of Warwick in the right of his wife, clashed with Somerset over custody of the

Despenser lands in Glamorgan, South Wales. Warwick had held these during the minority of his cousin, George Neville, Lord Bergavenney, but in June 1453 the king had granted the custody to Somerset. By the autumn Warwick was holding them by force against Somerset and Lord Dudley to whom the earl had been ordered to surrender them. While tensions simmered in the midlands, south Wales and the West Country, it was in the north that matters came to a head. Early in 1454 the Duke of Exeter allied himself with the Percy Lord Egremont and in the spring, having opposed York's appointment and claimed the office of protector for himself, he went north to join his Percy allies. The renegade lords attempted to seize the city of York in May, but fled as the Duke of York travelled north with a large retinue to enforce justice. Exeter claimed sanctuary in Westminster abbey, but the judicial proceedings failed to punish the Percies and their servants. Instead, they were defeated by Sir Thomas and Sir John Neville at Stamford Bridge at the end of October; Egremont and his brother, Sir Richard Percy, were captured and imprisoned in Newgate in London, while Exeter was taken from sanctuary and incarcerated, under Salisbury's guard, in Pontefract Castle.

The king's illness, and York's protectorate, had thus been marked by an alarming breakdown in order. While later Yorkist chroniclers would conclude that 'for a whole year he governed most nobly and in the best way' and modern historians can congratulate him on his commitment to 'rule consultatively and representatively with the lords', the fact remains that a significant proportion of the political nation regarded the protectorate as partisan government at its worst, driven by self-interest rather than the good of the commonweal.[16] In part this was the inevitable conclusion of any government that was not led by the impartial authority of an active king, but it was also an impression reinforced by York's activities and the decisions made during his protectorate. On 2 April 1454 he secured the appointment of the Earl of Salisbury as Chancellor of England to replace the recently deceased Archbishop of Canterbury, Cardinal John Kemp. Kemp was a stalwart of the Lancastrian regime, a churchman who had served Henry V and been a voice of moderation throughout the 1440s and early 1450; the contrast with Salisbury could not have been lost on the regime's opponents. York's record at dealing with local disorder was mixed. Although he moved quickly and forcefully to quell disorder in Yorkshire, elsewhere he was less successful. The Derbyshire gentry who had sacked Sir William Blount's manor of Elvaston simply refused to answer the protector's summons, making the unfortunate messenger eat the writ, seal and all, while in Wales York failed to control Gruffydd ap Nicholas, whose violent behaviour made a mockery of the protector's authority. Even where he did intervene forcefully, such as in the West Country where he bound over his erstwhile ally, the Earl of Devon, to keep the peace, York's policies backfired and lost him much-needed support. More damning perhaps was the long imprisonment of Somerset without a trial. In the autumn of 1454 the protector attempted to instigate proceedings against his rival, but found little support among the other lords.

The end of York's first protectorate was signalled by the recovery of the king around Christmas 1454. The basis for the Duke's government dissolved and calls for the release of Somerset grew. On 26 January Duke Edmund was released from the Tower on condition that he remained at least 20 miles distant from the king. This was probably small consolation to York who surrendered his office, possibly at the same council meeting that settled terms for Somerset's release. Power now passed back to the king and his household. On 4 March the council, with the king present, lifted the restrictions on Somerset's movement and repudiated the charges against him. York was forced to submit the matters between him and his rival, now reduced to a private squabble rather than a fundamental question of public government, to the arbitration of his fellow peers. Moreover, the office of captain of Calais, granted to York in July 1454, was taken back into the king's hands only to be bestowed on Somerset two days later. This was a deliberate affront to York, who had accused Somerset of military incompetence and worse only to see the most important command in the realm given to his rival, but it also demonstrated a reassertion of the royal authority. York's influence about the king was now gone: on 7 March Salisbury resigned the Great Seal; a week later Exeter was released from Pontefract Castle; and on 15 March the Earl of Wiltshire, Somerset's ally, replaced the Earl of

Worcester as Treasurer of England. Grants of office and patronage that had been made to York and his allies during the protectorate were now cancelled and redistributed among men close to the king. In mid-April Henry and his council resolved to summon a Great Council to meet at Leicester, in the heart of the Duchy of Lancaster lands. York and his Neville allies, perhaps justifiably, feared a repeat of the events of February 1447 when Humphrey, Duke of Gloucester, had been summoned to the Bury parliament only to be arrested on charges of treason. They decided to withdraw from Westminster, leaving without apparently asking permission of the king. The battle lines for the opening engagement of the Wars of the Roses were now drawn.

The period from the autumn of 1449 until the spring of 1455 drew together the various strands that made civil war virtually inevitable. Defeat in France led to recrimination at the centre of the Lancastrian regime, shattering the broad consensus that had maintained stability since the death of Henry V. It also triggered a popular backlash against the government, driven both by peculiar local circumstances and a vaguer belief, fuelled by rumour and fear, that the commonweal was under attack. The commons of Kent, Essex, Wiltshire and elsewhere who rose in the summer of 1450 did so not because they had been victims of an oppressive regime and tyrannical king but because they had no other explanation, other than the widely understood discourse of good and bad counsellors, traitors and greedy courtiers, for the fiscal, military and political calamity that had befallen them. The Lancastrian regime that had looked to and engaged the commons in a bid for legitimacy now found itself reacting to their calls for change. The commons were not the only part of political society that took up the existing discourse of 'clamour' and the call for reform. Richard, Duke of York, returned from Ireland not as the champion of reform but as one fully implicated in the regime's decisions and actions of the past decade and fearful that the accusations levelled against the Duke of Suffolk and other leading counsellors might also be directed against him. York may or may not have been convinced by the rhetoric of opposition in 1450, but by the time he made his stand at Dartford in 1452 he appears to have believed that his political opponents were determined to destroy him. Moreover, he was prepared to use force to defend himself and assert his rightful place in the king's counsels. In all these events Henry VI remains an enigmatic figure. It seems unlikely that he was a mere cipher, first of the Duke of Suffolk, then Somerset, and his interventions at key moments of crisis changed the course of events as did, in a very different way, his collapse in the summer of 1453. Up until that moment he was to all intents and purposes an adult, ruling king and, although clearly lacking in many of the qualities needed of a medieval monarch, his greatest subjects respected his authority. For some seventeen months, however, the restraints of kingly government were removed. York's authority as protector proved insufficient to maintain order among his fellow magnates. The duke's government was thus necessarily partisan and collapsed, leaving a deadly legacy of mistrust and fear, when Henry, albeit briefly and probably only partially, recovered his faculties around Christmas 1454.

Part 2

COURSE

3

FIRST BLOOD:
THE BATTLE OF ST ALBANS
1455 AND ITS AFTERMATH

Something fundamental happened in the streets of St Albans on 22 May 1455. An attack by Richard, Duke of York, and his Neville allies, the Earls of Salisbury and Warwick, upon the king's party transformed the nature of politics. By coming *vi et armis* ('with force and arms') against King Henry VI, his banner unfurled, their actions had removed the restraint on violence against the monarch. As in 1452, York protested that he acted not against the king but against the traitors in his midst, namely York's arch-rival the Duke of Somerset. At the end of the skirmish Somerset was dead (alongside the Nevilles' rivals, the Earl of Northumberland and Lord Clifford) and York had imposed his will upon the king by force of arms. Yet in many ways the first Battle of St Albans was a false beginning to the Wars of the Roses; it heralded a period of 'phoney war' in which the partisans of each side ostensibly sought reconciliation and compromise, while the majority of the political elite attempted to maintain the broad consensus that had ensured stability during the already long and troubled reign of Henry VI. This chapter will explore both the preparations for war and the efforts for peace. The period between the first Battle of St Albans and the next outbreak of open conflict, at Blore Heath on 23 September 1459, witnessed a steady hardening of attitudes on both sides which threatened to force more and more of the political nation into making a choice between the Houses of Lancaster and York.

THE BATTLE OF ST ALBANS AND YORK'S
SECOND PROTECTORATE

As they had been in 1450, the Duke of York's actions in May 1455 were determined by concerns over his own safety. The king's council had met at Westminster in April and determined to summon a Great Council to meet at Leicester the following month. Its ostensible purpose was to provide for 'the king's safety', but it was most probably designed to settle the dispute between York and Somerset, almost certainly in the latter's favour. According to their letter to the chancellor, Archbishop Bourchier, on 20 May, the Yorkist lords feared they had been deliberately excluded from the meeting and complained that 'we conceyve a jelosy had ayenst us'.[1] York may also have been haunted by the spectre of Humphrey, Duke of Gloucester, summoned to a parliament at Bury St Edmunds in February 1447 only to be there arrested and die in mysterious circumstances. Duke Richard's whereabouts in early May are obscure, but he probably went north to his castle at Sandal in Yorkshire and set about raising an army with the help of his Neville allies. The court's response was dilatory and confused. The king remained in Westminster and only on 18 May despatched letters asking for armed men to be sent to him in all possible haste. The following day York, Salisbury and Warwick received letters under the great seal ordering them to disband their forces under pain of forfeiture. On 21 May the king and his household, accompanied by the Dukes of Somerset and Buckingham and a handful of other lords, left Westminster for Leicester. By this time the Yorkists were encamped at Ware from where they answered the chancellor's orders for them to disband and wrote directly to the king. They protested their loyalty, their concern for Henry's safety and their determination to have justice against their enemies and traitors to the commonweal who sheltered 'undre the wynge of your mageste roiall'.[2] The letter was handed to the king's confessor who delivered it to the Earl of Devon in the king's quarters in the early hours of 22 May. It was later alleged that this communication was concealed from the king by Somerset and two household servants, Thomas Thorpe and William Joseph.

At this point Henry appears to have made one of his characteristically idiosyncratic interventions. Perhaps in a forlorn attempt to appease York and his allies, he replaced Somerset with the Duke of Buckingham as Constable of England and commander of the royal forces. Buckingham argued against meeting the Yorkists in open battle and instead the royal party prepared to travel the seven miles from Watford to St Albans, with plans to be there around midday. Buckingham perhaps hoped that in this way York would put off his attack and instead negotiate when more lords and bishops arrived from London. Duke Richard, however, had already moved to St Albans and his forces, superior to the king's in both number and prowess, awaited the royal party's arrival in the town. A brief attempt at further negotiation followed but it seems that York, and perhaps more importantly the Nevilles, had decided that their ends were only to be met by violence. The fighting, in which the earl of Warwick and the northerners led by the Neville retainer, Sir Robert Ogle, played a leading role, was short-lived. The king's banner was unfurled in the market place but it seems that his household showed little taste for the fight (indeed, it is possible that some of those close to the king were sympathetic to York). The battle soon developed into a rout with some of the king's men shedding their armour and fleeing. Henry was himself wounded in the neck, while Somerset was cut down attempting to flee the house in which he found himself besieged. There were probably few other casualties, but the Earl of Northumberland and Thomas, Lord Clifford, were cut down, perhaps targeted in a deliberate act of vendetta by the Nevilles. Indeed, after the battle while York was ordered to provide obits and pay compensation to Somerset's widow, Warwick was ordered to compensate the children of the dead Lord Clifford. Moreover, the aspect of personal feud is further highlighted by one later Yorkist chronicler who observed that 'when the seyde Duke Edmonde [of Somerset] and the lordes were slayne the batayle was ceased'.[3]

The king's return to London highlighted the new political order imposed by the Battle of St Albans. Henry entered the capital flanked by York and Salisbury with Warwick ahead of them bearing the royal sword. On 25 May York placed the crown on Henry's head in a solemn crown-wearing ceremony at St Paul's. The following day the king despatched writs summoning a parliament for 9 July. The mood was ostensibly one of conciliation. All discussion of the battle was forbidden and among the king's men only Lord Dudley and the Duke of Exeter were arrested; a special parliamentary pardon exonerated the Yorkist lords and blamed the battle on the deceit of Somerset, Thorpe and Joseph. Yet the parliamentary Commons contained a significant minority of men loyal to York; the speaker, Sir John Wenlock, had been dismissed as chamberlain to Queen Margaret in 1454 because, as the king had told him, 'in the untrewe troubelous tyme ye favored the duc. Of .Y. and suche as longed to hym'.[4] Moreover, as one well-informed contemporary noted, after the bill attributing blame to Somerset had passed 'mony a man groged full sore'.[5] A major redistribution of offices demonstrated that political power had been transferred to York, at least temporarily. The duke was made Constable of England and given command of castles in Wales formerly held by Somerset. Most importantly, Somerset's captaincy at Calais was granted to Warwick and he and York now began the tricky business of negotiating with the soldiers and wool merchants for the payment of the garrison's wages to secure the earl's entry into the strategically vital town. One final piece of business, probably enacted in the first session of the new parliament, testified to the partisan agenda of the assembly. The Commons introduced a bill, which passed both Houses, rehabilitating Humphrey, Duke of Gloucester, and asking that proclamation be made to the effect that he had been the king's faithful liegeman until the day of his death. By associating himself with Gloucester, fast-emerging as the erstwhile champion of reform and leader of the opposition to Henry VI's corrupt counsellors, York staked his own claim to lead the commonweal to better things.

Nevertheless, York was not king nor was he the 'only authority' in the realm as some historians have claimed.[6] Henry VI was still king, even if his royal presence and will were felt increasingly seldomly. York's government appears to have enjoyed little support among his fellow peers, at least if their parlous attendance at parliament is any measure of their commitment to the new regime. It may have been to consolidate his position and transfer real power to an aristocratic council led by himself that York engineered the events of the second session of the parliament of 1455. This assembled at Westminster on 12 November amidst news of further, violent disorder in the localities. In the West Country the Courtenays continued their feud against Lord Bonville, notoriously murdering his servant, the locally prominent lawyer Nicholas Radford, while trouble also flared up in the midlands and in London. In the king's absence York was named as his lieutenant in parliament, but the Commons demanded that the duke once more be appointed protector to deal with the disorder; the hearing of petitions for justice, they argued, 'shuld be overe grevous and tedious to his highnesse'.[7] There is no contemporary evidence that the king had again lapsed into a state of full mental collapse similar to that which had necessitated York's first appointment as protector, and it is probable that the duke and his followers in the Commons pressed for his reappointment regardless of any sudden change in the king's position. The Commons' request, communicated not by Speaker Wenlock but by York's servant William Burley, was at first refused by the lords. On 17 November, however, the lords reluctantly agreed to his appointment as protector until such time as the king, with the advice of the lords in parliament, ended it. In effect power was now in the hands of the council, with York at its head, but even under these circumstances the duke's ability to govern was circumscribed by the presence of the king. In all matters touching 'the honour, wurship and suertee' of the king's person, a deliberately broad and undefined term, the council was to notify Henry of its decisions, presumably so he might, if he chose to, alter them.[8] On 13 December parliament was prorogued to allow York to travel west to deal with the Courtenays and the Bonvilles. Both parties were soon under arrest and, although York himself never made it as far as Devon, the protector and council, on the face of it at least, had restored order.

York's ambitions, however, did not stop there. The Commons were once again pressing for an act of resumption of royal grants. Ostensibly this was a familiar attempt to restore sound royal finances, but it also sought to limit expenditure on the royal household and interfere in enfeoffments made of Duchy of Lancaster lands. This threatened to curtail the independent power of the crown. Perhaps emboldened by his apparent success in restoring order in the West Country, York threw his weight behind the Commons' call for resumption when parliament reassembled on 14 January 1456. Attendance among the lords seems to have been no better than before and York and the Earl of Warwick turned up with large, armed retinues. The suggestion that York's authority rested on military might cannot be ignored and contemporaries appear to have accepted that the continuation of his position as protector and 'chief and princepall councellor' depended on his ability to push through the Commons' call for resumption and limits on the freedom of future royal patronage.[9] The proposed act of resumption found little support among the lords. It eventually passed, but those aspects of the original petition designed to curtail royal freedom were omitted. The Duchy of Lancaster lands in the hands of feoffees were excluded, the plan to limit the queen's dower to 10,000 marks (£6,666 13s. 4d.) was dropped, and the king was not required to submit exemptions from the act to the scrutiny of the Commons. This was a clear failure for York. He did not, as some historians have suggested, resign from his office as protector; rather, in accordance with the terms of his appointment, on 25 February he was removed by the king in person, acting upon the advice of his lords spiritual and temporal. Although the duke was compensated financially (to the tune of £1,806, sums owed to him both from his first protectorate as well as for his duties during the present parliament), this may have been designed by the more moderate among the lords to placate him and remove a potential source of grievance rather than a genuine expression of thanks for his service. York, however, may have read his dismissal in other ways. His support for the Commons' call for resumption had failed, nor had he been able to establish the type of political ascendancy his victory at St Albans had promised. According to one source, the duke and king argued soon after his dismissal from office and York had certainly left Westminster before the parliament ended on 9 March.

QUEEN MARGARET AND THE LANCASTRIANS

The period following York's dismissal as protector in February 1456 and the outbreak of renewed conflict in September 1459 is one of the more obscure of the entire fifteenth century. One thing seems certain, however: the political role of the queen, Margaret of Anjou, increased in importance during this time and she emerged as the focus of Lancastrian loyalism and of the opposition to the Duke of York. Margaret (b.1430) was the younger daughter of René, Duke of Anjou and king of Naples, a direct relation of the kings of France. As such her espousal to Henry VI in 1444 was a vital part of the diplomatic rapprochement between England and France, culminating in the truce of Tours sealed just four days after their formal betrothal. Until 1453 she appears to have played a conventional role as queen consort, acting as mediator and patron, as well as developing close connections to the Duke of Suffolk and other leading members of the Lancastrian affinity. The king's illness in the summer of 1453 and the birth of their first son, Edward (created Prince of Wales on 15 March 1454), transformed her situation. Her attempts to establish a regency in January 1454 were thwarted by a lack of support among the lords, probably a reflection of her inability to provide the necessary military leadership, and led to the establishment of York's first protectorate. There can be little doubt that from this time Margaret considered York to be a threat to the Lancastrian dynasty in general and to her son in particular. These fears can only have been exacerbated by the death of her close ally, the Duke of Somerset, at the Battle of St Albans and the deliberately meddlesome offer made by the Scottish king, James II, in May 1456 to support Duke Richard's claim to the throne. Contemporaries recognised her importance in the opposition to York's second protectorate. This centred upon defeating the Commons' demands for resumption, and one observer characterised her as 'a grete and stronge laboured woman, for she spareth noo peyne to sue hire thinges to an intent and conclusion to hir power'.[10]

By the spring of 1456 what little authority still resided in the person of Henry VI was rapidly disappearing. Although government was naturally carried out in the king's name and he continued to sign council warrants and other instruments of government until 1460, real power was widely assumed to lie with Margaret. The queen and prince retired to her dower lands in the midlands shortly after the dissolution of parliament. Thereafter, Lancastrian power was centred upon the Duchy of Lancaster honours of Tutbury, Leicester and Kenilworth, and the city of Coventry emerged as the Lancastrian 'capital'. In the middle of August Henry moved to join his queen. Bertram Wolffe characterised this retreat to the midlands as 'the actions of the rash and despotic queen',[11] but it can equally be seen as a desperate attempt to secure what remained of Henry's authority and protect Lancastrian interests from the increasingly aggressive designs of the Duke of York. Henry, despite his increasingly evident short-comings, was still king and control of his person and the process of counsel was of paramount importance. The summer and autumn of 1456 were characterised by fear and rumour. Tales spread of an armed clash in which Viscount Beamount had been killed and the Earl of Warwick injured, while the violent actions of York's servants and supporters in Wales only served to justify the defensive measures taken by the Lancastrian court. The defences of Kenilworth Castle were strengthened and, in December, the London merchant, John Judde, was commissioned to procure and manufacture ordnance and other weapons of war.

It was almost certainly to further secure the reins of royal govern-ment that a Great Council was summoned to meet at Coventry on 7 October 1456. York and Warwick did attend, but key changes in the major administrative offices signalled that they were becoming marginalised in the decision-making processes. On 26 September the queen's chancellor, Lawrence Booth, was named as the new keeper of the privy seal, the prime instrument of government business (espe-cially in regard to finance and the distribution of patronage). On 5 October the Earl of Shrewsbury replaced Viscount Bourchier as treasurer, and six days later Archbishop Bourchier surrendered the Great Seal to William Waynflete, Bishop of Winchester, king's confes-sor and a man devoted to the personal service of Henry VI. Further institutional changes sought to protect the interests of the Lancas-trian royal family. In February 1457 the newly established council of the Prince of Wales was given formal control of his patrimony. It included Booth, his brother Archbishop Robert of York, Waynflete, Humphrey Stafford, son and heir of the Duke of Buckingham, the Earls of Shrewsbury and Wiltshire, Viscount Beaumont, and Lords

Dudley and Stanley. There can be little doubt that this body sought to extend Lancastrian control at the expense of the Duke of York and his followers. In April, for example, the disputed castles of Aberystwyth and Carmarthen were taken from York and granted to the king's half-brother, Jasper Tudor. Money remained an overriding concern for the Lancastrians. The parliament of 1455 had not granted supply and the royal households were forced to rely on their prerogative of purveyance (the compulsory purchase of foodstuffs and other supplies below their market price). This, of course, risked engendering popular opposition and it may be these fears that explain why the king spent at least a third of his time between August 1456 and July 1460 enjoying the hospitality of various religious houses. In many ways the normal mechanisms of public, royal finance broke down in these years. The Lancastrian court retreated into itself, the volume of government business diminished and what remained, particularly in terms of financing the royal households, depended increasingly on the private resources of the Duchy of Lancaster. A good example of this is the increased importance of William Grimsby, the treasurer of the king's chamber and keeper of his jewels, who from the autumn of 1456 until September 1457, when Henry returned to the Home Counties and London, regularly travelled between the midlands and the Exchequer at Westminster taking cash for the use of the king. In October 1458 he became deputy-Treasurer of England, an indication of how ostensibly public offices were being subjugated to the private needs of the Lancastrian royal family. When the king returned to the midlands in May 1459 Grimsby emerged as the principal messenger between the government at Westminster and the court in Coventry.

It is, however, too simplistic to assume that power had passed completely to the queen and the group of committed Lancastrians who now emerged to support her and her son, the Prince of Wales. Many, if not most, of the lords remained uncommitted to either the Duke of York or to the Lancastrian party solidifying around the queen. The council at Westminster continued to meet regularly and transact business, even if this had contracted in volume. Judicial business, in particular, seems to have continued under the guidance of the council, with special commissions of inquiry attempting to dispense impartial justice on a range of local disputes. The Earl of Salisbury, absent from the council since the middle of 1456, had returned in November, while York also played a prominent part in its deliberations. In February or March 1457 a large and representative Great Council met at Coventry. It was the occasion for a concerted attack on the Yorkist lords, led by Chancellor Waynflete, probably at the queen's instigation. Nevertheless, the French raid on the Kentish port of Sandwich at the end of August that year that put the brake on any immediate slide into faction. The French attack coincided with the king's return to London and the issue of commissions of array for most of the southern and midland counties. It was, as John Watts suggests, most likely the broadly based, inclusive council of nobles and leading churchmen then gathered at Westminster who initiated the attempt at reconciliation between the Yorkist lords on the one hand and the queen and the relatives of those lords killed at St Albans on the other.[12] This process culminated in the so-called 'Loveday' of March 1458. In November 1457 the Percies had already been persuaded to submit their dispute with the Nevilles to the arbitration of the council, and this prepared the ground for a further Great Council meeting on 28 February 1458, attended by both the Yorkist lords and their enemies, where a settlement was brokered.

If the majority on the council had high hopes for the projected reconciliation they were soon to be disappointed. One reason for this, as we shall see, was the continued fear and suspicion of each other that dominated the thoughts and actions of the principals. A more immediate reason was that both the settlement brokered by the lords (and encouraged, it seems, by the king himself) and its formal recognition at the 'Loveday' ceremony at St Paul's on 25 March 1458 highlighted the essentially private and personal nature of the dispute between the rival camps. This in turn further undermined the king's government which had conspicuously failed to offer the higher authority to which both sides were willing to submit. The council's award in effect attributed blame to York and his adherents, going some way to reversing the account presented in the parliament of 1455. The Yorkists had been the first to draw blood and the award required them to make amends by endowing a chantry chapel at St Albans for the souls of the deceased. Both Somerset's heir and widow and Clifford's heir were compensated, while the damages due to the Nevilles from the Percies for their actions in 1453/4 were forgotten in an effort to end that dispute. While the Earl of Salisbury seems to have acquiesced in the council's decision, for York it represented his failure to convince his fellow lords of the justice of his cause. His platform for reform, his stand against Somerset as a traitor, and his defence of the common-weal were reduced to a petty, personal squabble. The symbolism of the 'Loveday' itself was telling. Salisbury processed to St Paul's hand-in-hand with the new Duke of Somerset, and York likewise with Queen Margaret. This charade both explicitly recognised the existence of two, rival armed camps and ignored the public nature of York's grievances, presenting the political crisis purely and simply as one of private feud. Thus it was a triumph for Queen Margaret and the Lancastrians in as much as it upheld the legitimacy of Henry VI's government and its ability to resolve conflicts between the king's greatest subjects. Ironically, however, this reconciliation also ended once and for all any prospect of a peaceful resolution of the crisis.

YORKIST FEARS AND FAILURE

Since his returned from Ireland in the autumn of 1450, one consistent motive had dominated Richard, Duke of York's decisions and actions: fear. In the first instance his return from Ireland had been to counter any allegations of wrongdoing on his part and rumours that connected him to Cade's Rebellion. The attempted coup at Dartford two years later was motivated by his failure to remove the Duke of Somerset from the king's confidence, and a justified fear that his political eclipse would lead to financial ruin or worse. His first protectorate and Henry VI's mental collapse allowed York to fulfil his own perception of himself as the king's leading subject, but it also provided his enemies with more grievances against him once the restraining hand of the king was removed. When Henry recovered his limited faculties, however, York's fortunes were even more tied to the idiosyncratic behaviour of an increasingly enfeebled monarch. The attack on the royal party at St Albans was made out of sheer desperation.

Duke Richard simply could not allow the unfavourable settlement of his dispute with Somerset which the Great Council due to meet at Leicester threatened. While York may have been heralded by some at the time (and by many more after his death) as the champion of reform and he may have grown to see his own priorities as consistent with the better government of the commonweal, it was his failure to achieve his ends by 'constitutional' means and a genuine fear of his own security that led him to take up arms against the House of Lancaster.

Once the king and queen had moved to Coventry in the autumn of 1456 it was not hard to escape the perception of their growing hostility towards the duke of York and his allies. Even if Duke Richard did not at first respond himself with violence, the actions of his servants could be certainly be construed as direct assaults on royal authority. The most notorious incident came in South Wales. By the summer of 1456 the king's half-brother, Edmund Tudor, Earl of Richmond, had successfully wrested control of several key Welsh strongholds from the notorious ruffian, Gruffydd ap Nicholas. The problem was that command of two of these, Carmarthen and Aberystwyth, had been granted to York. In August two of the duke's retainers, Sir William Herbert and Sir Walter Devereux, assembled a force of some 2,000 men and took both castles by force, imprisoning Richmond. Both men were summoned to answer the king for their actions, but Herbert escaped and attempted to raise men from York's and the Nevilles' marcher lordships in the winter of 1456/7. It was not until June 1457 that Herbert finally submitted himself to the king. How far York was behind his servants' actions is unclear, but events in South Wales certainly heightened tensions between the Yorkist lords and their rivals. There were rumours that both York and the young Duke of Somerset, Henry Beaufort, would be 'distressed' at the Great Council meeting in October 1456.[13] In November the Dukes of Exeter and Somerset and the Earl of Shrewsbury allegedly tried to ambush Warwick as he rode to London, while the following month the mayor of Coventry had to intervene to prevent Somerset attacking York. It was Herbert's continued resistance that almost certainly led to York's summons to a further Great Council meeting at Coventry in February 1457.

Although the evidence for its proceedings comes principally from the later attainder of the Yorkist lords in the parliament of November 1459, there is no reason to doubt that it was anything other than a concerted attempt to humiliate and punish the Duke of York. The new chancellor, Bishop Waynflete, accused York of jeopardising the safety of both the realm and the king's person. The Duke of Buckingham and the other lords pleaded with the king to intervene and warn York and any other lord who again resorted to violence that they would be punished 'aftre ther deserte'. Duke Richard and the Earl of Warwick (whose father, Salisbury, did not attend the meeting) swore on the gospels not to attempt anything in future by 'wey of fayt'.[14]

For the Yorkist lords the message was clear: their enemies at court were gathering their resources for a final attack. For York himself it was particularly dangerous as groups and individuals unconnected to him continued to advance his name as the champion of reform and a rival to Henry VI for the throne itself. In May 1456 a new uprising in Kent, led by one John Percy of Erith, had again linked the duke with the Mortimer claim to the throne, while James II's mischievous offer to help him gain the throne of England can only have poured fuel on the fire. In September, while York stayed in London, a particularly grisly comment was made on his political ambitions: five dogs' heads were impaled on stakes outside the Bishop of Salisbury's house where he lodged. Each had a verse held in its jaws, suggesting that York, the son of a traitor, was 'that men that all men hate/ y wolde hys hede were here for myne/ ffor he hath caused all the debate.'[15] The Yorkist lords faced a dilemma: they could either absent themselves totally from the processes of government and counsel, leaving the field clear for their enemies, or they could attempt another coup along the lines of that initiated at St Albans in 1455. Although Warwick could, and did, retire to his command at Calais (from where he conducted a campaign of piracy against foreign merchants that ingratiated himself with the Londoners and men of the south-east), absence from the political spotlight was not really an option for the Duke of York. He may have genuinely believed his rhetoric that the king was surrounded by traitors and corrupt counsel who planned his destruction and the subversion of the commonweal, but his wealth and 'worship' as a great lord and his ability to command the obedience of his servants also depended on his position at the centre of government. To do nothing was not an option.

Thus when York, Salisbury and Warwick arrived in London early in 1458 to attend another Great Council meeting they did so at the head of large armed retinues, implicitly threatening to impose their will by force as well as to defend themselves from the rival retinues of the Dukes of Somerset and Exeter and the Percies. Strenuous efforts were made by the city authorities to keep the rival camps apart, including 5,000 soldiers employed to patrol London's streets. Nevertheless, as we have seen, the Great Council meeting did not descend into violent chaos and, perhaps out of deference to the king's wishes, the sham reconciliation of the 'Loveday' took place on 25 March. The Yorkist lords remained in and around the capital in the wake of the 'Loveday' while the queen retired again to the midlands (leaving Henry to itinerate pointlessly between St Albans, Windsor and various royal lodges in the Thames Valley), but soon active preparations were afoot against York and his allies. The queen returned to London in the autumn. Purchases of weaponry continued to strengthen the royal household, while appointments to local office attempted to secure the provinces against the Yorkist lords. In November an attempt on Warwick's life by members of the royal household almost succeeded. Around the same time the Earl of Salisbury committed himself formally to the Duke of York. He met his counsellors and retainers at his seat of Middleham in Yorkshire and agreed that they 'sholde take ful partie with þe ful noble prince the Duke of York'.[16] Salisbury's decision at this time is evidence of the justifiable need for self-preservation among York and his allies. Although, following the death of Salisbury's brother, Bishop Robert, in 1457, Lawrence Booth had been translated to the important see of Durham, there is little evidence that the court had otherwise attempted to undermine Neville power in the north. Nevertheless, the prominence of the new Percy Earl of Northumberland in the queen's counsels and the violence planned against both his son, Warwick, and the Duke of York, were enough to convince Salisbury that only York's eventual victory could safeguard his own position and power.

In May 1459 Henry VI joined Queen Margaret in the midlands. Royal letters were sent to several counties ordering the gentry to attend upon the king at Leicester on 10 May with as many men defensibly arrayed as they could muster. The king ordered the purchase of three thousand bow staves 'considering thennemies on every side aprochinge upone us, as welle upon the see as on lande'.[17] This was the prelude to another Great Council meeting summoned to meet at Coventry the following month. The assembly, to which the Yorkist lords and their allies (such as Archbishop and Viscount Bourchier and Bishop Neville of Exeter) had not been summoned, proceeded to accuse them of treason. The parallels with 1455 are obvious, but this time the initiative lay with the Lancastrians. It was not until 20 September that Warwick arrived in London from Calais. The queen and her party were now anxious to prevent a rendezvous between the Yorkist lords. Somerset was sent to track Warwick's progress north, which he did from a safe distance, while another royal army attempted to prevent Salisbury from reaching the Duke of York at Ludlow. The earl escaped their clutches, yet on 23 September another royal force, perhaps 10,000 men strong and led by the elderly James, Lord Audley, and the staunch Lancastrian, Lord Dudley, halted Salisbury's progress at Blore Heath, just south of Newcastle-under-Lyme. The battle lasted some four hours, but the Yorkists eventually prevailed, killing Lord Audley in the mêlée. The fighting was fierce, however, and Salisbury only narrowly escaped capture; his two younger sons were less fortunate and were imprisoned in Chester Castle.

Salisbury now pressed onto Worcester, where he was joined by the Duke of York. There York and Salisbury entered into a solemn agreement, an indenture signed and sealed in the cathedral, the contents of which are now unfortunately lost but which presumably bound them to assist one other saving only their allegiance to the king. This agreement, along with their demands, was now taken to the king by the prior of Worcester cathedral priory and other churchmen. The Yorkist articles repeated the charges that had formed the core of criticism levelled at the Lancastrian regime for the past decade. They accused the traitors about the king of subverting justice, impoverishing the crown, and ignoring the king's wishes. Their remedy was an equally familiar and unconvincing one: York and the Nevilles offered to set aside their personal grievances and insisted the king once again took advice from 'the grete lords of his blood.'[18] Once Warwick had joined his father and York at Worcester, the three lords retreated to the duke's stronghold of Ludlow. Now there could be no hope of compromise. York and Warwick declined the offer of a royal pardon if they surren-dered within six days. Although the pardon had omitted Salisbury for his part in Audley's death and would thus have been unthinkable given the lords' recent commitments to each other, its acceptance would also have admitted some guilt on their part. The Yorkists had now played their hand, yet despite their military successes their cause had attracted little support from their fellow peers. As they marched cross-country to Ludlow they were accompanied only by York's two sons, the Earls of Rutland and March, and Lords Clinton and Grey of Powis. On 9 October writs went out summoning a parliament to gather at Coventry on 21 November. York, Salisbury and Warwick were not summoned and it seems certain that the intention was to attaint the Yorkist lords of treason. Three days later the royal host found itself confronted by the Yorkists in defensive positions at Ludford Bridge, on the River Teme just south of Ludlow. The Yorkists faced the king's army, drawn up with banners displayed and accompanied by at least twenty members of the parliamentary peerage. This proved too much for many, including a contingent of professional soldiers from the Calais garrison led by the veteran soldier Andrew Trollope, and they promptly went over to the king in return for a pardon. This, as one chronicler observed, 'made the duke [of York] fulle sore a-frayde when he wyste that sum olde soudyers went from hym unto the kynge'.[19] Duke Richard and his allies decided that discretion was the better part of valour. They returned to Ludlow, leaving their army in the field leaderless, and from there went their separate ways. York and his second son, the Earl of Rutland, fled to Ireland, while Salisbury, Warwick and York's eldest son, the Earl of March, travelled, via Devon and the Channel Islands, to the safe haven of Calais.

It was a slow and tortuous journey from the streets of St Albans to Ludford Bridge. There were few partisans on either side: the Duke of

York, of course, on one side and the queen and the relatives of those noblemen killed in 1455 on the other. Even the Earls of Salisbury and Warwick only committed themselves to armed opposition against the king (as opposed to armed defence against their noble enemies) in 1458. Few other lords were willing to commit themselves to anything other than a defence of Henry VI's position as king. Even political allies of the Nevilles and the Duke of York, such as the Duke of Norfolk, Lord Bonville or Viscount Bourchier, were unwilling to question openly the king's authority. Equally, however, they were unprepared to bear arms against their erstwhile friends. Moderate nobles, like the Duke of Buckingham or the Earl of Arundel, remained steadfast in their loyalty to the king and in their abhorrence of disorder, taking the field against the Yorkist lords in the autumn of 1459. Nevertheless, the partisans on both sides were sufficiently powerful and committed to each other's destruction that, without an intervention from the king, armed conflict was inevitable. Indeed, Henry's failure to provide even a modicum of royal leadership in the years after 1455 must be the principal factor in explaining the outbreak of renewed and ultimately decisive conflict in 1459. While the king had made intermittent, and occasionally disastrous, interventions in politics since attaining his majority in 1437, he made next to no impact on events between 1455 and 1459. The one exception may have been the 'Loveday' of March 1458, reflecting Henry's personal desire for peaceful reconciliation. Yet this only served to make matters worse, highlighting the personal grievances of the principals rather than the wider, constitutional issues at stake regarding the nature and location of royal authority. As parliament gathered at Coventry in November 1459 to attaint the Yorkist lords, it must have seemed that the Lancastrian regime had finally triumphed. While London remained uncertain in its loyalties and the problem of the Yorkist stronghold at Calais was unresolved, the political nation as a whole had proved itself unwilling to support the Duke of York and his claim to represent the commonweal. It was a startling train of events that would, in little more than sixteen months, lead to the overthrow of Henry VI and the accession of the Earl of March to the throne as Edward IV.

4

THE TRIUMPH OF YORK:
THE FIRST WAR 1459–64

There can be little doubt that the period following the flight of the Yorkist earls in October 1459 until the defeat of the Lancastrian army at Hexham in May 1464 was among the most fast-moving and confused of the entire fifteenth century. To use a metaphor that would have been familiar to contemporaries, the Wheel of Fortune turned suddenly and significantly in these years. They began with the Duke of York and his allies in apparent disarray, only for their position to be turned on its head at the Battle of Northampton in July 1460. This was followed by York's extraordinary bid for the throne and his unexpected death at the Battle of Wakefield that December. The duke's death pushed his eldest son, Edward, Earl of March, into the limelight. He displayed many of the qualities lacking in his father to become Edward IV in March 1461, defending his claim by his decisive victory later that month at the Battle of Towton. There then followed three difficult years in which Edward attempted to consolidate his kingship in the face of Lancastrian resistance. The eventual defeat of the Lancastrian rebels in May 1464 owed much to the military prowess of Edward's greatest subject, Richard Neville, Earl of Warwick. Yet even in victory the king and earl sowed the seeds of a new round of civil unrest and war.

FROM COVENTRY TO WAKEFIELD

The parliament that met at Coventry on 20 November 1459 had been summoned before the defeat of the Yorkist lords at Ludford Bridge. It had been called to condemn them and their allies, but it was not an overtly partisan gathering. Although York, Salisbury and Warwick were not summoned, attendance by the remaining peers was strong and, while many of the known 186 members of the Commons were to emerge as supporters of the House of Lancaster, a significant minority are known to have remained neutral or even supported the Yorkists. It was decided to proceed against the rebellious lords by way of attainder: they were to be stripped of their estates and their heirs disinherited. In all 27 rebels were attainted, but this was certainly fewer than had originally been mooted and some notable Yorkist supporters, such as Sir Walter Devereux, William Herbert and William Hastings, were pardoned. The conclusion must be that most of the lords wished to maintain the broad consensus that had kept the peace during most of the 1450s. In this, they had the crucial support of the king, whose

Plucking the Red and White Roses in the Old Temple Gardens (1908) by Henry Arthur Payne captured the popular image of the civil wars as a dynastic struggle between the Houses of Lancaster and York.

professed willingness to pardon all those willing to submit must have tempered the mood. There may also have been disquiet about the process of attainder itself. Although not unknown previously, its use on this scale was unprecedented and its consequences may have unnerved several among the lords and Commons. It was probably to counter growing disquiet over the process of attainder that the so-called *Somnium Vigilantis* was written. It set out the case against York and his allies in no uncertain terms. No matter how grave the problems facing the realm, rebellion against the king could never be justified. Moreover, the Yorkist lords had broken their oaths of allegiance to the king on more than one occasion and failure to punish them severely would now dangerously undermine royal authority. The author of this tract is unknown, but its intended audience may well have been moderate lords, like the Duke of Buckingham, and perhaps even the king himself. Significantly, the tract dismissed the 'foolish commons' who still sympathised with the Yorkist lords' call for reform despite their broken oaths and rebellion.[1] The final form of the attainder, however, which reserved the king's right to pardon those who would submit, confirmed the opinion that Henry too was more inclined towards mercy than justice.

The effect of the somewhat ambiguous message of the Coventry parliament was reinforced by the regime's utter failure to turn the military victory at Ludford Bridge into a decisive strategic advantage. In Calais, where the Duke of Somerset had been appointed captain on 5 October, Warwick successfully defeated all attempts to dislodge him. In January 1460 Lancastrian attempts to reinforce Somerset were thwarted by a raid on Sandwich, led by John Dynham, the West Country esquire who had helped Warwick and March escape from England the previous October. Warwick's ships, impounded at Sandwich in November 1459, were retaken, giving an important strategic boost to the Yorkist earls. Warwick then defeated Somerset at Newembridge just outside Calais and the duke was forced to retire to the Lancastrian-held Castle of Guînes, where he remained, impotent to intervene in English affairs, until the autumn of 1460. Similarly, Jasper Tudor, Earl of Pembroke, responsible for re-asserting royal authority in Wales enjoyed little success in attempting to reduce the Yorkist-held Castle of Denbigh. In the north, although Salisbury's lands were seized by the crown they were in fact given to his kinsman and former retainer, Sir Ralph Gray, to meet the costs of defending the Anglo-Scottish marches. Elsewhere in the north, the Neville retinue remained remarkably intact. York remained safe in Ireland, supported both militarily and financially by the Anglo-Irish establishment, and in March 1460 the Earl of Warwick travelled to Waterford to meet with Duke Richard and discuss their next move.

Warwick returned to Calais in June. Shortly afterwards, his kinsmen and deputy, William Neville, Lord Fauconberg, led another raid on Sandwich, destroying a Lancastrian fleet poised to sail to Calais and securing the port for a Yorkist invasion. On 26 June the Earls of Salisbury, Warwick and March landed in Kent and begun their march on London. The Yorkist agenda was a familiar one: their lives endangered by traitors about the king, they were marching for justice, both for themselves and the commonweal. This message was reinforced by their re-issue of one of Jack Cade's manifestos of 1450. The so-called 'Articles of the Commons of Kent' may have been an attempt to garner popular support as they marched to London, but it also revealed the constitutional poverty of the Yorkist position. Nothing had changed since 1450: Henry VI still failed to offer any effective royal leadership and the realm remained impoverished and ungoverned. The Yorkists' explanation for this parlous state of affairs was the corrupt government of the 'traitors' who remained at court and the fact that lords loyal to the commonweal were excluded from counselling the king. The Earls of Shrewsbury and Wiltshire and Viscount Beaumont had replaced the Dukes of Suffolk and Somerset as the villains of the Yorkist imagination, but the language of complaint had a depressingly familiar tone. The rebel lords' protestations of loyalty to the king must have been wearing thin but, as yet, there was still no alternative on the political horizon. On 10 July the Yorkists met the royal army, led by the Duke of Buckingham and Earl of Shrewsbury in the presence of the king, at Northampton. Once again, treachery influenced the outcome and Lord Richemont-Grey's timely defection led to a crushing Yorkist victory. Buckingham, Shrewsbury and Lord Egremont were killed and Henry once again fell under the control of the Yorkist lords. Queen Margaret and her son, who had wisely remained in Coventry, fled north. By 16 July the victors were back in London and in the same position they had found themselves five years earlier; in control of the king and government by force of arms. Their response was similar: George Neville, Bishop of Exeter replaced Archbishop Bourchier as chancellor, while Viscount Bourchier was appointed treasurer in place of the dead Shrewsbury. On this occasion, however, the king's household was also purged and Salisbury's younger son, John Neville, was appointed chamberlain. On 30 July the chancellor despatched writs summoning a new parliament to assemble at Westminster on 7 October. In the meantime the realm awaited the Duke of York's return and his response to this latest turn in events.

For reasons unknown York delayed his return from Ireland until early September. This may have been because he was aware of the difficulty and unpopularity of the course of action he had now decided upon. As he made his way to Westminster he carried a sword borne upright before him, usual practice for the king's lieutenant in Ireland but unknown in England. As neared his destination he adopted the undifferentiated royal arms, dropped Henry VI's regnal year from the dating clause of his letters, and retained individuals in his service without the usual clause reserving their allegiance to the king. The message was clear: Duke Richard had come to claim the throne, rightfully his by inheritance based upon his maternal descent from Lionel, Duke of Clarence, the second son of Edward III. Quite when York had decided to claim the throne remains one of the great unanswered questions of the fifteenth century. Rumours, of course, had circulated since 1450 and the duke's own recognition of his position had been implicit in his claim to exercise the office of protector of the Realm and in the production of several elaborate genealogies stressing his royal blood. The act of attainder passed against him in 1459 had claimed that one of the duke's servants, Robert Radcliff, had with his dying breath revealed that York had designs on the crown. Once back in Ireland after the debâcle of Ludford Bridge, York had exercised his quasi-regal powers without reference to Henry VI's regime, summoning a parliament that had passed a law making rebellion against the governor treason and initiating a separate coinage for Ireland. If, however, Duke Richard had revealed his intentions to his allies at their conference in March 1460 he may have met with little immediate support. Warwick, in particular, appears to have emerged as a conciliatory force in the wake of the victory at Northampton. In July the Milanese ambassador praised his efforts to 'keep the country in peace and unity', while four months later one of John Paston's correspondents warned that the realm would be 'vttirly on-done' without Warwick's guiding hand.[2]

When York arrived in Westminster on 10 October 1460 he immediately made his way to parliament. There, in the presence of the lords, he laid his hand on the throne and announced 'that he purposed nat to ley daune his swerde but to challenge his right . . . and purposed that no man shuld haue denyed the croune fro his hed.'[3] But instead of popular acclamation Duke Richard met with general consternation. Archbishop Bourchier asked if he wished to see the king to which York replied that he could think of no one who ought not rather come to see him. The duke's bold, even brash, move had backfired; it did not meet with the public support of even his closest friends, never mind the many lords hostile to him then present in parliament, and on 16 October he was forced to submit a formal, written case. This was based entirely on his descent from Lionel of Clarence, but the lords hesitated and passed the matter to the king. Henry, needless to say, prevaricated further: 'in so moche as his seid highnes had seen and understouden many dyvers writyngs and cronicles', he asked York to do the same and present more evidence in support of his claim.[4] Two days later the lords passed the matter to the judges who claimed that matters touching the king's estate were for the lords not them. The lords turned next to the sergeants of law who, unsurprisingly, said that matters outside the competence of the judges were also too high for them. Finally, on 25 October the lords came up with a compromise, reminiscent of the treaty of Troyes in 1422. Henry was to remain king but on his death the throne was to be settled on York and his heirs. The process recorded dispassionately on the parliament roll obscures what was a probably a bitter row between York and his erstwhile allies. His desire to be crowned king was probably in the first instance undone by the refusal of Archbishop Bourchier to participate in any coronation, but Duke Richard almost certainly also faced opposition from Warwick. It seems certain that the two men had discussed York's claim to the throne in their meeting the previous March, and Warwick may initially have backed the duke's action. Nevertheless, when faced with overwhelming opposition from the bishops and the rest of the parliamentary peerage, it seems that the earl may have wavered in his support for York. Indeed up to the Battle of Northampton, the whole platform upon which the rebel lords had campaigned was one of loyalty to the king and a determination to work for the commonweal. This was at once undone by York's actions; his opponents were now confirmed in their opinion that the entire decade of resistance had been driven by the duke's ambition and pride. His own defence of his position was feeble; York was absolved from breaking the oaths of allegiance and promises to eschew 'the wey of fayt' he had made throughout the 1450s because they were against God's law. He had, in fact, been rightfully king all along. It was a sentiment that few appear to have shared.

Meanwhile the Lancastrians had not been idle. Queen Margaret had been negotiating with the Scottish king, James II, for assistance against the rebels; the price of Scottish support was the town of Berwick-upon-Tweed. In October the Duke of Somerset returned from the continent and, with the Earl of Devon, mustered his forces alongside the Earls of Northumberland, Westmorland and other Lancastrian lords at Hull. York and Salisbury had little choice but to move north to face the Lancastrian threat and restore order and stability in Henry VI's name. York and Salisbury left London on 2 December, while Warwick remained in the capital. It seems likely that York misjudged the size of the Lancastrian army and he soon took refuge in his castle at Sandal. On 30 December 1460 Duke Richard's army was caught in the field by a much larger Lancastrian force. The Battle of Wakefield was a disaster for the Yorkists. Duke Richard, his son the Earl of Rutland, and Salisbury's son, Sir Thomas Neville, all fell in the mêlée. Salisbury was taken alive and beheaded at Pontefract the next day. Their remains were then taken to York and their severed heads

The only surviving wall of Sandal Castle, Yorkshire, from where Richard, Duke of York, sallied out to meet his death at the hands of the Lancastrians in December 1460.

displayed on the city's walls. York's, in mockery of his royal pretensions, was adorned with a paper crown.

THE YORKIST TRIUMPH

Edward of Rouen, Earl of March, the eldest surviving son of Richard, Duke of York, was born in the Norman capital on 28 April 1442. Little is known of his childhood, but by 1454 he was resident at his father's castle at Ludlow. He does not feature among the opposition to Henry VI's regime until October 1459 when he was among those who fled England after the Battle of Ludford Bridge. March, as we have seen, accompanied his uncle, the Earl of Salisbury, and cousin, the Earl of Warwick, to Calais. He appears to have played a secondary role in affairs during the crucial months that followed and he did not travel to Ireland in March to meet with his father. In Calais, however, he had his first taste of combat, apparently taking part in the defeat of the Duke of Somerset at Newembridge, and by the time the 'Calais earls' landed in Kent that June March's reputation and

King Edward IV by unknown artist oil on panel, *c.*1540
© National Portrait Gallery, London

importance had clearly grown. He was present at the Battle of Northampton in July, but remained in London throughout the autumn, neither travelling to the midlands with Warwick in September nor accompanying his mother to meet the Duke of York, when the latter returned from Ireland. March's reaction to his father's claim to the throne is unknown: the Burgundian chronicler, Jean de Waurin, states that March initially opposed York's claim and he certainly kept a low profile during the negotiations that resulted in the Accord of October 1460. On 1 November, at the solemn crown wearing to mark the settlement, March carried Henry VI's train, while York walked in procession alongside the king.

Edward was spending Christmas at Shrewsbury when he received news of his father's death. He had been sent west in December to raise men from the family estates in Wales and the Marches, while Warwick had remained in London to guard the capital. On receiving of the news of the disaster at Wakefield, Edward, now Duke of York himself, prepared to intercept the Lancastrian army marching south. News, however, reached him of a second Lancastrian force, commanded by the Earls of Pembroke and Wiltshire, coming from Wales. Now Edward demonstrated the vigour that would characterise his actions over the coming months. He turned his army around and on 2 or 3 February he intercepted the Lancastrian earls at Mortimer's Cross, on the old Roman road to Wales between Leominster and Wigmore. Ably assisted by those old servants of the House of York, Sir William Herbert and Sir Walter Devereux, he routed the Lancastrian army. Pembroke and Wiltshire escaped, but Henry VI's step-father, Owen Tudor, was taken and later executed. The day before the battle three suns had allegedly appeared in the sky, disquieting the Yorkist soldiers. Edward, it was said, had made this ominous portent into a virtue, likening it to the Holy Trinity and declaring it a symbol of divine support for their cause. He then adopted the 'sun in splendour' as one of the most important Yorkist badges. Whatever the truth behind this story, there can be no doubt that Edward's dynamism and his resulting victory energised the flagging Yorkist cause.

That cause was to be dealt another blow on 17 February when Warwick suffered a heavy defeat at the hands of Queen Margaret's army at St Albans. This Battle of St Albans was a much larger affair than its predecessor some five years earlier. Warwick was accompanied by the Duke of Norfolk, the Earls of Arundel and Suffolk, and six other lords. The Yorkist army had a self-consciously chivalric character to it, with many of its leading figures having distinguished themselves in the French wars: Warwick's uncle, Lord Fauconberg, had been one of the leading English war captains, while the Kentish knight, Sir Thomas Kyriell, recently returned from imprisonment following his capture at the Battle of Formingy in 1450, had enjoyed a long and distinguished career in France. On 8 February, before leaving the capital to face the Lancastrian host, Warwick, Kyriell and another old supporter of York, Sir John Wenlock, were elected as knights of the Garter. Warwick also, of course, had in his custody Henry VI himself. The Lancastrian army on the other hand had a distinctly northern character: it numbered among its ranks the Dukes of Exeter and Somerset, the Earls of Devon, Oxford, Shrewsbury, Northumberland and Westmorland, and five other lords. Its legitimacy as truly representative of the House of Lancaster and proper royal authority was conferred by the presence of Henry, the disinherited Prince of Wales. The Yorkists, it seems, were defeated by sheer weight of numbers as much as anything, although poor communication may have meant that many, perhaps including Warwick himself, were never engaged. By the end of the day, Warwick was in flight and the king had been reunited with his Lancastrian supporters.

The way now seemed clear for the Lancastrians to enter London and regain the reins of royal government, but at this crucial juncture the city authorities stood firm and barred the gates. The principal reason for this was probably fear of the northerners, who had quickly gained a reputation for pillage from their passage along the Great North Road into Hertfordshire. Another possibility is that the mayor and aldermen of London had already committed themselves firmly to the Yorkist cause. Instead Edward and Warwick, who had met at Chipping Norton in Oxfordshire, entered the capital themselves on 27 February. Only one course of action now lay open to them: by killing the Duke of York the Lancastrian had broken the Accord negotiated the previous October. Edward had to make amends by claiming the throne for himself. Thus, on 1 March Bishop Neville of Exeter declared Edward's just title to the throne to a presumably select and sympathetic gathering in St John's Field. The assembly was asked if Henry had forfeited his rights to be king and Bishop Neville demanded to know if they would accept Edward in his stead as their king. The answer, of course, was affirmative. Two days later the people were summoned to gather outside St Paul's on the morning of 4 March. Edward processed to the cathedral and at St Paul's cross the people were again asked if they accepted him as their king. Having been universally acclaimed he made his way to Westminster Hall, where he took his place upon the king's seat and assumed the royal regalia. Edward then made a declaration of his own title to the throne to the further acclamation of the gathered crowd. The reign of Edward IV had begun.

Edward's accession was sudden and its manner novel. The Accord of October 1460 had, in effect, recognised the Duke of York's *de jure* right to the throne; it was a compromise that would probably have proved unworkable while Henry remained *de facto* king. It was this principle, that the crown of England was in effect the personal property of the new Duke of York and his right inheritance that formed the basis of Edward's kingship. The most significant aspect of the series of events that led to Edward's accession was not his 'election' as king, but the judgment made by the assembled crowds at St John's Fields on 1 March that Henry VI, an anointed king and representative of a dynasty universally accepted as rightful kings until only a few months before, should be deposed for his recent misdeeds (principally breaking the Accord and murdering the Duke of York). The assembled crowd then merely assented to Edward's *de jure* right to be king of England. His 'election', if it can be called such, was the decision by the small Yorkist council, which met at Baynard's Castle two days later, that they would support and defend his right. On 4 March the crowd assembled at Westminster Hall acclaimed Edward's accession, much as they would have done at a more regular coronation; in no sense was he king by election of the people. Nevertheless, the notion of popular support for the new king emerged as an important principle of Yorkist propaganda. York himself, and later Warwick, had staked their claim for political power on the basis that they were representing the commons and the commonweal; it played into the new regime's hands to foster the idea that Edward had 'toke upon hym the crowne of England by the avysse of the lordys spyrytual and temporalle, and by the elexyon of the comyns'.[5]

Edward now needed to establish his authority and this meant defeating the Lancastrians in battle. On 11 March Lord Fauconberg went north with an army funded by generous loans from the Londoners and two days later the king himself left the capital, accompanied by the Duke of Norfolk and joining forces with the Earl of Warwick in the midlands. By 28 March Edward had reached Pontefract and the following day, Palm Sunday, the Yorkist host clashed with the Lancastrians between the villages of Saxton and Towton. Towton was the largest and bloodiest battle of the civil wars and may well be the largest to have ever been fought on English soil. Chroniclers (and some historians) have suggested the unlikely number of 76,000 men present on the field, and although this is certainly an exaggeration it is probable that the combined armies numbered in the tens of thousands. It was the decisive battle of this first stage of the Wars of the Roses and the mass participation of the political elite (some three-quarters of the English nobility were present on the field) was testimony to its significance. The Lancastrian army was larger than Edward's and contained the majority of the nobles and gentlemen present on the field. Edward was accompanied by Norfolk, Warwick and Lords Montagu, Scrope of Bolton, Fauconberg and Fitzwalter.

There is little contemporary evidence for what happened during the battle. There are no eye-witness accounts and many historians have relied on the colourful version of events written by the sixteenth-century chronicler, Edward Hall. It is clear, however, that the battle took place in a blizzard and the Yorkist archers appear to have been assisted by the strong wind which speeded their arrows towards the Lancastrians, while ensuring their enemy's volleys fell short. It was also notable for the aggressive tactics employed by the Yorkist army. It seems that Edward himself may have been responsible for this dynamic approach and he was certainly in the thick of the fighting: Bishop Neville wrote to the papal legate, Bishop Coppini, that the king and the other Yorkist lords had won the battle through their prowess 'first fighting like common soldiers, then commanding, encouraging and rallying their squadrons like the greatest captains'.[6] At first it seemed that a cavalry charge led by the Duke of Somerset and the Lancastrians' advantage in numbers would carry the day, but the arrival late in the afternoon of the Duke of Norfolk's men turned the tide of battle in favour of the Yorkists. Eventually, the Lancastrian lines broke and their retreat towards Tadcaster soon developed into a chaotic and bloody rout. The result was a catastrophe for the Lancastrian cause: the Earl of Northumberland and Lords Clifford, Dacre, Neville, Richemont-Gray and Welles were killed in action, alongside many of their retainers, while the Earls of Devon and Wiltshire were taken and subsequently executed. The Earl of Wiltshire's luck finally ran out a few days after the battle when he was captured near Newcastle and executed. The slaughter was immense and contemporaries were shocked at the scale and significance of the

Lancastrian defeat. Unfortunately for Edward, the Lancastrian royal family had decided to await news of the battle's outcome in York and, upon hearing of the defeat, they managed to slip quietly across the border into Scotland. Edward entered the city of York the next day and the following weeks were spent touring those northern counties still loyal to the House of Lancaster. On 26 June Edward returned to London in state, amidst great celebrations, and two days later he was crowned king at Westminster Abbey.

EXPLAINING THE YORKIST VICTORY

The Yorkist triumph had been sudden and in many ways had been achieved against the odds. There are a number of factors, both immediate and longer term, that explain Edward IV's success. The first must be the dynamism shown by Edward himself. His kingly demeanour in London had impressed the city and those asked to acclaim his accession. Most importantly, as David Saintiuste has recently argued, it was the new king's abilities as a military leader

Very little survives to mark the battlefields of the Wars of the Roses. This monument commemorates the Battle of Towton and the death of Randolf, Lord Dacre in 1461.

that proved crucial in February and March 1461. At both Mortimer's Cross and at Towton he fought manfully, earning the respect of those around him and of contemporary chroniclers. More than one source states that the king's personal intervention at a moment of crisis saved the day for the Yorkists. At Towton Edward also delivered a pre-battle speech that lifted the flagging spirits of his army, while at Mortimer's Cross his re-interpretation of a celestial omen soon passed into Yorkist legend. Moreover, Edward's military leadership was complemented by the experience and skill of old soldiers, such as Lord Fauconberg. At Towton Fauconberg's skilful use of archery fooled the Lancastrians into loosing their arrows out of range of their Yorkist opponents. At both battles the Yorkists appears to have successfully goaded the Lancastrians into making ill-judged assaults on their lines. Equally, the Earl of Warwick, despite his defeat at St Albans in February 1461, proved a brave and effective military leader, while at Towton the intervention of the Duke of Norfolk also played an important role in the Yorkist victory.

The Yorkists had also benefited from their command of royal military resources even before they had taken over the reins of government in July 1460. York's lieutenancy of Ireland conferred legitimacy and power upon him in his relations with the Anglo-Irish aristocracy, even if his salary of £2,500 p.a. was seldom paid in full. Warwick's command at Calais and his keepership of the sea allowed him to collect taxation and gather loans by employing the public authority of the crown alongside his own private lordship. Equally, the Nevilles' command of the West March against Scotland allowed them to recruit men to their service with royal wages. Salisbury's fee of £1,250 p.a. from 1455 equalled his net income from land calculated in 1436. As Michael Hicks has pointed out, their control of ostensibly public resources made the Yorkist earls into 'overmighty subjects' and provided the resources with which they could successfully challenge the crown.[7] The Yorkists may also have enjoyed a military advantage in terms of the quality of their soldiery. The self-consciously chivalric identity fostered by the Yorkist lords in the early 1461 may have played an important role in attracting military-minded men to their banner. Sir Robert Ogle, a Durham knight experienced in border warfare under both the Nevilles and the Percies, played a vital role under the Earl of Warwick at St Albans in 1455 and probably also brought a significant contingent of borderers to fight for the Yorkists at Towton. Equally, the success of Warwick and Edward in attracting Burgundian knights, men-at-arms and gunners to their service should not be underestimated and reflects the Yorkist lords' chivalric and military reputation. The Burgundian gunners also played an important role in the reduction of the Lancastrian strongholds in Northumberland in 1462–64. Finally, the military expertise and manpower of the Calais garrison, where Warwick had been captain since 1455, played an important role in giving the Yorkists a decisive military advantage. Despite Andrew Trollope's defection at Ludford Bridge and the resistance of Lancastrian soldiers in the castles of Hammes and Guines, a sizeable contingent of the Calais garrison accompanied the Yorkist earls when they landed in Kent in June 1460. Similarly, the military resources of Calais, which was the largest arsenal available to the English kings with a vast quantity of artillery of all descriptions, were instrumental in securing the Yorkist regime against Lancastrian rebels between 1461 and 1464.

The military and chivalric reputation of the Yorkists stands in contrast to that of the Lancastrians. With the exception of Somerset and Andrew Trollope, who had a European-wide reputation as a 'tres soubtil homme de guerre', there were few effective military commanders among the Lancastrian lords.[8] Moreover, their armies quickly gained a reputation as the antithesis of chivalry and reinforced contemporary opinions of ordinary soldiers as criminals and enemies of the commonweal. Queen Margaret's Lancastrian army apparently plundered its way along the Great North Road, creating fear among the southerners and Londoners in particular. Abbot Whethamstede records how they plundered the town of St Albans and it was the only the protection of the martyr himself that had saved the monastery. This fear and the perception of the Lancastrian soldiery as predatory and criminal were instrumental in the Londoners' decision to bar the capital to Margaret's army in February 1461. Moreover, the actions of the Lancastrian commanders after the second Battle of St Albans reinforced their reputation as cruel and unchivalric. The summary execution of Sir Thomas Kyriell, a veteran of the Hundred Years War, and Lord Bonville, who had both stayed behind with King Henry once the rest of the Yorkist host had fled, aroused general condemnation.

These differing perceptions of the motivations and actions of the Yorkist and Lancastrian armies in the first months of 1461 demonstrate one of the most important reasons for the Yorkists' success. Simply put, they won the propaganda war. Edward and, perhaps to an even greater extent, the Earl of Warwick were 'idols of the multitude' and the Yorkists owed their success in no small part to the support they enjoyed from the commons. This was particularly true in London and the south-east and derived in part from Warwick's actions as captain of Calais. From 1457 onwards he had encouraged piracy out of Calais, clearly a boon to the ailing economies of the Kentish ports. The earl was also lavish in his hospitality: he exchanged gifts with the leading townsmen in Kent and London and his household was noted for its hospitality. More importantly, however, in 1459 and 1460 Warwick made a self-conscious appeal as champion of the commonweal. His manifesto, issued as he crossed from Calais to rendezvous with York at Ludlow in 1459, echoed many of the familiar complaints that had first come to prominence in 1450. He demanded that the traitors about the king be removed and that Henry VI 'by thadvice of the grete lordis of his blood' address the realm's problems. To the calls for the 'due and evunly minestering of justice and rightwisnesse', however, Warwick added a target piece of propaganda. Clearly with London's merchant community in mind (who had already lent him money to defend the seas in the wake of the French descent on Sandwich in August 1457), he added 'the cours and recours of merchandise' and 'novelries by oon waye into the grete hurte of merchauntes' to the list of problems the Yorkist lords planned to address. Similarly, when the Earls of March, Salisbury and Warwick and Lord Fauconberg landed in Kent in June 1460 they re-issued one of Cade's petitions of 1450 almost verbatim. They claimed, in effect, to have invaded England at the request of the commons of Kent and vowed to reform both the general ills of the commonweal and the specific grievances of the county through which they marched to London.[9] Indeed, the support of the Kentish gentry was instrumental in allowing them to march on London and confront the Lancastrians at Northampton the following month.

This popularity was also crucially transformed into tangible expressions of support in terms of men and, more importantly perhaps, money. In the aftermath of York's victory at St Albans in 1455 Warwick had been appointed captain of Calais and he succeeded in guaranteeing the payment of the garrison's wages and the discharge of their arrears through a complex series of negotiations with the wool merchants. By February 1456 the crown owed the merchants of the Calais staple some £39,000 and in March they lent another £40,000 to cover the garrison's wages to secure Warwick's entry into the town. In reaction to the support given to Warwick by the staplers the Coventry parliament of 1459 banned exports of wool to Calais; the merchants were thus forced to support the Yorkist lords if they wished to recover their debts. The willingness of the wool merchants, in effect, to underwrite Warwick's command at Calais also reflected their belief that their own interests would be best served by a government led by the Yorkist lords. As well as their 'public' loans to fund the Calais garrison, the staplers and London merchants made private loans to the Yorkist lords, especially Warwick, and, it was alleged, their desire to secure eventual repayment was one of the reasons they were so steadfast in their support of the earl throughout the 1460s. Crucially, from July 1460 until April 1461 the mercantile community of London financed the Yorkist war effort. These included corporate loans, sums advanced by individual livery companies, and private loans (such as the £100 lent by the Mercers' company to Warwick) and totalled at least £11,000. Equally, the Yorkist lords ensured that the income from the customs was not diverted to the royal household but paid directly to the merchants for the swift repayment of their loans.[10]

THE ESTABLISHMENT OF THE YORKIST REGIME

Edward's victory at Towton and his coronation did not end opposition to the new regime. There was still the inconvenient fact that the Lancastrian royal family were at large, while substantial proportions of the political nation remained loyal to the old dynasty. One of Edward's first moves was to reward his stalwart supporters: Viscount Bourchier was created Earl of Essex, Lord Fauconberg was promoted to Earl of Kent, while several prominent Yorkist and Neville retainers (Sir Humphrey Bourchier, Sir Walter Devereux, Sir William Herbert, Sir Thomas Lumley, Sir John Neville, Sir Humphrey Stafford of Southwick, Sir Robert Ogle, Sir John Wenlock and Sir William Hastings) were also ennobled. The initial attempts to secure the realm seemed successful. In Wales, Herbert and Devereux (now Lord Ferrers) launched a successful campaign against the rebels and by May 1462 they had captured the Lancastrian strongholds of Carreg Cennen, Pembroke, Caernarvon and Denbigh, only leaving Jasper Tudor holed up in Harlech Castle where he remained for another seven years. In the north Lord Ogle soon secured Alnwick and Dunstanburgh, while in October the last Lancastrian outpost in Calais, Hammes Castle, fell to Warwick's men. Edward's first parliament, which assembled at Westminster on 4 November 1461, formally declared the legitimacy of the Yorkist claim to the throne, tracing the endemic 'unrest, inward werre and trouble, unrightwisnes, shedyng and effusion of innocent blode, abusion of the lawes, partialte, riotte, extorcion, murdre, rape and viciouse lyvyng,' to the usurpation of Henry Bolingbroke in 1399 and stressing the 'princely prowesse' of Edward in avenging his father's death and defeating the usurping Lancastrians.[11] 130 prominent Lancastrians were identified and many were attainted, including fourteen peers many of whom were still in arms against the king. To underline the new regime's commitment to the commonweal and to distance himself, rhetorically at least, from Lancastrian excesses, Edward did not ask for a grant of taxation and promised to be a good and gracious sovereign.

These initial successes, however, masked the fact that Edward's regime faced serious challenges. In November 1461 the Lancastrian Sir Wiliam Tailboys had managed to recapture Alnwick Castle in Northumberland. Local unrest also betrayed Lancastrian sympathies in the south-west, while early in 1462 the Earl of Oxford was arrested for a treasonable plot in East Anglia. Edward's response was a judicial progress in the spring to affirm the authority and legitimacy of the new regime. More serious, however, were the efforts of Margaret of Anjou to raise a French army to invade England in return for the secession of Calais. The French king, Louis XI, at first seemed willing to support such an endeavour but raids on the French coast by the Earl of Kent may have persuaded him against a wholehearted support of the Lancastrian cause. Nevertheless, in October 1462 some 800 French soldiers, under the command of the experienced captain, Pierre de Brézé (already infamous for his raid on Sandwich in 1457), landed at Bamburgh in Northumberland. Before long both Dunstanburgh and Alnwick had fallen to the invaders and their Lancastrian allies. This met with a swift response from Warwick and his brother, Lord Montagu, who immediately invested the Lancastrian-held castles and by December their defenders had surrendered and Alnwick, Bamburgh and Dunstanburgh were back in Yorkist hands. These developments had probably convinced Edward of the efficacy of a policy of reconciliation towards the leading Lancastrian rebels, most notably Henry Beaufort, Duke of Somerset, and Sir Ralph Percy, head of that family during the minority of the fourth Earl of Northumberland. Historians have been divided over Edward's motives in accepting his erstwhile enemies back into the fold, but the initial moves may in fact have been made by Somerset late in 1462 as the Lancastrian campaign in the north faltered. Indeed, the duke's rehabilitation was gradual: he first proved his loyalty campaigning in the north in the winter of 1462 before being included in the general pardon issued in March 1463. The decision was certainly unpopular, however, and in 1463 Somerset retreated to his estates in North Wales amidst riots and popular disquiet over his new role in the Yorkist regime.

If Edward had hoped that his reconciliation with his erstwhile enemies would bring stability to the north he was soon to be proven wrong. In March 1463 Queen Margaret crossed the border at the head of a joint Lancastrian and Scottish army. Sir Ralph Percy immediately returned to the Lancastrian fold and surrendered Bamburgh and Dunstanburgh, while Sir Ralph Gray, another recently pardoned Lancastrian, also changed sides and betrayed Alnwick. In June a large royal army, well equipped with ordnance from Calais and the Tower of London, marched north under Warwick to join Lord Montagu, the recently appointed warden of the east and middle marches. Faced with an overwhelming royal response and without the prospect of Scottish support, Queen Margaret fled for France and negotiations for a truce began between Warwick and the Scottish ambassadors. In December 1463 the two parties agreed a truce which was to last until October the following year, leaving the Lancastrian rebels isolated. In January, however, the rebels received a boost when Somerset reneged on his oath and travelled north, eventually (after a narrow escape at Durham) joining the defenders of Bamburgh. Between the beginning of February and the end of March, accompanied by Sir Ralph Gray, Sir Ralph Percy and Lords Hungerford and Roos, Somerset conducted a campaign which resulted in the capture of Norham Castle as well as several Northumbrian towns. However, fortune would soon intervene once more: on 25 April Lord Montagu was en route to meet representatives of James III when he was intercepted by a Lancastrian force, commanded by Somerset, at Hedgley Moor. The battle was a short-lived affair: Lords Hungerford and Roos quickly fled, while the Lancastrian vanguard, commanded by Percy, was overwhelmed and Percy himself killed. Somerset and Gray escaped and regrouped at Alnwick, but on 15 May they were surprised at Hexham by a Yorkist force commanded by Lords Montagu, Greystoke and Willoughby. The duke was captured and executed the following day. Only Gray evaded capture and made for Bamburgh, which he held with another rebel, Sir Humphrey Neville. Following an artillery bombardment, the garrison surrendered, delivering the treacherous Gray to his fate. On 10 July 1464 he was beheaded at Doncaster. His head was symbolically displayed on London Bridge; the fall of Bamburgh Castle marked the end of Lancastrian resistance to Edward's rule in the north and brought the curtain down on the first stage of the Wars of the Roses.

Edward IV had shown remarkable skill and courage in winning the throne in March 1461. Indeed, the period from October 1460, when Duke Richard had laid claim to the throne, had been marked with a determination and ruthlessness on both sides that had not been apparent throughout the previous decade. In July 1460, when they had

The gatehouse and curtain wall of Dunstanburgh Castle, Northumberland, scene of some of the last Lancastrian resistance to Edward IV in 1464 (Tim Simpson)

captured Henry VI at Northampton, the Yorkist earls had maintained a fiction of loyal opposition that was ultimately untenable given their own actions and the implacable hostility of Margaret of Anjou. Nevertheless, York's justifications for his claim to the throne could not be accepted at first by a majority of his peers and the rest of the political elite. The resulting Accord was another of those unworkable compromises that had characterised the politics of the 1450s. Paradoxically perhaps, his death at the hands of Queen Margaret and her followers made the prospect of replacing Henry VI a more viable possibility. Edward was untainted by the squalid politics of the 1450s, a true champion of the commonweal who could avenge the death of his father and Lancastrian perfidy. His victories at Mortimer's Cross and Towton were, in effect, a trial by battle and the legitimacy of the Yorkist cause was affirmed by his victories. Nevertheless, Edward's honeymoon period as king was short-lived. Rebellion continued due to the simple fact that the majority of the political nation had not supported his cause in 1461. His policy of reconciliation with former Lancastrians, most notably the Duke of Somerset, was, with hindsight, probably the right one, but it backfired spectacularly and appeared, by 1464, to underline the weakness of the new regime. Moreover, the final defeat of the Lancastrian cause had not been achieved by the 'princely prowess' of the king but by the resources, expertise and determination of the Earl of Warwick and his brother, Montagu. In 1463, in a letter to the French diplomat, Jean de Lannoy, Lord Hastings praised the achievements of the 'noble and valiant' Earl of Warwick in suppressing Lancastrian resistance in the north. The king, on the other hand, Hastings reported, had continued to enjoy the pleasures of the chase. While the precise meaning of this remark may be unclear, one conclusion stands out: Edward had abrogated one of his key responsibilities. The security of the Yorkist regime depended not on his efforts but on those of Warwick. The earl's importance was something not lost to contemporaries and Edward's most important subject expected reward and recognition.

5

REBELLION AND READEPTION:
THE SECOND WAR 1469–71

The end of Lancastrian resistance in the north and the capture of the fugitive Henry VI in July 1465 should have brought peace and stability. While dissident Lancastrians continued to plot both at home and abroad, they lacked the resources necessary to challenge the rule of Edward IV. K.B. McFarlane famously claimed that only 'an undermighty ruler had anything to fear from overmighty subjects'.[1] Unlike Henry, Edward was not undermighty in terms of his personal attributes or his fitness to govern, but his royal authority was circumscribed by the political culture and institutions of government in which he operated. Throughout the 1460s the public authority of the crown sat uneasily alongside the private power of the Earl of Warwick and his Neville relations. Ironically, Warwick's status as an 'overmighty subject' (and there can be little doubt that he was indeed so during that decade) derived principally not from his own lands but from the resources and influence he derived from office granted by the crown. Edward's determination to decide upon his own foreign policy, to take counsel from whom he chose, and, crucially, to marry whom he wanted was not unreasonable for a king, but it challenged and undermined Warwick's power and lay at the heart of the renewal of civil war in 1469. The earl's ability to play 'Kingmaker', to depose Edward in favour of the discredited and incapable Henry, points to the structural problems that consistently undermined royal authority for much of the fifteenth century. Yet Edward's victory in 1471 demonstrates the powerful desire for strong, effective royal government that was also characteristic of late-medieval England.

EDWARD IV, WARWICK AND THE WOODVILLES

There was little doubt among contemporary observers that the young Edward IV owed his throne to his cousin, Richard Neville, Earl of Warwick, and that during the early 1460s Warwick was the most powerful man in the kingdom. Bishop Kennedy of St Andrews considered him 'the governor of England under Edward IV', while a French observer quipped that the English 'have two rulers M. de Warwick and another whose name I have forgotten.'[2] Warwick's position depended in part on his private power as a great magnate, his midland estates held in the right of his wife (and from whom he derived his title) and his northern Neville patrimony inherited on the death of his father in 1460. More importantly, however, it also depended on the public authority he wielded on behalf of the king. By 1464 Warwick's array of offices was unprecedented. Since 1455 he had been captain of Calais and his control of the town's military resources had played a vital role in the events of 1459–61. In December 1457, in response to the French raid on Sandwich, he had been appointed keeper of the seas, funded by the subsidy of tonnage and poundage in all ports except Sandwich and Southampton. New responsibilities followed the accession of Edward IV. His power in the south-east of England was cemented by his appointment as warden of the Cinque Ports and constable of Dover Castle, while he was also made admiral of England. In the north, where he inherited his father's Neville connection, he was made king's lieutenant, and on 5 May 1461 he received a confirmation of all offices held jointly with his father or brothers for life. These included the wardenship of the west march, the chief stewardship of the northern and southern lands of the Duchy of Lancaster, as well as a host of wardships and the custody of the estates of minors and rebels. His relations were also rewarded: his uncle, William Neville, Lord Fauconberg, was made Earl of Kent and became steward of the king's household, while Warwick's brother, John, Lord Montagu, was made a knight of the Garter in 1462 and warden of the east and middle marches the following year. In May 1464 Montagu was elevated to the earldom of Northumberland in recognition of his service in the north; a year later he received a grant of the forfeited Percy estates and in 1466 the Duchy of Lancaster honours and Castles of Tickhill, Knaresborough, and Pontefract in recompense for his unpaid wages as warden of the march. As Michael Hicks has observed, what these grants 'demonstrate is the Nevilles' determination – and Warwick's in particular – to hang on to whatever they already possessed and to amplify it.'[3]

These rewards provided Warwick, as premier earl and as head of a powerful family, with the means to be an overmighty subject. His income from his own estates was in the region of £7,000 p.a. in the early 1460s, while his fees from office amounted to at least £5,000 p.a. This provided him with an income probably twice that enjoyed by the Duke of the York in the 1450s. Moreover, due to his personal capital he was able to command loans from the mercantile community, particularly the Calais staplers, and their agreement to fund the Calais garrison from the wool customs in 1466 removed a financial headache that had been the undoing of several previous magnate captains. Warwick's income allowed him to embark on a massive campaign of retaining, giving his badge of the ragged staff out freely, and to establish his household as a byword for hospitality and conspicuous shows of good lordship. As one later London chronicler remembered: 'The which Erle was evyr had In Grete ffavour of the commonys of this land, By reson of the excedyng howshold which he dayly kepid In alle Cuntrees where evyr he sojourned or laye.'[4] Moreover, even those who had not partaken of the earl's liberality could not help but be impressed by his exploits in defending the seas, the magnificence of his embassies to France and the Low Countries, and his commitment to justice and the commonweal. Thus the Earl of Warwick was 'an idol of the multitude', loved by the commons, with the resources and popularity to challenge royal policy if it went against his interests and those of his Neville family.[5]

From 1464 there were two areas where the developing thrust of royal policy could be seen to threaten Warwick's interests. The first of these was the issue of counsel. The king's right to listen to and act upon the counsel he deemed most appropriate had been challenged throughout the 1450s, yet it was a fundamental principle of English political culture. The Duke of York and his allies had characterised their political opponents as 'evil counsellors' who subverted the commonweal from within by monopolising the institutions of counsel. There can be little doubt that in the opening years of the reign Warwick and the Nevilles were Edward IV's leading councillors. Their proximity to the king arose from both their personal, familial relationship to Edward and by virtue of their formal office. The lists of witnesses to royal charters in the first half of the decade reveal the dominance of the Earl of Warwick, the Earl of Kent (until his death in 1463), Lord Montagu and Archbishop George Neville. Together the king and the Nevilles formed a formidable alliance in the early years of the reign. Other councillors and courtiers played a lesser role in these years, although they too were well rewarded for their service. The king's chamberlain, Lord Hastings, was prominent, while Lords Herbert, Mountjoy and Stafford of Southwick were also important courtiers. Nevertheless, it is difficult to escape the impression that in the early years of the reign it was the Nevilles, particularly Warwick, who dominated the government of England.

This changed abruptly in the autumn of 1464. At a council meeting at Reading Abbey in September Edward announced that he had, in the previous May, married Elizabeth Woodville, daughter of the Lancastrian peer, Sir Richard Woodville, Lord Rivers, and widow of Sir John Grey, eldest son of Lord Ferrers of Groby. The king's marriage dismayed contemporaries. First, Elizabeth was a commoner (albeit her mother, Jacquetta of Luxembourg, was a foreign princess) and a widow. Second, the match meant that Edward was no longer a prize to be dangled before foreign princes eager for alliances with England. Finally, Elizabeth's large family (her two sons from her previous marriage and no fewer than 12 surviving siblings) would certainly affect the domestic political balance. Moreover, the marriage was a snub to Warwick who was pursuing negotiations for a French or Castilian bride when Edward announced his nuptials to Elizabeth. There is plenty of evidence that the Woodville marriage was greeted with unease.

John, Lord Wenlock, himself close to the Earl of Warwick, told a Burgundian correspondent that the king had married out of love 'without the knowledge of those who should have been called for council; for that reason it is to the great displeasure of the several great lords, and also of the greater part of his council.' Foreign observers picked up the mood of disquiet. Venetian merchants observed that 'the greater part of the lords and the people seem very much dissatisfied at this', while the German merchant, Caspar Weinrich, wrote that 'this winter King Edward in England took to queen a nobleman's wife, and she was also crowned (in May 1465) against the will of the lords.'[6] Warwick may have escorted the queen on her first public outing at Michaelmas 1464 and, on the face of it, accepted his cousin's decision, but in reality he could do little else. Yet in the years that followed the growing influence of the queen and her family in Edward's counsels threatened to undermine the earl's influence and power.

The rise of the Woodville family was the most important political development in England in the second half of the 1460s. The rewards granted to them were lavish and reflected Edward's own determination to advance his wife's family. Elizabeth's dower was only some £4,500, smaller than the usual 10,000 marks (£6,666 13s. 4d.) allotted to previous consorts. However, it was assigned in the main on the Duchy of Lancaster estates in the south and was therefore a secure source of income. Her large household offered employment and patronage to her kinsfolk, yet it was her immediate family who benefitted most obviously from the marriage. Her brother, Anthony Woodville, Lord Scales in the right of his wife, was elected a knight of the Garter. In 1466 her own son, Thomas Grey, married Anne Holland, the daughter of the king's sister, Anne, duchess of Exeter, despite the fact she was already betrothed to George Neville, heir to the Earl of Northumberland. Her other siblings secured equally advantageous matches throughout the decade. Her sisters married the heirs to the earldoms of Arundel, Essex, Kent, and Pembroke, and the dukedom of Buckingham, while her younger brother, John, was betrothed to the 65-year-old dowager duchess of Norfolk. The most important recognition of the Woodvilles' new importance, at least in terms of its political significance, were the favours heaped upon the queen's father, Richard, Lord Rivers, who became an earl as well as Treasurer and Constable of England. In 1460, when Rivers and his son had been captured by the Yorkist earls at Sandwich, they had been brought back to Calais and there Warwick had berated him for his common origins and impudence in challenging the rights of 'lords of the king's blood' to counsel Henry VI.[7] Edward appears to have forgotten this incident amidst his amour for Elizabeth, but it seems that Warwick and other members of the Yorkist establishment had longer memories.

The second aspect of royal policy that developed to undermine Warwick's position in the second half of the 1460s was foreign policy. Since the beginning of the reign Earl Richard had been courted by the new French king, Louis XI, and he consistently championed a French alliance over a pro-Burgundian policy. There is evidence to suggest, however, that Edward had entertained notions of renewing the Hundred Years War from early in his reign. The election as knights of the Garter of the Duke of Milan and the king of Naples in 1463 may point to plans to encircle the French with hostile princes bound personally to Edward. It is noteworthy that Philip the Good, Duke of Burgundy, rejected the offer of the Garter, well aware of the chivalric commitment to Edward that it entailed. The king's marriage transformed the diplomatic situation. With a marital alliance now out of the question, Edward snubbed the French ambassadors when they arrived in England in September 1464. Moreover, there were powerful voices pushing the king towards a Burgundian alliance and away from France in the mid-1460s. The influence of the mercantile community, anxious to preserve its trade with the Low Countries, should not be underestimated, but the Woodvilles too were pro-Burgundian. They were, of course, related by marriage to the House of Luxembourg and the Edwardian court increasingly looked to the court of the Valois dukes for inspiration under their influence. Edward remained aloof from the conflict that erupted by France and Burgundy in 1465 (the so-called 'War of the Common Weal'), but the death in August of that year of Isabella of Bourbon, the second wife of Charles, Count of Charolais and heir to Philip the Good, saw a new round of diplomatic posturing. Despite embassies to both courts, led by Warwick, the tide was turning in favour of an English alliance with Burgundy. In June

1467 Antoine, the illegitimate son of Philip the Good, arrived in England for a spectacular display of jousting against Anthony, Lord Scales. In the same month Edward personally took the Great Seal from Archbishop Neville, replacing him as chancellor with Bishop Stillington of Bath and Wells.

In the event the jousts at Smithfield were cut short by the death of Philip the Good on 15 June 1467. This was the opportunity Edward had waited for in order to press ahead with his diplomatic encirclement of France. Alliances were cemented with Brittany and Castille and in November the king sealed a trade treaty with Burgundy. At the same time Edward's sister, Margaret, appeared before the council and agreed to marry Charles, the new Duke of Burgundy. This was duly ratified in February 1468 and in May the king announced to parliament his intention to invade France. The response was positive in the form of a substantial grant of taxation, but the king's policy was a risky one. He had made unpopular trade concessions to the Burgundians, borrowed heavily to pay his sister's dowry, and alienated his most powerful subject, the Earl of Warwick. By the end of 1468 Edward's policies at both home and abroad were beginning to destabilise the realm. Rumours of Lancastrian plots abounded: a major conspiracy involving the London alderman, Sir Thomas Cook, and several reconciled Lancastrians, such as Sir Gervase Clifton, was uncovered. More sinisterly, committed Yorkists and servants of the Earl of Warwick, like John, Lord Wenlock, were also implicated. Rumours spread on the continent that Warwick was in secret negotiations with the Lancastrians in exile or that he planned to place the king's younger brother, the Duke of Clarence, on the throne. These rumours Earl Richard refused to even grace with an answer when summoned to appear before the king. Local unrest broke out in Kent and in the midlands in 1468 and elsewhere disquiet arose over the influence of some of Edward's favoured courtiers. Early in 1469 Thomas Hungerford and Henry Courtenay were arrested in the south-west and subsequently executed, principally, it was rumoured, because Humphrey, Lord Stafford of Southwick, coveted the Courtenay earldom of Devon. The rumours appear to have been proved true in May when Stafford was created Earl of Devon.

REBELLION AND DEPOSITION

By the beginning of 1469 Edward IV's authority was seriously compromised. He had reneged on his promise to invade France (but kept the taxation granted for this purpose) and grasping courtiers were dominating the king's counsel and royal patronage, while powerful magnates of the king's own blood were excluded from their rightful position in the realm. If this litany of royal wrongdoing had a familiar ring to it, it was precisely because the king's opponents, principally the Earl of Warwick, decided to portray Edward's regime in this way, reviving the 'commonweal' language used by the Yorkist lords in 1459–61. Warwick decided to make his move in June. In April there had been a popular uprising in Yorkshire, led by one Robin of Redesdale. The rebels' grievances were the familiar ones (taxation, evil counsellors, and local misgovernment), but there is nothing to suggest that Warwick was involved. Indeed, his brother, the Earl of Northumberland, appears to have suppressed it without difficulty. However, as soon as this rebellion was suppressed the county rose again, this time led by one Robin of Holderness. The principal grievance this time was local clerical taxation, but the rebels also demanded the restoration of the Percy family to the earldom of Northumberland. Later Tudor chroniclers identified Warwick's hand behind these events but this seems unlikely and before long John Neville had crushed that rising too.

A third rising in June, however, was far more serious and seems certain to have been engineered by Warwick. It is unclear whether the earl had planned this rising in advance or, like the Duke of York before him, he had merely taken advantage of his own popularity among the commons and appropriated their grievances and political platform to his own ends. The rebel leader again called himself Robin of Redesdale, but on this occasion he appears to have been a member of the Conyers family, long-standing Neville servants. The head of the family, Sir John, was Warwick's steward in Richmondshire and the rebellion in effect mobilised the Nevilles' Middleham affinity against the king. At the same time Warwick put the second part of his plan into action. On 6 July he crossed to Calais in the company of Archbishop Neville, his daughter Isabel, and the king's brother,

George, Duke of Clarence. There, on 11 July, he married his daughter to Clarence against the king's express wishes, and on the following day the rebel lords issued a manifesto 'for the honoure and profite of oure seid sovereyn Lord and the comune welle of alle this his realme.'[8] It condemned the king's evil counsellors, naming Earl Rivers, William Herbert, Earl of Pembroke, and Humphrey Stafford, the new Earl of Devon, and several other courtiers, and accused them of rapacity and maintaining lawbreakers. Warwick and Clarence summoned their supporters to meet them at Canterbury on 16 July and from there they marched to London and onwards to Coventry. Edward seems to have been caught unawares. On 9 July he had written to his cousin and brother asking them to deny rumours of their treachery and had despatched the Earls of Pembroke and Devon north to meet the rebels. On 26 July Pembroke was routed at Edgecote near Banbury and later taken to Northampton and executed. Devon had fled before the battle but was soon afterwards lynched by a mob in Bridgwater. Worse followed: Earl Rivers and his son, Sir John Woodville, were captured and put to death, and then the king, whose followers seem to have deserted him, was intercepted by Archbishop Neville and taken to Warwick Castle.

In some ways the situation in early August 1469 mirrored that of July 1460, when the Yorkist lords had captured Henry VI at the Battle of Northampton. Then the rebels had been able, temporarily at least, to impose their rule on a weak king and govern in his name. Warwick and Clarence appear to have attempted to do the same, summoning a parliament to meet at York on 22 September. In reality, however, the situation was quite different: Edward IV was a young, active king, while the rhetoric of commonweal, used so successfully by the Yorkist lords in 1460, was wearing thin among the political elite. Warwick's rebellion may have been seen for what it was, essentially a thinly veiled plot to remove his enemies from court and the council to reassert his own position in the realm. The Kingmaker's inability to govern was demonstrated by escalating local disorder and, most seriously, a new pro-Lancastrian rebellion in the north led by Sir Humphrey Neville, Warwick's kinsman from the senior branch of the Neville family. The rebellion was motivated as much by Sir Humphrey's hatred of his

Middleham kinsmen as it was by any desire to see Henry VI returned
to the throne and Edward and Warwick moved north together to
suppress the rising, executing Sir Humphrey and his brother Charles
at York on 29 September. By October Warwick and Clarence were
forced to admit their failure: some sort of settlement was reached and
Edward was able to return to London, his royal power restored.
Between November and February 1470 the king redistributed royal
patronage. The appointment of William Grey, Bishop of Ely, as
treasurer may have been acceptable to Warwick, but other changes
reflected a diminution of the earl's power. Richard, Duke of Gloucester,
the king's younger brother, became Constable of England and justiciar
of South Wales and, most significantly, the young Henry Percy was
released from the Tower. On 1 March he was restored to his lands
and before the end of the month Warwick's brother, John Neville, had
been dispossessed of the earldom of Northumberland. Despite the
ostensible air of reconciliation, there seems little doubt that by the
spring of 1470 Edward had finally resolved to break Warwick's power.
Earl Richard's animosity to the Woodvilles and his murder of Earl
Rivers proved an insurmountable obstacle to any lasting settlement,
just as the Duke of York's rivalry with the Duke of Somerset had
dashed any hopes of reconciliation in the early 1450s. As Sir John
Paston had observed in October 1469 that while 'the Kyng hym-selffe
hathe good langage of the lordys of Claraunce, of Warwyk, and of my
lordys of York [Archbishop Neville], of Oxenfford, seyng they be hys
best frendys. But hys howsolde men paue other langage.'[9]

By March 1470, however, local disorder had again become endemic
as men took advantage of the instability of royal government to pursue
their private quarrels by violence. One such dispute occurred in Lincolnshire where Richard, Lord Welles, his son, Sir Robert, and his son-in-law
attacked Sir Thomas Burgh's manor house at Gainsborough. Burgh,
however, was also master of the king's horse and Edward chose this
dispute to reassert his royal authority. Lord Welles obeyed the king's
command to appear before him, but Sir Robert refused and instead
instigated a general rebellion. According to his later confession, he
claimed the county had risen amidst rumours that the king and Burgh
were planning to impose harsh justice on the commons of Lincoln-

shire. These rumours had been spread by servants of the Duke of Clarence, and it is clear that the rebel lords planned to use the unrest in Lincolnshire to their own ends. On 12 March the rebels were routed by the king at the Battle of 'Losecote Field', near Empingham in Rutland. Their battle cry had been "A Clarence! A Clarence! A Warrewike!" but they had proved no match for the disciplined royal host and fled after a preliminary artillery barrage.[10] Welles was captured and his confession damned the rebel lords, claiming that they planned to make Clarence king. Edward now moved north to confront Warwick's supporters, receiving the submission of Lord Scrope of Bolton and Sir John Conyers. On 24 March the king declared Warwick and Clarence traitors and promoted Warwick's brother, John Neville, to the title of Marquess Montagu, partly in compensation for his loss of the earldom of Northumberland but also in recognition of his continued loyalty. Warwick and Clarence, however, escaped Edward's wrath. They set sail from Devon and, after failing to drop anchor at Southampton, were refused entry to Calais (where Warwick's lieutenant, John, Lord Wenlock, had been confirmed in his offices by the king). Finally, on 1 May, the rebel lords landed in Honfleur where they sought the assistance of the king of France, Louis XI.

The events of the following months are among the most extraordinary of the entire fifteenth century. Louis now managed to convince the exiled Margaret of Anjou to accept reconciliation with her erstwhile enemies, Warwick and Clarence. He also persuaded the Kingmaker to support the restoration of Henry VI, still languishing in the Tower of London. Margaret agreed to a marriage between her son, Edward, and Warwick's younger daughter, Anne, while Clarence was to be content with the lands and title of the Duchy of York. On 22 July at Angers Warwick and Margaret were formerly reconciled. Earl Richard was made to beg theatrically for forgiveness on bended knee for fifteen minutes; he was after all 'the gretest causer of the fall of King Henry, of here and here soone'. Warwick defended his position, arguing 'he had not done but that a nobleman outrayed and disperred owghte to have done', but it was all mere posturing. Both parties to the Angers agreement were acting out of expediency; this was a marriage of convenience. The rebel lords composed an open letter addressed to the 'trewe commones' of England, justifying their actions in supporting Henry VI not in terms of dynastic legitimacy but through an appeal to the language of the 1450s. They highlighted their commitment to the 'wele of the crowne and thavauncyng of the commen weele of Englonde, and for reproving of falshod and oppression of the poore peopull.'[11] They can be little doubt that this was empty rhetoric, although the concern shown by the authorities back in England to suppress the letter demonstrates the power of the idea of the commonweal and continued popular appeal of the Earl of Warwick. Indeed, Edward IV was right to be concerned. Early in August rebellion broke out again in the north of England, led by Warwick's ally, Henry, Lord Fitzhugh. The king responded quickly, marching north with his household. The rebels faded away and on 10 September Edward granted pardons to the rebel leaders, including Fitzhugh. However, three days later, with the king still in York, Warwick and Clarence, accompanied by Jasper Tudor (the Lancastrian Earl of Pembroke) and the Earl of Oxford, landed in Devon.

Once in England, Warwick moved quickly. He recovered his artillery and marched to Coventry. His return to England was marked by a popular show of enthusiasm and the commons of Kent rose in support of the earl, while the Earl of Shrewsbury and Thomas, Lord Stanley, also joined the rebels' banner. Most important of all, Marquess Montagu (who had recently been replaced as warden of the east and middle march by the Earl of Northumberland) at first raised men on Edward's behalf but then ignored the king's summons and joined his brother. Edward's position was now hopeless; he was in no position to give battle to Montagu, let alone Warwick's growing army. Accompanied only by Anthony, Earl Rivers, William, Lord Hastings, William, Lord Saye, and a small household he fled to King's Lynn and from there took ship to the Netherlands on 2 October. Narrowly avoiding capture by a hostile Hanseatic flotilla, he landed on the island of Texel and was taken into the protective custody of Louis of Bruges, Lord of Gruthuyse, a former Burgundian ambassador to England. Meanwhile, on 3 October Bishop Waynflete escorted the feeble Henry VI from the Tower and, three days later, Warwick led his army into London and submitted himself to the restored King Henry.

Edward IV's deposition was a startling turnaround of events. Some contemporaries chastised Edward for his inactivity in allowing Warwick to gain the military advantage, but he could not have allowed Fitzhugh's rebellion to grow. The restoration of the Percy family to their ancient title of Earls of Northumberland alienated Montagu and may have ultimately led to his throwing in his lot with his brother Warwick, yet Edward had been able to count on his loyalty throughout the 1460s and he needed the Percy family to effectively govern the northern borders. Clearly the crisis of 1469–71 arose principally from the ambitions of the Earl of Warwick but to claim that 'Edward did not lose his throne . . . because he had misgoverned' during the 1460s is to ignore the popular perception, fuelled by the rebel lords' propaganda, that the king had allowed evil counsellors to subvert justice and the commonweal.[12] Edward had made an injudicious marriage and had been cavalier with parliamentary taxation, while his foreign policy had ignored the counsel of his greatest subject. Added to this was a rival focal point of authority in the person of Henry VI and a legitimate alternative to the Yorkist king. Nevertheless, the Readeption regime of Henry VI and Warwick lacked support among the nobility and landowning class; few were convinced by the Kingmaker's rhetoric and fewer still believed that Henry VI could be an effective king.

THE RESTORATION OF EDWARD IV

Initially at least Edward received a lukewarm reaction from his brother-in-law, Charles the Bold, Duke of Burgundy. He and his father had supported the Lancastrian cause in 1459–61 and, despite his marriage to Edward's sister in 1468, the ducal court now played host to the exiled Dukes of Somerset (Edmund Beaufort, brother of the duke killed at Hexham in 1464) and Exeter. Duke Charles, however, feared, quite rightly, that part of Warwick's agreement with Louis XI had involved a promise to commit England to war with Burgundy. By November he appears to have been warming to his Yorkist guests. The following month Louis repudiated the treaty of Péronne and declared Charles's French lands forfeit. The duke was left with no choice: on

31 December he granted Edward £20,000 to assist in his recovery of his throne and three days later Edward was invited to the ducal court at Aire. Assured of Burgundian support, Edward set about assembling an invasion fleet and by 19 February his fleet of 36 ships was ready to set sail from Flushing.

Meanwhile the Readeption regime in England struggled to assert its authority. Henry VI cut a pathetic figure; his few public appearances seem to have further undermined his subjects' confidence in him and he spent the five months of his second reign largely confined to the Bishop of London's palace. Warwick presided over the government, awaiting the return of Queen Margaret and Prince Edward. George Neville, Archbishop of York, was reinstated as chancellor and Marquess Montagu was again appointed warden of the east and middle marches. There were, however, few other demonstrations of partisanship. Several prominent Yorkists (including Queen Elizabeth) fled to sanctuary, but only the Earl of Worcester was executed and many more, including the Duke of Norfolk, the Bourchiers, Lord Dynham, and even the queen's younger brother, Sir Richard Woodville, were reconciled with the new regime. The Duke of Clarence occupied a curious position in the new structure of power: according to one source he was held in 'great suspicion, despite, disdeigne, and hatered' by the supporters of Henry VI who worked to 'procure the distruction of hym, and of alle his blode', and it was not until February 1471 that he was appointed Lieutenant of Ireland.[13] Warwick summoned a parliament in Henry VI's name to assemble at Westminster on 26 November 1470. Its records have not survived, but it seems to have achieved little and only Edward and his brother, Gloucester, were attainted. Many members of the political elite appear to have retreated from politics during the Readeption and hesitated to commit themselves in support of the new regime. Leadership of the county commissions of array and of the peace were concentrated in the hands of a few lords, notably the Duke of Clarence, Montague, the Earls of Oxford, Pembroke and Warwick, and Lord Scrope of Bolton, while many of Edward's prominent servants and those men ennobled during the 1460s were conspicuous by their absence. While for a few, like the Sussex gentleman Sir John Lewkenor, the Readeption provided an opportunity to recover the fortunes and position in local society that they had lost during the 1460s, most landowners chose to sit tight and await the return of the Lancastrian exiles from France.

Edward and his small band of supporters (probably less than 2,000) set sail from Holland on 11 March. The following day they were prevented from landing at Cromer by forces loyal to the Earl of Oxford, but on 13 March they finally dropped anchor at Ravenspur at the mouth of the Humber. Edward avoided immediate defeat at the hands of the Yorkshire levies by claiming, in a deliberate echo of the events of 1399, that he had returned merely to reclaim his Duchy of York and showing in his defence letters of support from the Earl of Northumberland. Edward gained entry to the city of York, but, as even the partisan account known as *The Arrivall* recognised, he attracted few men to his banner. Crucially, however, Montagu did not move against him, perhaps because of his own crisis of loyalty but more likely because the northern gentry would not obey his summons and looked to the Earl of Northumberland for leadership. By his inactivity Northumberland did Edward 'right gode and notable service' and allowed the Yorkist force to pass into the midlands. There Edward began to collect his supporters, Sir James Harrington and Sir William Parr with 600 men at Nottingham and 3,000 more men at Leicester, and marched to confront Warwick who was at Coventry.[14] Crucially, on 3 April, just outside Warwick, Edward met and was reconciled with his brother, Clarence. Faced with overwhelming force, the Kingmaker refused battle and retreated south. The Yorkists entered the capital on 11 April. Henry VI was soon captured and returned to the Tower (along with Archbishop Neville) and Edward was reunited with Queen Elizabeth. Reinforcements arrived from Kent and two days later the Yorkists marched out of London to confront Warwick, then at St Albans.

On the morning of 14 April, Easter Sunday, both armies were arrayed just outside the town of Barnet. Again, the numbers deployed by both sides are obscure, but Warwick probably held the advantage. The Yorkists had camped very close to the Warwick's lines in order to negate the effect of his artillery which kept up a constant, if ineffective, bombardment throughout the night. Shortly after four o' clock in the morning Edward, took the initiative, displaying the prowess and vigour that had characterised his actions in 1461, and attacked, despite a thick fog. Probably due to the Yorkists' night deployment, the two armies were not aligned perfectly. On the Yorkist left Lord Hastings was engaged by the Earl of Oxford in the flank, while on the Lancastrian left the Duke of Gloucester's battle crashed into the flank of the men led by the Duke of Exeter. In the centre, however, Edward himself stood firm: as *The Arrivall* tells us, the king 'mannly, vigorowsly, and vallianty assayled them, in the mydst and strongest of theyr battaile, where he, with great violence, bett and bare down afore hym all that stode in hys way, and than, turned to the range, first on that one hand, and than on that other hand, in lengthe, and so he bet and bare them downe, so that nothing myght stande in the syght of hym.' The battle was savage: on the Yorkist side Lords Cromwell and Saye were killed in the mêlée and Gloucester and Rivers injured, while for the Lancastrians Montagu was cut down and the Duke of Exeter left for dead. At the height of the battle Warwick's men had mistaken the Earl of Oxford's badge of the 'star with streams' for Edward's 'sun with streams' and attacked, causing Oxford's contingent to cry "Treason" and flee. The Kingmaker himself was killed as the battle turned against the Lancastrians, 'somewhat fleinge' according to *The Arrivall*.[15] The Earl of Oxford managed to escape to Scotland, but the Duke of Exeter fled to sanctuary in London from where he was taken on 26 May and imprisoned in the Tower of London. In three hours of fighting Edward had reasserted his kingly authority through a stunning demonstration of his own personal prowess.

Yet Edward could not rest on his laurels; there was still the small matter of Queen Margaret and her Lancastrian supporters to deal with. On the same day as Edward had defeated Warwick at Barnet, the Lancastrian exiles had finally returned from France, making landfall at Weymouth. Hearing of the Kingmaker's demise, she resolved to fight on and marched for Wales to join forces with Jasper Tudor. Once again, Edward demonstrated remarkable energy. Those who had fought at Barnet were tired and many injured, but the king galvanised his supporters by celebrating St George's Day in the Garter Chapel at Windsor. From there he left for the West Country with an army of some 5,000 men. The Yorkists were at Malmesbury by 1 May with the Lancastrians encamped at Bristol, where Margaret received rein-forcements and artillery. There then followed a race in order to prevent the Lancastrians crossing the Severn into Wales. The city of Glouces-ter refused them entry and Margaret was forced to attempt to make the crossing at Tewkesbury. Edward had kept pace his enemies, the Yorkists having marched an astonishing 35 miles in a day, and when the Lancastrians found the ford at Lower Lode impassable they were obliged to give battle. Edward had outmanoeuvred his opponents and forced Margaret to fight on his terms.

The Battle of Tewkesbury, fought on 4 May 1471, was a decisive victory for Edward IV. The Yorkist host was deployed in the custom-ary three 'battles' or formations: the vanguard commanded by Gloucester, the centre by the king himself, and the rearguard by Lord Hastings. The Lancastrians were similarly deployed: Edmund Beaufort, Duke of Somerset, commanded the battle facing Gloucester; Warwick's former lieutenant at Calais, Lord Wenlock, stood opposite Edward; while John Courtenay, the recently restored Lancastrian Earl of Devon, was arrayed against Hastings. A heavy artillery bombardment by the Yorkists goaded Somerset into the attack, the duke moving against Edward's own battle in search of a quick and decisive outcome. The king, assisted by the men of Gloucester's battle, blunted Somerset's initial attack. Then 200 mounted Yorkist men-at-arms fell upon the Lancastrians' flank and before long Somerset's attack faltered. A complete rout of the Lancas-trians ensued. Devon and Wenlock were killed in the fighting (Wenlock perhaps by Somerset who, enraged at his failure to support his attack, accused him of treason), while, most significantly of all, Edward, Prince of Wales, was cut down as he fled the field. Somerset himself sought sanctuary in Tewkesbury Abbey but two days later he was dragged out and summarily executed, along with other prominent Lancastrian pris-oners. Queen Margaret, her cause finally lost, attempted to find sanctuary but by 14 May she too was in Edward's custody.

The Battle of Tewkesbury did not immediately end opposition to Edward's restoration. At the end of April the men of Richmondshire had risen in support of Henry VI, but on hearing the news of the Lancastrian defeat they submitted themselves to the Earl of Northum-berland as Edward prepared to march north against them. More serious

Battle of Barnet (14 April 1471), from the Ghent manuscript, late 15th-century (Ghent University library, MS236). In this medieval interpretation Edward IV (mounted, crowned and on the left of the picture) is shown piercing the armour of the Earl of Warwick with his lance.

was the rebellion of the Bastard of Fauconberg, Warwick's illegitimate cousin. He had been charged with patrolling the Channel and on hearing the news of Warwick's defeat at Barnet he had returned to Calais. With 300 men of the garrison he had crossed to Kent, where he recruited support in the Cinque Ports and in the city of Canterbury, and on 12 May he attacked the city of London. The Tower and London Bridge were well-defended by Earl Rivers and Lord Dudley and Fauconberg retreated to Blackheath. Six days later he and his followers withdrew at the approach of the king's army. Edward entered the capital in triumph on 21 May. There was only one outstanding piece of business: what to do with Henry VI? The former king was lodged in the Tower and, according to *The Arrivall*, on hearing the news of the

Modern interpretation of the Battle of Barnet by Chris Collingwood. In the painting, which depicts the centre of the battle, Edward IV charges toward the banner of Henry Holland, Duke of Exeter, while in the foreground soldiers of the Houses of York and Lancaster engage at close quarters.

death of his son at the Battle of Tewkesbury 'he utterly despaired of any maner of hoope or releve.' In fact, 'he toke it to so great dispite, ire, and indignation, that, of pure displeasure, and melencoly, he dyed the xxiij. day of May.'[16] The truth is probably less melodramatic. Edward could not allow this alternative source of royal legitimacy to continue and almost certainly ordered Henry put to death.

The events of 1469 to 1471 demonstrated both the strengths and weaknesses of the late-medieval English polity. On the one hand the relative financial weakness of the crown and its reliance on the great magnates for the proper discharge of the kingly responsibilities of defence and justice provided the opportunity for 'overmighty' subjects to flourish and challenge the king's authority. Thus kings did not need to be 'undermighty' in mid-fifteenth century England to fall foul of the ambitions of their greatest subjects. Edward IV made mistakes in the 1460s and may have allowed his youthful passions to cloud his judgement, but his principal failing was simply to ignore the wishes and thwart the ambitions of the Earl of Warwick.

Richard Neville, Earl of Warwick, is one of most enigmatic figures of the Wars of the Roses. He was a man of great ambition. By the

late 1460s it is clear that he regarded himself as of international importance, standing shoulder-to-shoulder with princes and playing the role
of Kingmaker. He was certainly regarded by contemporaries as an
exemplar of knighthood and chivalry. In 1460 popular verse celebrated him as 'that noble knight and floure of manhode' and the earl
cultivated this image by his actions in both peace and war.[17] This
image, self-fashioned as it may have been, proved an enduring one
and persisted into the Tudor period. In reality, Warwick was a military commander of limited abilities, defeated by the Lancastrians at
St Albans in 1461 and by Edward at Barnet, and he showed little of
the personal prowess exhibited by many of his contemporaries. He
was, however, a skilled politician, well aware of the shifts in political culture that defined the mid-fifteenth century. More than any of
his contemporaries perhaps, he was able to exploit the idea of the
commonweal and mobilise the commons' sophisticated understanding of the constitution and the nature and duties of kingship in support
of his own aims. Yet in so doing, Warwick may have neglected his
traditional responsibilities as a territorial magnate. In 1471 the
Neville affinity in Cumberland, led by Sir William Parr, fought for
Edward IV, while some of midlands servants failed to serve alongside
him despite the earl's impassioned pleas for assistance.

Moreover, as the Duke of York had in the 1450s, the Kingmaker
discovered that no amount of personal charisma or largesse could
hide the fact that he was not king. In many ways the great strength
of the late-medieval English polity was the loyalty and respect shown
to crowned and anointed kings. This had accounted for the slow and
hesitant descent into civil war in the 1450s and was again evident in
1471. Once Edward IV returned to England his personal prowess
and kingly virtues, demonstrated first and foremost on the battlefield,
trumped the commonweal card played by Warwick. His rival for the
throne, Henry VI, was a mere shadow of the virile, virtuous Edward,
who displayed the necessary ruthlessness in ensuring that no serious
dynastic rival survived the events of that year. Unfortunately, for the
Yorkist dynasty and England in general, Edward failed to maintain
the vigour demonstrated in 1471 for the remainder of that decade.

6

FORTUNE'S WHEEL:
THE THIRD WAR 1483–87

In May 1471 Edward IV could look forward to the future with some degree of satisfaction. He was undisputed king, his right vindicated in battle, and his Lancastrian rivals, Henry VI and Edward, late Prince of Wales, were dead. So too was the Earl of Warwick, his major political rival of the 1460s. His own dynasty seemed secure in the person of his eldest son, Edward (born while the king had been in exile in November 1470), supported by his two uncles, Richard, Duke of Gloucester and the recently reconciled George, Duke of Clarence. Edward could also rely on the support of his wife's large family, led by Anthony Woodville, Earl Rivers, able lieutenants such as William, Lord Hastings, and an expanding network of Yorkist servants tied, more often than not, personally to the king through their membership of his household. Yet, less than fifteen years later the Yorkist dynasty had been decimated, the immediate family of Richard, duke of York, extinguished in the male line, while the wider Yorkist establishment had imploded with many of Edward's closest servants now committed to a new king, Henry Tudor, who had, in 1471, been an obscure Lancastrian exile. This dramatic reversal of Yorkist fortunes had taken place in a very short length of time, little more than two years elapsed between the death of Edward IV on 9 April 1483 and the victory of Henry VII at the Battle of Bosworth on 22 August 1485. This period witnessed usurpation and the probable murder of a legitimate king, the reappearance of noble rebellion, the direct and perhaps decisive involvement of foreign princes in English affairs, and the death of an English king in battle (the first since Harold Godwineson in 1066), before Henry VII finally brought down the curtain on the Wars of the Roses.

EDWARD IV'S 'SECOND REIGN'

After his victory at Tewkesbury, Edward moved to consolidate his authority over the realm. Although he had won the 'Second War' at the head of a political faction, there is little evidence that the re-establishment of Yorkist rule was unpopular nor that it faced serious challenges. Only that irreconcilable Lancastrian, John de Vere, Earl of Oxford, and Thomas Clifford, brother of the fugitive Lord Clifford, attempted armed challenges to the regime in 1473 and both were soon neutralised. One defining feature of Edward's kingship after 1471 was the extent to which he delegated local power to a small group of trusted noblemen. In the main these were members of his family or in some other way personally connected to him, most importantly through membership of the royal household. In the south-west the gap left by the death of Sir Humphrey Stafford, Earl of Devon, in 1469, was filled to some extent by that loyal servant of the House of York, John, Lord Dynham. Later, the king's step-son, Thomas Grey, Lord Groby (from 1475 Marquess of Dorset) emerged as a leading figure in the region. In Wales, William Herbert, the new Earl of Pembroke, replaced his father as the king's leading representative, but by 1473 his inability to keep order in the Welsh marches had led to the creation of a council, under the control of Earl Rivers, to govern the principality in the name of the young Prince Edward. In East Anglia authority devolved upon the Dukes of Norfolk and Suffolk and increasingly John, Lord Howard, treasurer of Edward's household since 1468. In Lancashire and Cheshire Thomas, Lord Stanley, dominated the region partly through his stewardship of royal lands, while in the midlands the lands and influence of William, Lord Hastings, the king's chamberlain, were augmented by the grant of the stewardship of the Duchy of Lancaster honour of Tutbury in Staffordshire which had been granted to the Duke of Clarence in 1471.

Indeed, initially at least, the king's brothers, Clarence and Gloucester, bore much of the brunt of this local responsibility for maintaining order and royal authority, dividing between themselves the lands and influence of Warwick 'the Kingmaker'. In 1471 Edward had granted Warwick's midlands estates, the larger part of the earl's lands, to Clarence, while the Neville lands in the north had been granted to Gloucester. In the north Gloucester worked alongside the Earl of Northumberland and other northern lords, while in the midlands and the south-west, Clarence too was expected to cooperate with local magnates. The division of this inheritance, however, exposed the dangerous fault lines within the Yorkist establishment. Neither brother was content with these grants from the king, and Clarence in particular pressed for the title to the entire Beauchamp inheritance in the right of his wife, Warwick's daughter Isabel. This disregarded the claims of the earl's younger daughter Anne, and, more importantly, those of Anne, the dowager countess of Warwick, the rightful heiress to the Beauchamp patrimony in the midlands. In 1472 Gloucester attempted to secure his share of the inheritance by seizing Anne Neville, then officially in Clarence's custody, and marrying her. Clarence agreed in principle to a division of the estates but little was done in practice and by 1473 the brothers were on the verge of open conflict. It took the king's personal intervention in December of that year and the threat of a parliamentary act resuming royal grants to force Clarence to submit. There were even rumours that the king would allow the dowager countess to enter into her Beauchamp inheritance and that she in turn would grant the lands to Gloucester. The settlement doubtless reflected the king's lack of trust in Clarence. In the midlands he was stripped of his grant of Tutbury, while in Ireland, where he was the king's lieutenant, his powers were curtailed by the appointment of the household knight, Sir Gilbert Debenham, as chancellor. Writing some years later and with the benefit of hindsight, the author of the Crowland Chronicle observed that 'These three brothers . . . the king and the dukes, possessed such outstanding talent that if they had been able to avoid dissension that triple cord could have been broken only with the utmost difficulty.'[1]

It was against this background of family squabbles and continuing problems of local disorder that Edward's French campaign of 1475 must be viewed. When parliament assembled in October 1472 the matter of war with France topped the agenda. The first session was taken up with efforts to convince the Commons to grant taxation. The sense of urgency around this was unusual 'with many speeches of remarkable eloquence' delivered in support of new taxation. John Alcok, Bishop of Rochester, deputising for the chancellor, Bishop Stillington of Bath and Wells, made a long and detailed address to the Commons with two main themes. First, he recalled the connection between peace and unity at home and war against foreign enemies. Although Henry VI, 'the grete occasion of trouble and long dis-ease of this londe' was now dead, yet 'many a grete sore, many a perilous wounde' still remained and large numbers of 'riotous people' remained at large. This had encouraged foreign enemies, especially the Scots allied with the French, and more recently the Danes, to attack England. Thus 'there can be founde noon so honourable, so necessarie, nor so expedient a werk, as to sette in occupacion of the were outward the forseid idell and riotous people'. Finally, by means of a quick lesson in English history, Alcok concluded 'that it is nat wele possible, nor hath ben since the Conquest, that justice, peax, and prosperite hath contenued any while in this lande in any Kings dayes but in suche as have made were outward'. The successful reigns of Henry I and II, Richard the Lionheart, Henry III, Edward I and III, and Henry V were given as examples for the members of the Commons to reflect upon. Alcok's second theme was the king's recovery of his rightful inheritance in France. He portrayed Edward as a virile, chivalric figure in the mould of Edward III and Henry V. The realm had been delivered from civil war by the 'moost victorious prouesse' of the King and his virtues were contrasted with vices of the French king. By his 'subtyll and crafty enterpruises' Louis sought to undermine England's stability, encouraging both the Scots and the Danes. Edward, by contrast, was the type of king that both his English and rightful French subjects could be proud of. Alcok asked the Commons 'to considre the knyghtly courage, grete proesse and dispocion of our Soverain Lord the Kyng, whoos good Grace will eschewe payne, perell, ne jeopardie, for thaccomplishment of the premises'.[2] This chivalric potrait of Edward IV as warrior and law-giver reveals the widely held contemporary belief that 1475 offered the opportunity to draw a line under the civil wars and refashion the Yorkist monarchy in the image of Edward III. As David Morgan has argued, it was the king's 'dual capacity of fighting and judging' that dominated Alcok's speech, and another text composed at the same time setting out a programme of law reform, suggests that the model for this renewal of Yorkist kingship was Edward III 'who diffyed kowertyse, avansed manhode, and magnyfied trouthe.'[3]

The result was an innovative grant to fund 13,000 archers, reminiscent of that granted to Henry VI in 1453. It was hoped to raise no less than £118,000 by this expedient, although in practice the sum raised was far less and in the spring of 1473 parliament granted a conventional fifteenth and tenth to make up the difference. In a demonstration of the Commons' suspicion of Edward's intentions, however, the money was to be held in special treasuries until the army was ready to embark. The lessons of 1463 and 1468, when the king had received generous grants for royal campaigns that failed to materialise, had not been lost. Diplomatic wrangling with Brittany, Scotland, the Hanseatic League and, crucially, the Burgundians delayed the beginning of the embarkation but in July 1474 Edward finally concluded the treaty of London with Duke Charles committing the English to a landing in France before 1 July the following year. Unfortunately for Edward, as the Burgundian ambassadors negotiated the treaty, his brother-in-law turned his attentions to the eastern borders of Burgundy proper, investing the town of Neuss on behalf of his ally and kinsman, Rupprecht, Archbishop of Cologne. The siege dragged on through the winter and Charles was still there when Edward joined his army in Calais on 4 July 1475. The duke finally met Edward ten days later, although he was not accompanied by his own army and he made little effort to assist the English army. Duke Francis of Brittany also failed to take the field alongside his English ally. By 12 August Edward had had enough and made the first diplomatic overtures to Louis XI. Less than two weeks later, much to the consternation of Duke Charles, the two kings met in person and agreed the terms of the treaty of Picquigny. By this agreement Louis was to make a down payment of some £15,000 and an annual pension of £10,000. Thus the king's 'great enterprise' ended in an honourable and financially lucrative peace.

Even though some contemporary chroniclers considered the settlement to have been honourable, it was not a sentiment universally shared. The acquiescence of the king's leading captains was bought with French gold: Hastings received an annuity of 2,000 crowns (some £330), John, Lord Howard 1,200 and others 1,000 crowns each. Many of the soldiers, however, voted with their feet and entered Burgundian service. One Gascon servant of Earl Rivers quipped that Edward IV had won nine victories and lost only one battle, this present campaign. Sir John Paston, a soldier in the Calais garrison, had written to his mother, Margaret, full of enthusiasm for the coming campaign. His letter of 11 September telling his mother that 'thys wyage off the Kyngys is fynysshyd', is matter of fact, but revealing nonetheless. He finished his letter by explaining that 'I was in goode heele whan I come hyddre (to Calais), and all hooll, and to my wetyng I hadde never a better stomake in my lyffe, and now with-in viij dayes I am crasyd ageyn.'[4] The promise of July had faded into a dull September; Sir John's exuberance had given way to a jaded sense of disappointment which would never quite fade. Indeed, the French were in no doubt that Edward's settlement was less than honourable. Popular verse lampooned the English, while the vicomte de Narbonne mocked the two English sureties, Lord Howard and Sir John Cheyney, kept in Paris to ensure Edward's observance of the treaty: 'you English were so anxious to return home that 600 pipes of wine and a pension which the king gave you sent you post-haste back to England.'[5]

The sense of chivalric disappointment evident in 1475 was to be further reinforced two years later. On 5 January 1477 Charles the Bold was killed at the siege of Nancy. His daughter by his marriage to Isabella of Bourbon, Mary, was now heiress to the second most powerful state in Western Europe and her step-mother, Margaret, set about securing an English marriage to safeguard her inheritance from Louis XI. Margaret pushed the case for her favourite brother, the

Duke of Clarence, to marry the young Mary (his own wife, Isabel, having fortuitously died just weeks earlier). Edward, however, would not countenance the match, even suggesting Earl Rivers as an alternative. Yet as Commynes observed, he 'was only a minor earl, and she the greatest heiress of her time'.[6] Nevertheless, a Great Council assembled in February and rumours were soon rife of a military expedition to assist Duchess Margaret. Sir John Paston again sensed the opportunity for some great act of chivalry: 'It semythe þat worlde is alle qwaveryng. It wil reboyle somwher, so þat I deme yonge men shall be cherysshyd; take yowre hert to yow'.[7] Paston expected to be sent to France with Lord Hastings, the Lieutenant of Calais and, indeed, the following month Hastings set sail with sixteen men-at-arms, including Sir John, and over 500 archers. Sir John was not the only one anxious to assist the Burgundians: the Duke of Gloucester personally oversaw the despatch of English archers and hoped perhaps to lead a larger expeditionary force. In May Hastings, almost certainly with Gloucester's support, attempted to bypass the king's lukewarm response to Burgundian requests for help and sent English troops to the besieged town of Boulogne. This earned an angry rebuke from Louis XI and the king ordered him to write to the French king assuring him of his support for the treaty of Picquigny. In 1477, as in 1475, the chivalric aspirations of Gloucester, Hastings and others in the Yorkist establishment had been disappointed by Edward. Whether the king ultimately decided to remain idle to thwart Clarence's designs on the Duchy of Burgundy or merely because, as the Burgundians thought, he was too lazy to commit himself, the effect was the same. It widened the rift between the three brothers and further undermined the stability of the Yorkist regime.[8]

The immediate consequence of the events of 1477 was probably the arrest and eventual execution of the Duke of Clarence on 18 February the following year. Clarence was clearly aggrieved at the way in which his brother had dismissed his plans to marry Duchess Mary; matters were made worse when soon afterwards when the king also vetoed a proposal by James III of Scotland that Clarence marry his sister, Margaret, as part of a wider Anglo-Scottish marriage alliance. The duke retired to Warwick Castle and in April arrested Ankarette

Twynho, one of his late wife's servants, John Thursby and Roger Tocotes. They were accused of poisoning Duchess Isabel, found guilty by a packed jury and the first two soon executed (although Tocotes managed to escape). Their real crime was probably to have carried news of Clarence's grumblings to the king's servants. Edward responded by arresting and torturing the Oxford academic, Dr John Stacy. He was accused, along with one of Clarence's servants, Thomas Burdet, of necromancy and encompassing the king's death. Clarence in turn made an extraordinary declaration of Burdet's innocence before the king's council. Edward's patience had finally run out on his brother and in June he was arrested and committed to the Tower. Edward hesitated to bring Clarence's career to its inevitable conclusion, but in January 1478 parliament assembled to determine the duke's fate. The parliament was packed with royal supporters and no-one spoke out in Clarence's defence. The charges against him (that he had secured an exemplification of his nomination as heir to the throne made in 1470, that he had spread seditious rumours of Edward's bastardy, that he had encouraged his servants to raise rebellion, and that he usurped royal authority by the judicial murder of Ankarette Twynho) may well have been true but they hardly constituted treason. Indeed, his attainder had progressed slowly and when he was condemned on 7 February Edward delayed his execution for a further ten days and only moved when the Commons, led by their Speaker Sir William Allington, demanded justice.

If the king's household and the wider royal affinity may have approved of Clarence's execution, it is unclear whether it was greeted with any enthusiasm by the Duke of Gloucester. The younger brother was, however, the most obvious beneficiary of his demise besides the king: he received back the office of Great Chamberlain of England which he had surrendered to Clarence six years earlier and was allowed to reorganise and consolidate his estates in the wake of his brother's fall. Moreover, Edward increased Gloucester's power in the north: he was allowed from 1480 a virtual freehand in pursuing an aggressive policy against the Scots which culminated in the capture of Berwick-upon-Tweed in August 1482 and the grant of a hereditary palatinate in Cumberland and Westmorland in January the

King Richard III by unknown artist oil on panel, late sixteenth century
(late fifteenth century) © National Portrait Gallery, London

following year. Nevertheless, the Clarence episode did not reflect well on the House of York. While it allowed Edward to consolidate his authority and enjoy domestic stability and prosperity for the remainder of his reign it also revealed the contradictions and tensions at the heart of the Yorkist regime.

THE USURPATION OF RICHARD III

Edward IV died on 9 April 1483 after a short illness. There is no doubt that as Edward lay *in extremis* at Westminster many of his policies were beginning to unravel. Nowhere was this more apparent than in the collapse of his foreign policy. Since 1477 Edward had attempted to play France off against the Burgundians. In August of that year Duchess Mary had married Archduke Maximilian of Austria, the son of the Holy Roman Emperor, Frederick III. Edward had promised a secret Anglo-Burgundian treaty as long as Maximilian promised to make good any shortfall in the French pension. In May 1480,

111

following the Burgundian victory over the French at the Battle of Guinegate the previous August, Edward had promised his daughter, Anne, to Philip, son and heir of Maximilian and Mary. Louis XI had as a result defaulted on the pension, but Edward did not revoke the treaty of Picquigny. Indeed, the king was reluctant to burn his boats with Louis and resisted Maximilian's call for an invasion of France. In part, this was due to England's commitment to war with Scotland in support of James III's estranged brother, Alexander, Duke of Albany, but it also reflected Edward's desire to try and maintain relations with both European powers. This desire was thwarted, however, by the death of Mary of Burgundy in a riding accident on 27 March 1482. The estates of Flanders and Brabandt, whose provinces had borne the brunt of the war with France, immediately sued for peace and in December Louis XI and Maximilian came to terms at the treaty of Arras. The Dauphin was betrothed to Mary, the daughter of Maximilian and Duchess Mary, while Artois and Picardy were ceded to France as her dowry. England was excluded from these negotiations, the French pension lost and Calais surrounded by hostile territory. Edward may have been enraged and threatened renewed war with France, but the truth was that his foreign policy had been characterised by indecision and motivated by greed rather than any principle or pre-Machiavellian cunning. Moreover, the strains of war with Scotland were beginning to show and the royal finances, which had been restored during the 1470s, were creaking under the pressure. Indeed, by April 1483 funds were so scarce that there was barely enough to pay for the king's funeral.

Despite these difficulties, few could have imagined that within little more than ten weeks of Edward's death his son would have been deposed and declared illegitimate, and that the Duke of Gloucester would be acclaimed Richard III and the true heir of Richard, Duke of York. Yet these developments were made possible by the manner of Edward's rule and the contradictions at the heart of the Yorkist polity. In mid-April simmering tensions between Lord Hastings and the queen's Woodville and Grey kinsmen erupted into open conflict in the council. Hastings proposed that the king's uncle, Gloucester, be appointed protector until Edward came of age; the Marquess of

Dorset argued for an immediate coronation with the young king guided by a council and household in which the dowager queen, Elizabeth Woodville, and her kinsmen would play the leading role. On 29 April Gloucester, who had been in York when he received news of his brother's death, met Henry Stafford, Duke of Buckingham (a young noble who had been conspicuously sidelined during Edward's reign), at Northampton. They were joined by Anthony Woodville, Earl Rivers, who had accompanied the king from Ludlow. The two dukes promptly arrested Rivers and the following day, at Stony Stratford, intercepted Edward V and arrested his chamberlain, Sir Thomas Vaughan, and Sir Richard Grey. Edward's own reaction towards the dukes seems to have been lukewarm at best, while the queen and Dorset, all too aware of dangers facing them, fled to the sanctuary of Westminster Abbey. The king, accompanied by his uncle and Buckingham, arrived in London on 4 May and six days later the council appointed Gloucester as protector. Crucially, however, it failed to support his demand that Rivers and the others be condemned for treason.

The reasons for this *coup d'état* against the Woodvilles and Greys are not difficult to fathom. Since 1471, when they had shared Edward IV's exile, Gloucester and Hastings had been political allies; their alliance had been cemented by their common cause over France and Burgundy in 1475 and 1477 and Hastings's support for Gloucester's Scottish campaigns in the early 1480s. Hastings's rivalry with the Woodvilles can be traced back to May 1471 when he had been appointed Lieutenant of Calais despite a grant made to Rivers of the same office the previous June. Both Hastings and Gloucester shared a military-chivalric outlook which was at odds with the more courtly character of the Woodvilles. Their disdain for Rivers in particular may have been based on his perceived lack of courage. In 1476 Rivers's reputation had suffered when he deserted the Burgundian camp on the eve of the Battle of Morat. According to the Milanese ambassador, having offered his services to Charles the Bold, he made his excuses and left when told of the approach of the enemy. As Duke Charles told the ambassador, Rivers had left 'because he is afraid'.[9] Further evidence of Rivers's unpopularity at Calais came in August 1482 when it was rumoured that he and the Marquess of Dorset had planned to betray the town to the French; the author of these rumours was forced to confess they were 'utterly false & untrue' before the king and council.[10] Neither Gloucester nor Hastings could share power in the new regime with such men. Gloucester may have also held Rivers and his kin responsible for the death of Clarence. Hastings was also motivated by his long-running feud with the Marquess of Dorset. The precise nature of their dispute is obscure, but it may have been over sums outstanding for Dorset's marriage to Hastings's step-daughter, Cecily Bonville, heiress to the Bonville estates in the south-west and barony of Harrington in the north-west. According to Mancini, Edward IV had been so concerned over this bitter dispute, which had involved mutual accusations of treason, that he had effected a deathbed reunion between them. Moreover, both Gloucester and Hastings would have had cause for concern by the arrangements made in early 1483 that would have made Dorset and his brother, Sir Richard Grey, among the wealthiest magnates in the realm. From June 1481 Dorset had enjoyed the wardship and marriage of Clarence's heir, the Earl of Warwick, but his power was to be further augmented by the plan to marry his own son and heir, Thomas, to Anne St Leger, heiress to the Duchy of Exeter. The agreement promised to divide the Exeter estates between Dorset and his brother during the lifetime of Anne's mother, the duchess of Exeter.

Everything changed suddenly on 13 June 1483. At a further council meeting Gloucester announced details of a plot involving the queen and other leading members of the Yorkist establishment. Hastings was arrested and summarily executed, while Thomas Rotherham, Archbishop of York, John Morton, Bishop of Ely, and Thomas, Lord Stanley were imprisoned. A sudden alliance between Hastings and the Woodvilles seems improbable to say the least, and the inescapable conclusion must be that Richard moved against his erstwhile allies because he now planned to usurp the throne. As Charles Ross concluded: 'Whether or not they (Hastings and the others) already had well-formed suspicions as to his (Gloucester's) intentions, they would oppose his scheme to the last.'[11] Contemporaries were clearly shocked by the violence of this act and the rest of the council was cowed into submission. Events thereafter moved quickly. On 16 June Queen Elizabeth agreed to surrender her younger son, Richard, Duke of York, from sanctuary and he joined his brother in the Tower. The reason given was that the coronation could not go ahead without him, but in any case it was soon postponed to November. Around the same time orders were sent north for the execution of Rivers, Grey and Vaughan, and Clarence's son, the Earl of Warwick, was placed under the care of Anne, duchess of Gloucester. On 22 June, the day originally scheduled for the coronation of Edward V, Dr. Ralph Shaw, a Cambridge theologian, outlined Richard's claim to the throne at StPaul's Cross. Two days later the duke of Buckingham rehearsed the claim to the mayor and alderman of London and on the next day to a select gathering of lords, knights and esquires. The parallels with the way in which Edward IV had claimed the throne in 1461 were striking. The precise grounds upon which Richard justified his usurpation in June 1483 are unclear. Dominic Mancini states that the claim was based originally on the fact that Edward IV was a bastard; other sources, perhaps with the benefit of hindsight, suggest that only the late king's sons were deemed illegitimate.[12] In the circumstances, the former perhaps seems more likely. As in 1461, the acclamation of Richard as king by his peers on 26 June suggested that he was the true heir of Richard, Duke of York, and that he had been rightful king all along. On 28 June writs were despatched to the Calais garrison announcing that Richard had been acclaimed king 'by the concord assent of the Lords and Commons of this Royaume.'[13] On 6 July, in a ceremony presided over by his two closest supporters, the Duke of Buckingham, high steward of England, and John, Lord Howard, newly created Duke of Norfolk and Earl Marshall of England, Gloucester was crowned King Richard III. Any murmurings of discontent over the nature of his accession were probably quietened by the nearby presence of an army of some 4,000 northerners.

Richard III's usurpation was one of the most shocking and audacious acts of the entire Wars of the Roses. It seems unlikely that Richard had long cherished the throne and there is every indication that he was the most loyal of his brother's lieutenants during Edward IV's reign. What is clear, however, is his antipathy towards the queen's family, the Woodvilles, and a probable belief in April 1483 that he was the only man capable of ensuring stability and domestic peace during a royal minority. Exactly how his claim to be protector of the realm during Edward V's minority came to be transformed in the space of some six weeks into a claim to be rightful king himself is likely to remain one of the great unanswered questions of English history. It is possible, perhaps even likely, that he came to be persuaded of either the illegitimacy of Edward IV's sons or even of the late king himself. Philippe de Commynes suggests that these ideas had been put in Richard's mind by Robert Stillington, Bishop of Bath and Wells, 'that wicked bishop'.[14] Stillington, who was briefly arrested and lodged in the Tower in March 1478, might have revealed to the Duke of Clarence some legitimate doubts about the validity of Edward IV's marriage to Elizabeth Woodville, while rumours of Edward's own illegitimacy had been in circulation since at least 1469 and were repeated in 1475. Moreover, there is evidence that in support of Richard's claim his mother, Duchess Cecily, made a statement before witnesses that Edward IV was illegitimate. Whatever the truth of these rumours and allegations, whether Cecily gave her testimony freely or under coercion, the possibility that in June 1483 Richard believed himself to be rightful king of England cannot be ignored. Rather than being the scheming villain of Tudor propaganda, Richard had been convinced the throne was rightfully his and the violence of his usurpation was the inescapable consequence of asserting that right.

BUCKINGHAM'S REBELLION AND HENRY TUDOR

Whatever Richard's convictions in 1483, it appears they were not widely shared by his contemporaries. By the time Dominic Mancini left London in mid-July the princes in the Tower had disappeared from public sight and by the autumn there was a widely held conviction that they had been murdered. For Richard the murder of Edward V and his brother, the Duke of York, was a necessity, yet it was also an act of barbarity which prevented many of his subjects from accepting him as a legitimate and lawful king. Following his coronation Richard began the customary royal progress through his realm. This took him through the Thames Valley to Gloucester (where he parted company with the Duke of Buckingham who returned to his estates in the Welsh Marches), then to Duchy of Lancaster estates in the midlands, and finally to York where the royal party arrived on 29 August. Richard remained in the city for three weeks, investing his son as Prince of Wales, but even at this triumphant moment there were reminders of the problems that confronted him in legitimising his rule; Archbishop Rotherham, only recently released from imprisonment, was one notable absentee from the proceedings. Far more threatening, however, was news of a conspiracy involving both Elizabeth Woodville and Margaret Beaufort, countess of Richmond and mother of Henry Tudor. By the time Richard began his journey south from York the rebellion had spread to encompass his erstwhile ally, the Duke of Buckingham, who had probably been persuaded to join the conspirators by his captive, John Morton. While the involvement of the volatile Buckingham in the plot may have come as a surprise and personal blow to Richard, more serious still was the role played by many of Edward IV's former household servants, men such as Sir John Fogg, Sir John Cheyney, Sir Richard Guildford, Sir Giles Daubeney and William Brandon. Their involvement in the rebellion signalled the narrow base of Richard's support and how the manner of his usurpation, and the growing conviction that he had murdered the sons of Edward IV, had placed him outside the bounds of acceptable political behaviour. According to the Crowland Chronicler, the conspirators asked Henry Tudor to marry Elizabeth, the eldest daughter of Edward IV, and for him to challenge Richard's throne as the true political heir of the House of York.[15]

The rebellion when it broke on 10 October was a damp squib. The risings in Kent, Wiltshire and the south-west were poorly co-ordinated and failed to mobilise popular support. Key nobles, such as John, Lord Cobham, in Kent and George Talbot, Earl of Shrewsbury, in the midlands, failed to support the rebels. Crucially, Thomas, Lord Stanley (who was married to Margaret Beaufort), backed Richard, perhaps because of the involvement of the Duke of Buckingham in the rebellion. The duke had proved himself a fickle character and his own designs on the throne were something few were minded to encourage. Richard arrived in Salisbury at the beginning of November. Buckingham, who had raised his standard in Exeter on 18 October, found his route into Wales blocked by floods and was eventually deserted by even his own servants. On 2 November he was executed in Salisbury. The king then pushed westwards. Henry Tudor, who had belatedly set sail from Brittany at some point after 30 October, arrived in Plymouth, buffeted by storms, with a party of some 500 men. Seeing Richard's men on the shore and hearing news of Buckingham's execution, Henry soon turned his little flotilla around and headed back to Brittany. Richard had seen off a serious challenge to his throne but in so doing he had exposed the weakness of his position. Before long as many as 500 English exiles, including the Marquess of Dorset and many former members of Edward IV's household, had arrived in Brittany seeking to pledge their allegiance to Henry Tudor.

Henry Tudor was an unlikely claimant to the throne. Born in 1457, he was the son of Edmund Tudor, Earl of Richmond, and Margaret Beaufort. His father had been half-brother to Henry VI and a committed Lancastrian, while his mother was the great-granddaughter of John of Gaunt. Henry himself had been an exile in Brittany since June 1471 when he and his uncle, Jasper, had fled England in the wake of Edward IV's victory. Tudor's Lancastrian credentials had made him a potential rallying point for opposition to the Yorkist Edward IV, although there seems little evidence that anyone took his claim particularly seriously. In exile Henry had been the plaything of princely diplomacy. In 1471 he and Jasper had probably planned to go to the court of Louis XI, but storms had forced them onto the coast of Brittany. There Tudor proved a useful bargaining counter for Duke Francis II who sought English help against the French king. In 1475 Edward IV had requested the return of the exiled Tudors, ostensibly to marry Henry to one of his own daughters, and Henry had even been put aboard a ship at St Malo bound for England. At the last minute he feigned illness and escaped capture and an uncertain fate. Thereafter the diplomatic situation changed and Tudor seemed destined for a comfortable exile until his position was transformed in the summer of 1483. It is difficult to ascertain his role in the various conspiracies that revolved around his mother and John Morton, and it was not until 24 September that Buckingham wrote to him to make common cause against Richard. Indeed, Tudor did not become a serious threat to Richard until he had the committed support of the Woodvilles and other former servants of Edward IV. At Rennes cathedral on Christmas Day 1483 Henry solemnly promised to take Elizabeth of York as his queen and was acclaimed king of England by those who had joined him in the wake of Buckingham's rebellion.

Richard's response to Buckingham's rebellion and the emergence of Henry Tudor as a credible challenger to his throne was threefold. First, he had to secure those parts of his realm most affected by the rebellions. Richard could command the loyalty of a significant following, but these were in the main the men who had served him as duke of Gloucester. These men, large numbers of them from Yorkshire, were now transplanted into positions of local authority in the southern counties and granted the offices and lands recently forfeited by rebels. In Kent, for example, the Yorkshire knight, Sir Ralph Ashton, received the office of Lieutenant of Dover Castle and he exercised an important influence in the county, alongside several other northern servants of the king, from his newly acquired home at Westenhanger. Ashton at least had connections by marriage in the county, but elsewhere Richard's 'plantations' disrupted existing power structures and caused significant disquiet. The author of the Crowland Chronicle considered them evidence of the king's tyranny.[16] Richard's actions in the autumn and winter of 1483/4 suggest a man cautious of all but his most intimate servants. On the Scottish borders, for example, he failed to reward the Earl of Northumberland as he had promised. Although he granted the earl the new title of warden-general of the marches, he retained effective control of the west himself and made Lord Dacre his deputy there. Equally, in Durham, following the death of Bishop William Dudley in November 1483, the palatinate was ruled by a council of the king's men, stifling the ambitions of both Percy and the Neville Earls of Westmorland.

Second, Richard used his first (and only) parliament in an attempt to legitimise his rule. The assembly had been delayed from November 1483 by the rebellion and eventually gathered at Westminster on 23 January 1484. Little is known of the composition of the Commons, but the choice of William Catesby, one of the king's esquires for the body, as Speaker in his first parliament is perhaps a measure of its subservient nature. Nevertheless, even here Richard was cautious to portray himself as a virtuous king, anxious not to overburden his subjects with unnecessary taxation and rule in the best interests of the commonweal. The parliament abolished 'benevolences', the practice of extra-parliamentary taxation that had developed in Edward IV's last years, and it also revoked an act of the January 1483 parliament that had preserved royal rights on the estates of the Duchy of Lancaster against enfeoffments by individual royal tenants. Richard forewent the obvious profits to the Crown as the act had been to the 'grete hurte and thraldome of his subgiettes' and annulled it, 'havyng more affeccion to the commen wele of this his realme and of his subgiettes then to his owne singler profit.'[17] Nevertheless, the royal finances were a pressing concern and the Commons made the generous gift of the subsidy of tonnage and poundage for life. The grant of tonnage and poundage may have come at the end of a protracted period of negotiations between the king and parliament and it was not until 20 February that the real business, the legitimisation of Richard's usurpation, began. The so-called *Titulus Regius* stated that although Richard had taken the throne the previous June at the request of the three estates of the realm it had not been done 'in fourme of parliament'. Doubt thus lingered over its legitimacy, and so, to clarify matters, Richard's right to the throne should now be rehearsed and ratified by parliament. The document claimed that since Edward IV's marriage to Elizabeth Woodville the realm of England had fallen into disrepute:

'the ordre of all poletique rule was perverted, the lawes of God and of Goddes church, and also the lawes of nature and of Englond, and also the laudable customes and liberties of the same, wherin every Englisshman is inherite, broken, subverted and contempned, ayenst all reason and justice, soo that this land was ruled by silf will and pleasur, fere and drede, almaner of equite and lawes leide apart and dispised, wherof ensued many inconvenientes and myschefes, as murdres, extorsions and oppressions, namely of poore and impotent people, soo that no man was sure of his lif, land ne lyvelode, ne of his wif, doughter ne servaunt, every good maiden and woman standing in drede to be ravysshed and defouled.'[18]

The reason for this was quite simple: Edward's marriage had been unlawful and his children were therefore bastards. Richard was the rightful king by inheritance and, moreover, the only man capable of restoring good government. Once the *Titulus* had been passed Richard dissolved parliament and in a highly unusual step gathered the lords and leading members of his household to swear a public oath to uphold his son's rights should anything happen to him.

Finally, Richard waged an aggressive diplomatic campaign to neutralise Tudor's support from hostile foreign powers. He continued the unofficial naval war against France that had begun in the last months of Edward's reign and began preparations to extend hostilities towards Scotland and Brittany. The aim may have been to unite the realm behind him in 'werre outward' but he may also have hoped to intimidate foreign princes against supporting challengers to his throne. In May 1484 the death of the Prince of Wales delayed plans for a royal expedition against Scotland and by July Richard had accepted James III's calls for peace. A three-year truce with Scotland, concluded in September, allowed Richard to concentrate his efforts against France and Brittany. In the same month he concluded a deal with the unpopular Breton chancellor, Pierre Landais, to surrender Tudor. Henry, however, got wind of this and fled to France. While Tudor had enjoyed the support of the ailing Duke Francis of Brittany he may have been an irritant to Richard, but with the support of the French he was transformed into a credible threat. The French regency government of Charles VIII, under the control of his aunt Anne of Beaujeu, feared that the English would support the Duke of Orléans who was attempting to enlist Breton and Burgundian support against the Beaujeu regime. They were thus inclined to be favourable to Tudor if only to keep Richard guessing. In November the French declared Henry the rightful heir of Henry VI and the House of Lancaster and promised help in the form of 4,000 soldiers and some £4,500. In the same month Tudor's cause was further bolstered by the escape of the Earl of Oxford from imprisonment in Hammes Castle and the defection of part of the Calais garrison. However, in March 1485 Orléans submitted to the regency government and in June a group of pro-French nobles overthrew Pierre Landais (hanging him from the wall of Nantes Castle). At a stroke the potential usefulness of Tudor to the Beaujeu regime disappeared and French enthusiasm for his cause wavered. Moreover, Richard's attempts at reconciliation with Queen Elizabeth Woodville and her servants around Christmas were beginning to pay dividends. In January and February 1485 several Woodville servants, most notably Sir John Fogg, were pardoned and even the Marquess of Dorset was persuaded to reconcile himself to Richard. He was captured trying to leave France and returned to Henry a virtual prisoner. In the spring of 1485 there was every sign that Richard's domestic policies were beginning to bear fruit, while the vagaries of European politics were also beginning to swing back in his favour.

What then went wrong to explain Henry's successful landing at Milford Haven on 7 August 1485 and his defeat of Richard at Bosworth only two weeks later? By the middle of July it was clear that the French regarded Tudor merely as a possible distraction for Richard; they were certainly no longer willing to honour the agreement they had made the previous November. For Henry, chastened by news of the growing rapprochement between Richard and the Woodvilles and even rumours of a marriage between the king and his niece, Elizabeth of York, it was now or never. On 13 July he secured a private loan from Philippe Lullier, captain of the Bastille and one of Charles VIII's councillors, that allowed him to hastily recruit around a thousand recently disbanded French soldiers. These men were veterans, trained in the use of the pike and fighting in close formation, and when Tudor's small force of seven ships sailed from Honfleur on 1 August they formed the core of his army. Tudor's small force marched through Wales uncontested yet attracting only a small number of men to his banner, and arrived at Shrewsbury on 17 August. The town initially barred its gates to the pretender, but eventually Henry's army was allowed to pass through and a small contingent joined its ranks. The next day he met Sir William Stanley, his step-uncle, at Stafford. Stanley's force of some 3,000 did not join Tudor's army but he gave Henry vital information of Richard's disposition and covered the rebels' advance into the midlands.

If Henry Tudor's force was small and he had been unable to convince many of the legitimacy of his claim to the throne and his advanced into England, King Richard had fared little better. Immediately on receiving the news of Tudor's landing he had dispatched letters to his servants summoning them to muster at Nottingham. Crucially, Thomas, Lord Stanley, refused to answer Richard's summons despite the fact his son and heir, Lord Strange, was held hostage and his younger brother, Sir William, was proclaimed a traitor. On 20 August Richard led his army south to Leicester to cut off Tudor's route to London. His army was almost certainly larger than Henry's, probably twice its size, but it was still probably little more than 5,000 strong and the number of men engaged on his behalf may have been even less. On 22 August the two armies faced other across the Leicestershire countryside on Ambion Hill, near the village of Dadlington. The vanguard of Tudor's army was led by the Earl of Oxford and contained Phillibert de Chandée's mercenaries, while the wings were commanded by Sir Gilbert Talbot and Sir John Savage. Probably to the south of Tudor's position the Stanleys waited with their large force. Richard's vanguard was led by the Duke of Norfolk, while the Earl of Northumberland remained in the rear with a large contingent of northerners. Estimates of the number of noblemen with Richard vary from six to about twenty, although a figure towards the lower end of the spectrum seems most likely. As with all of the battles fought during the Wars of the Roses, accounts of the fighting that followed are confused and, at times, contradictory. Oxford took the initiative and closed on Norfolk's vanguard. Tudor's mix of French, Scots, Welsh and a few Englishmen appears to have had the best of the mêlée, but then Richard saw the opportunity to end the challenge to his rule once and for all. He made a headlong cavalry charge, in itself an unusual occurrence during the civil wars, towards Tudor's standard. It nearly succeeded: Henry's standard-bearer, Sir William Brandon, was killed and Sir John Cheyne, a formidable knight, bested by Richard himself. Yet, Henry's French mercenaries kept their discipline and protected him from Richard's onslaught. As the king's attack faltered, Sir William Stanley committed his men, tipping the battle decisively in Henry's favour. Richard died fighting in the thick of the action and even Polydore Vergil, the Tudor historian, testified to his bravery: 'and king Richard alone was killyd fyghting manfully in the thickest presse of his enemies.[19]' Among his lieutenants, the Duke of Norfolk was cut down, while his son, the Earl of Surrey, was captured. The Earl of Northumberland, on the other hand, appears to have watched events unfold from the sidelines. Richard's body was stripped, tied to a horse and taken to Leicester, where it was displayed for three days. This gruesome performance was necessary to convince the political nation of his death.

The Battle of Bosworth, the most decisive battle of the civil wars of the fifteenth century, was also paradoxically one of the smallest. In terms of numbers engaged, both nobles and commoners, it did not compare with Tewkesbury or Barnet and certainly was nowhere near the scale of Towton. The disengagement from politics that this suggested was probably the most damning indictment of Richard III's short reign. Henry Tudor, who had been a political nobody in 1483, was able to march across Wales and into England virtually unopposed and defeat in battle a king who should have been able to deploy the loyalty of his subjects and the resources of the realm against the pretender. Moreover, Tudor had launched his invasion not with the backing of the French crown, but on the back of a private loan, hastily arranged, and with the assistance of only a thousand French mercenaries. Richard may have, in the final analysis, perished in a display of chivalric bravado, but his defeat revealed the divisive and unpopular nature of his regime. It is surely mistaken to claim that the events of August 1485 were not 'a response to the outrage caused by the murder of the princes of the Tower'. [20] While many members of the Yorkist establishment had been willing to support Richard against the Woodvilles in April 1483, far fewer had acquiesced in the murder of Hastings and the usurpation. Fewer still could countenance the murder of Edward's sons and the support given to Buckingham's

King Henry VII by unknown artist oil on panel, 1505
© National Portrait Gallery, London

Rebellion and eventually Henry Tudor's claim to the throne by so many former supporters of the House of York was a direct result of the manner in which Richard became king. Once king, whatever his personal commitment to justice and good government, his base of support was too narrow and he could not even command the loyalty of men, like the Earl of Northumberland, who had been his committed supporters during the 1470s. There is no doubt that the usurpation itself had further weakened kingly authority, making challenges to the throne more likely, even probable. This manifested itself in two ways: the willingness of men to support claimants for their own short-term political ends and a general disengagement from politics that made these unlikely candidates for the throne all the more likely to succeed. These were the most important challenges that faced the new king, Henry VII.

THE ESTABLISHMENT OF THE TUDOR REGIME

Henry Tudor secured his throne by a mixture of conciliation and careful repression and threat. On the one hand his policy of conciliation was unavoidable; like Edward IV and Richard III he had triumphed at the head of a small faction and it was not enough to run a kingdom. Professional administrators, such as those who staffed the central law courts, the exchequer and chancery, were largely kept in place, while many men who had not actively opposed his capture of the throne continued to hold high office. For example, Henry appointed John, Lord Dynham, Richard's Lieutenant of Calais, as Treasurer of England at the end of 1485. Henry followed the policy established by Edward IV and appointed his friends and family to positions of

Elizabeth of York by unknown artist oil on panel, late sixteenth century (*c*.1500) © National Portrait Gallery, London

regional authority: Giles, Lord Daubeney in the south-west, Jasper Tudor, now Duke of Bedford, in the Welsh marches, and the Stanleys in the north-west. Yet Henry could not rule without the active support of a broad section of the political nation. Thus the Earls of Northumberland and Westmorland, who had submitted themselves to the king in the aftermath of Bosworth, were eventually released from prison in December and welcomed Henry when he began his tour of the north in March 1486. The new king's most important conciliatory act, however, was his marriage on 18 January 1486 to Elizabeth of York, the daughter of Edward IV. This was, in the language of Tudor propagandists, the union of the red rose of Lancaster with the white rose of York. It needed a papal dispensation (they were related within the prohibited degrees), secured by Bishop Morton while in Rome earlier that year. This marriage, which Henry had solemnly undertaken to enter into while in exile, was symbolic and practical in importance. It promised to unite the political supporters of both Tudor and York (removing the stigma of bastardy that Richard III had placed upon his brother's children) and offered dynastic security, something seemingly assured by the birth of a prince and legitimate male heir to the throne, Arthur, on 18 September 1486, just eight months after the marriage of his parents. Nevertheless, it was not necessary to legitimise his kingship, a point the new regime was anxious to make, and it is significant that Henry did not formally announce his intention to marry until 10 December 1485, after his title had been confirmed in parliament.

Indeed, Henry's first parliament signalled the nature of the new Tudor regime. It was summoned to meet at Westminster on 7 November, just a week after his coronation on 30 October. Once again, the composition of the Commons is obscure, but the choice of Speaker, Sir Thomas Lovell, another parliamentary novice and one of the new king's most trusted companions, suggests its nature. Henry did not ask for parliamentary ratification for his title. Instead, he presented his right and title as a *fait accompli*; his previous attainder was simply nullified by virtue of becoming king. Even the attainder of Richard (achieved by sleight of hand through dating the beginning of his reign to 21 August, the day before Bosworth) offered no justification for

Henry's title; it needed no validation. The *Titulus Regis* simply stated that 'thenheritaunce of the corounez of the realmes of England and of Fraunce . . . be, rest, remayne and abyde in the most royall person of our nowe soverain lord Kyng Henry the .vij.th, and in the heires of his body laufully comyng . . . and in noon other.'[21] Significantly, there was no mention of his impending marriage to Elizabeth of York. The parliament made a generous settlement of the crown's finances: while no direct taxation was requested, Henry received the subsidy of tonnage and poundage for life, £14,000 was set aside for the yearly maintenance of the royal household, and in the New Year parliament passed a sweeping act of resumption, resuming all royal grants made since 1455. This latter act may have been tempered by a staggering 461 exemption clauses (compared to 288 in 1465), but it at least afforded Henry the opportunity to be magnanimous towards his new subjects.

Henry also ruled through repression and fear and nowhere was this more apparent than in his rule of the north of England. The north was especially important for the new king: its powerful magnate families, such as the Percys, the Stanleys and the Cliffords, commanded powerful military resources and it was a region that had been fulsome in its support for Richard III. Moreover, its coastline offered opportunities for invasion (as it had for Henry Bolingbroke in 1399 and for Edward IV in 1471), while its proximity to Scotland could not be ignored. Henry's policy was two-fold. First, he offered rewards to those who had previously supported Richard: the city of York received a reduction in its fee-farm in return for the election of pro-Tudor officials, while the Earl of Northumberland was eventually allowed to return to his old offices in return for submitting to the new king. Second, Henry established a system of bonds (known as recognizances) which bound the northern gentry and nobility to one another and to royal servants at Westminster. These threatened crippling financial penalties at the slightest hint of disloyalty (such as not appearing before the king's council when summoned), yet they also offered a means to reconcile former opponents. Lords Scrope of Bolton and Masham, for instance, who joined the Earl of Lincoln's rebellion in 1487, were spared but placed under such bonds.

The success of these policies is evident in the reaction to the rebellions against Tudor rule between 1485 and 1487. Early in 1486 Humphrey Stafford of Grafton, Worcestershire, attempted to raise the midlands in the name of Clarence's son, Edward, Earl of Warwick, while Francis, Viscount Lovell, Richard III's former chamberlain, tried to raise the area around Richard's former lordship of Middleham, Yorkshire. Both risings turned out to be nothing more than an inconvenience, and by the time Henry reached York on 20 April Lovell's army had dispersed. He fled to the Low Countries where he was joined by John de la Pole, Earl of Lincoln. De la Pole, who was Edward IV and Richard's cousin, had been heir apparent following the death of the Prince of Wales in 1484, but despite being present at Bosworth on Richard's side he had escaped any punishment. It seems his motivation for rebellion was loyalty to the House of York, rather than any personal commitment to Richard, and he was probably drawn into the conspiracy by Margaret of Burgundy. In February 1487 he suddenly fled to the Low Countries and the following month he and Lovell arrived in Ireland at the head of a small army provided by the dowager duchess of Burgundy. There they joined with the Irish Earls of Kildare and Desmond in proclaiming an obscure young man, Lambert Simnel, as the Earl of Warwick and King Edward VI. In June Lincoln, Lovell and Simnel landed in Lancashire but, as in the previous year, the rebels failed to rally those men with Yorkist sympathies to their banner. On 16 June the rebels met Henry, his army strengthened by a large contingent supplied by the Stanleys, at Stoke near Newark in Nottinghamshire. The battle ended in a swift and bloody defeat for the rebels. Lincoln was killed, Lovell went missing and Simnel was put to work in the royal kitchens, a measure of the very limited appeal his rebellion appears to have had. Stoke marked a watershed for Henry and confirmed the fact that while individuals would continue to plot against him, the realm as a whole had no more stomach for rebellion and civil war. On 25 November 1487 Elizabeth of York was finally crowned queen of England. It was this symbolic act, rather than their marriage which had taken place nearly two years earlier, that marked the end of the Wars of the Roses.

*   *   *

Recent commentators have seen little continuity between the wars of 1459–64 and 1469–71 and the events of 1483–87. Edward IV's victory in 1471 and the twelve years of stable government that followed ended the dynastic uncertainty and political instability that had caused the collapse of Lancastrian kingship. Yet fundamental tensions remained. Despite recent claims to the contrary, Edward's style of kingship was neither as dynamic nor as effective as Henry V's. In 1475 and 1477 he disappointed influential segments of the Yorkist establishment and by 1483 his policies, both at home and abroad, were beginning to unravel. He most certainly did not 'leave his dynasty securely settled on the throne' for within less than two months of his death Edward V has been removed as king and probably murdered by his own uncle, while many of his closest supporters had deserted the House of York for an obscure claimant distantly related to the House of Lancaster.[22] Richard of Gloucester's usurpation was one of the most shocking and unwarranted misuses of power in a century that abounded with them. His seizure of the throne debased the monarchy and undermined further the already shaky foundation of royal power in fifteenth-century England. Henry Tudor became king of England in August 1485 through a combination of good fortune (battles are risky affairs as both Richard III and his father, the Duke of York, discovered to their cost) and the disengagement of a large segment of the political nation. This lack of engagement in the political process would paradoxically allow Henry to build a new edifice of royal authority, a distinctly Tudor method of governing and political culture that would survive more than a century of change even more radical than that experienced during the 1400s.

Part 3

CONSEQUENCES

7

WAR AND SOCIETY:
THE IMPACT OF THE WARS

There seems a general consensus among recent historians that the Wars of the Roses had little immediate and even less long-lasting impact on English society.[1] The Tudor portrait of gloom and doom (which saw 100,000 Englishmen slaughtered, the nobility decimated, and the nation impoverished) has been replaced by one in which gentry culture flourished and the domestic economy grew while fighting was limited in both duration and intensity. Estimates for the period of actual campaigning range from 'little more than twelve or thirteen weeks in thirty-two years' to some two years. However long the battles lasted, most historians agree with the verdict of the contemporary French observer, Philippe de Commynes, that, in comparison to their continental neighbours, the population of England escaped the worst excesses of war. Fifteenth-century England was 'the most peaceful country in Europe'.[2] This chapter will question that basic assumption. To what extent was England really a society organised for peace, one in which the warlike proclivities of the minority could safely by ignored by the majority? What was the communal and individual experience of war? Were the battles of the Wars of the Roses mere skirmishes in which fighting, and dying, was limited to the political elite or did they impact more widely across all strata of society? Most important, however, is the question of whether the impact of and engagement in the civil wars changed during their course.

David Grummitt

WAR IN FIFTEENTH-CENTURY ENGLAND

Both contemporary Englishmen and foreign observers could agree that fifteenth-century England had been spared the worst horrors of war. Sir John Fortescue contrasted England with France and argued that the inhabitants of the latter were oppressed by heavy taxation designed to maintain a standing army and that the country was subject to the predations of the soldiery. England on the other hand, a mixed monarchy where parliament upheld the liberties of the subject, was free of the burdens of war and tyranny. Commynes, ever anxious to criticise the government of the Valois kings, drew attention to the short duration of campaigns in England, the absence of pillage, and, initially at least, the limitation of casualties to the political elite.[3] Most modern commentators have accepted that the Wars were limited in both their duration and the impact they had on English society. But if fifteenth-century England was a demilitarised society organised for peace, in which political violence was short-lived in duration and surgical in its execution, then something quite extraordinary had occurred in the years following the accession of Henry IV in 1399.

The late thirteenth and fourteenth centuries had witnessed an unprecedented militarisation of English society. The wars of the three Edwards had been fought by large armies, which had mobilised the wealth of the nation through ever-increasing levels of taxation and drew more and more of the king's subjects into direct involvement in his wars. The armies of Edward I and Edward III in Wales, Scotland and later France were comprised of well-to-do commoners and an increasingly militarised aristocracy. Moreover, these armies were large: 3,000 heavy cavalry and over 25,700 infantry for Edward I's Falkirk campaign of 1298, while in 1294–95 Edward probably had at least 35,000 infantry and three to four thousand knights, squires and sergeants in the various English armies in Wales. Changes in the art of warfare in the fourteenth century, away from massed infantry armies, diminished the size of armies but even in 1360 the army that Edward III led to the gates of Paris still numbered in excess of 10,000 men. The number of men-at-arms, heavily armed soldiers wearing full armour either on horseback or on foot and recruited from the landowning classes, remained impressive: at least 4,000 for the Crecy campaign of 1347 and as many as 4,500 in the expedition Richard II led to Scotland in 1385. In the fifteenth century the size of English armies fighting in the Hundred Years War continued to diminish (around 10,500 for the Agincourt campaign but more typically around 3,000), but this represented further developments in the nature of warfare and not a wholesale demilitarisation of English society. The short chevauchées and small standing garrisons of Normandy necessitated smaller armies, deployed more frequently and with a greater ratio of archers to men-at-arms. Nevertheless, the frequency of these expeditions (no less than 40 expeditionary forces crossed the channel between 1415 and 1450) ensured that the demand for soldiers, supplies and money was an omnipresent one in late-medieval England.

The demands of war during the reigns of the three Edwards had important and long-lasting consequences that continued to be felt during the fifteenth century. The first of these was the practice of raising armies by commissions of array. In 1277 the recruitment of infantry for Edward I's first Welsh war had been delegated to county sheriffs, but by the 1290s this responsibility was in the hands of specially appointed commissioners, usually led by the leading nobleman of the county and made up of prominent landowners. Throughout the fourteenth century the commissioners of array also developed a system of quality control, checking the war-readiness of the county levies and enforcing the 1285 Statute of Winchester which ordained that each able-bodied man between the ages of 16 and 60 be able to serve for forty days a year and should have arms and weapons appropriate to his wealth and social status. The practice of raising armies by indenture meant that the importance of the commission of array for assembling expeditionary forces diminished during the later fourteenth century, but they continued to be issued frequently, especially in the coastal and border counties, and they were vital in maintaining English society at some degree of military preparedness. The statute of Winchester was reissued in 1437 and again in 1442. In 1450 the seventeen villages of Ewelme half-hundred in Oxfordshire could assemble 85 soldiers, seventeen of whom were capable archers, although the commissioners reported that many men were deficient in both arms and armour. From 1458 the frequency of commissions of array increased, in effect preparing the realm for the outbreak of civil war. The effectiveness of the commission of array in mobilising a nation for war should not be underestimated. In the summer of 1450 it was the mechanisms of the commission, without either royal warrant or effective noble leadership, that enabled the commons of Kent to assemble a well-armed force of several thousand to march on London. Similarly, it was essentially the same system, albeit one overhauled and reinvigorated by the early Tudors, that allowed the leaders of the Pilgrimage of Grace to assemble a rebel army of at least 30,000 men in 1536.

A second important consequence of the militarisation of English society under the three Edwards was the willingness and ability of the English to pay for war. While estimates of the crown's income in the late middle ages are notoriously difficult to make, it is clear that that its ability to tax its subjects rose dramatically from the late thirteenth to the mid-fourteenth century. New forms of taxation, both direct (in the form of parliamentary subsidies) and indirect (in the form of new taxes on trade, particularly wool), allowed Edward I and Edward III to fund ambitious, expansionist policies at home and abroad. Moreover, through the development of the notion that parliament was the proper place to seek authority for taxation, the community of the realm gave its approbation to this expansion of royal power. Although the levels of taxation appear to have dwindled in the late fourteenth century, they rose again in the early fifteenth century and peaked to fund Henry V's conquest of Normandy. Surprisingly little is known of the systems through which these taxes were collected at a local level, but it is clear that local communities usually regulated their collection and often took measures to ensure that the tax burden fell in a reasonably equitable manner. In the mid-fifteenth century local arrangements for the collection of war taxation had been in place for over a century and these were employed to fund the campaigns of the Wars of the Roses. Early in 1460 John Paston described how the towns and villages of Norfolk had paid the wages of 400 men assembled by the commissioners of array, while numerous English towns raised local taxes to send contingents to serve in the civil wars. From the 1360s the English were also used to subsidising royal government through loans. Edward I and Edward III had, of course, funded their wars on credit and by 1307 Edward I's debts stood at £200,000. By 1339 a debt of £300,000 had threatened the collapse of Edward III's foreign ambitions. The crucial difference, however, was that from the 1360s these loans came not from foreign bankers but from the crown's own subjects. In the fifteenth century it was English mercantile capital, dependent on the fortunes of the wool trade, rather than the loans of the great southern European banking houses, that maintained royal government. Thus in the mid-fifteenth century English merchants (such as the wool merchants who bankrolled the Earl of Warwick's takeover of the Calais garrison in 1455 or the Londoners who supported the Yorkist earls in 1460) had a vested interest in a swift and decisive conclusion to political conflict and uncertainty. Even reluctant lenders, such as the men of the palatinate of Durham who contributed to the Lancastrian cause in December 1460, still provided cash to enable the rival parties to put men in the field.

The conflicts of the thirteenth and fourteenth centuries ensured that English society was equipped to wage war, but they had also imbued the realm with a deeply militaristic culture. Many recent historians have taken contemporary complaints of military decline at face value. William Worcester, writing in the 1450s, lamented the fact that recently those that had been 'descinded of noble bloode and borne to armes' had neglected these skills, turning instead to the law and a life of idleness.[4] J.R. Lander dismissed Worcester as 'the arch-conservative spokesman of the vanishing group of veterans of the Hundred Years War' while still broadly accepting his conclusion that the nobility and gentry of fifteenth-century England were less martially inclined than their grandfathers had been.[5] Yet Lander was probably wrong on both counts. Worcester's concerns about a decline in martial ability may have been misplaced but he was certainly not alone in the second half of the fifteenth century in advocating a military/chivalric revival. Between 1450 and 1475 a number of military texts, such as Vegetius's Roman classic *De Rei Militari*, Christine de Pizan, Ramon Lull and Alain Chartier, were translated and re-written for an English audience.[6] Moreover, military and chivalric texts generally appear to have enjoyed a resurgence of interest in this period. Far from being regarded as anachronistic and unfashionable, ambitious men continued to aspire to a military and chivalric definition of gentility. When the family of the York merchant Nicholas Blackburn (d.1432) commissioned his likeness in a stained glass window in the church of All Saints North Street they had him depicted in full armour, testimony to the enduring appeal of the martial image even among the urban, mercantile elite.

It is also by no means clear that the landowning classes had turned their backs on their traditional military roles by the mid-fifteenth century. The extent to which the gentry had withdrawn from an active role in the Hundred Years War has been greatly exaggerated. This argument had been made largely on the basis of the increasing ratio between men-at-arms and archers in the expeditionary forces of the fifteenth century. In the mid-fourteenth century the ratio appears to have been equal between men-at-arms and archers. By 1415 a ratio of 1:3 appears to have been the norm, but in 1430 this rose to 1:12 and throughout the 1430s and 40s a ratio of 1:5 was the average. A number of explanations have been advanced. First, a change in the nature of campaigning away the chevauchée towards static garrisons lessened the opportunities for plunder and ransom thus making the prospect of service abroad less enticing. Second, the gentry were less eager to serve in armies comprised of a majority of non-aristocratic soldiers and, finally, the burdens of shire administration meant it was simply not possible to combine a successful domestic career with service in war overseas.

Nevertheless, it is clear that service in war remained an important part of the *cursus honorum* of a significant minority of the English gentry in the years after 1422. This differed from county to county, with some counties, such as Essex where lawyers made up a substantial component of the county elite, contributing less than others. Elsewhere, however, military service continued to define the county elite up until the outbreak of civil war. In Kent, for instance, men such as Sir William Haute, Richard Woodville and Sir Thomas Kyriell combined careers as sheriff, MP and justice of the peace alongside active service in France. Individuals identified by most historians as courtiers and domestic administrators, such as James Fiennes, Lord

Saye and Sele, in Kent, Sir Richard Haryngton in Lancashire or Sir Robert Vere in Devon, continued to serve in Normandy to end of the English occupation in 1450. As Simon Payling has recently shown, their campaigning in France was not mutually exclusive with service in England.[7] Moreover, there is no evidence that these old soldiers represented a core of disaffected opponents of the Lancastrian regime and their careers during the Wars of the Roses demonstrate that existing loyalties and a degree of personal choice determined their decision to fight for Lancaster or York.

THE IMPACT OF THE WARS: (I) THE ARISTOCRACY

There can be little doubt that in the 1450s and 1460s a good proportion of the political nation were willing to risk their lives and livelihoods in the the civil wars. This was particularly apparent among the nobility. Colin Richmond's figures demonstrate the extent of their involvement, particularly in 1459–61. At Ludford Bridge, for example, six lords fought alongside the Duke of York, while as many as 21 were present on the Lancastrian side. At St Albans in February 1461 12 Yorkist lords faced 15, possibly 17, Lancastrian peers, while at Towton no fewer 21 Lancastrian lords fought against at least .nine Yorkists. In all at least 58 of the 70 men who received a personal summons to parliament or a patent of creation between 1459 and 1461 played an active role in the Wars of the Roses. Moreover, they appear to have led from the front. Fourteen of the 36 Lancastrian peers were either killed in battle or executed shortly afterwards, while five of the 22 Yorkist lords lost their lives.[8] Although McFarlane was undoubtedly correct to point out the Wars *per se* did not lead to the extinction of any more than a handful of noble houses, the battles of 1459 to 1461 undoubtedly took a savage toll on the nobility, with over a quarter of the parliamentary peerage being wiped out in less than two years.

The scale of involvement in the events of 1459–61 on the part of the gentry was no less impressive indeed; according to Richmond, it was their involvement on the Yorkist side that tipped the balance in favour of Edward IV. Precise figures are impossible to determine, but the attainder of Lancastrians in the parliament of 1461 and other evidence suggests that at least 32 men who had sat in the Commons during Henry VI's reign were present on the Lancastrian side at the Battle of Towton, while at least fifteen (almost certainly an underestimate) fought for Edward IV. The catastrophic Lancastrian defeat certainly took a heavy toll on the gentry who fought for Henry VI. Servants of the Nevilles, like the Northumberland esquire John Bere, and those of the Percys, such as the Bertrams and Sir Thomas Crackenthorpe (possibly knighted by the Earl of Northumberland on the eve of the battle) died fighting alongside their lords at Wakefield and Towton. A further 42 Lancastrian knights and esquires were executed after the battle. Yorkist casualties were obviously far fewer, with the Kentish esquire Robert Horne among the most prominent of the dead, but clearly large numbers of knights and esquires were present on Edward IV's side. Several men, like John Howard (later Duke of Norfolk), William Hastings, Walter Blount and Humphrey Stafford, were knighted on the Yorkist side and service in the battles of 1459 and 1461 was a common thread that ran through Edward's household servants and the political elite of Yorkist England. The impact and trauma of the civil war of these years, and in particular the period from the Battle of Wakefield to the Battle of Towton, should not be underestimated. It is evident that the reports of contemporary chronicles of between 28,000 and 38,000 men slaughtered on Palm Sunday 1461 were a wild exaggeration, but such claims were also a rhetorical device designed to underline their authors' horror at what had happened.

It is possible therefore that Tudor commentators like Sir Thomas Smith, who claimed that the Wars of the Roses decimated the English aristocracy, were not as far from the truth as we might suppose. The trauma of 1459–61 lived on in the national consciousness into the sixteenth century and the bloodletting, which continued until the defeat of the last Lancastrian stalwarts at the Battle of Hexham in 1464, may have been instrumental in persuading many members of the aristocracy to take a step back from politics when conflict broke out again in 1469. Professor Lander's figures provide an instructive comparison. Only four peers (the Earl of Oxford and Lords Fitzhugh, Scrope of Bolton and Willoughby and Welles) fought for the Earl of Warwick between 1469 and 1470, while only seven (the Earls of Devon, Pembroke, Rivers, Northumberland and Arundel and Lords Hastings and Ogle), turned out for the king. John Tiptoft, Earl of Worcester, was also executed on Warwick's orders in 1470. In 1471 only eighteen peers (ten Lancastrian and eight Yorkists) actually took part in the Battles of Barnet and Tewkesbury. Indeed, many of the peers who fought in 1471 had no choice: Warwick, like his erstwhile rival, Henry Beaufort, Duke of Somerset, was fighting for his life, as were partisans of Edward IV like William, Lord Hastings, or the king's brother, Gloucester. Most, however, felt they could stay at home. According to Lander this indifference grew largely from Edward's own policies, particularly his favour shown to his Woodville in-laws and his rather ungrateful treatment of Warwick, but this does not fully account for a disengagement from politics that was 'remarkable'.[9]

This disengagement from politics was starkly apparent in 1485. Only six nobles definitely fought for Richard III at Bosworth, with another six possibly being present. Even those who had benefited directly from Richard's patronage, such as Lord Scrope of Bolton, or who had been retained by him as Duke of Gloucester, as had the Earl of Northumberland, failed to fight alongside him. Less than a quarter of the parliamentary peerage turned out to support their king in battle. Tudor's assembly was even less impressive: the exiled earl of Oxford, his uncle Jasper, Duke of Bedford, John, Lord Welles, and, possibly, Thomas, Lord Stanley (although the Stanley contingent, led by his brother Sir William, proved decisive). In 1487 the roll call of nobles who turned out to support Henry VII at the Battle of Stoke was a little better: the duke of Bedford, the Earls of Devon, Kent, Oxford and Shrewsbury, Viscount Lisle, and between four and nine barons. The rebels counted among their number the earl of Lincoln, Francis, Viscount Lovell and, possibly, that old campaigner, Lord Scrope of Bolton. This still meant that the vast majority of the English peerage was absent. But does this mean that the late-fifteenth century nobility were representative of a wider aristocracy that no longer had the enthusiasm or the ability to take an active role in war, whether a civil war or a campaign against the Scots or French? It would be a mistake to assume that this disengagement was evidence of a less warlike attitude among the nobility or indeed the aristocracy in general. The martial ideal continued to define notions of nobility well into the sixteenth century and war in the prince's service was, by the end of the fifteenth century, accepted as the most honourable service any aristocrat could perform. Twenty-three peers could still stir themselves to lead contingents in Edward IV's French expedition of 1475, while in 1492 eight earls, a viscount and sixteen lords accompanied Henry VII to Boulogne. In Henry VIII's reign noble participation in war reached an even greater percentage: in 1513 twenty-three peers served in France in person with the king and another three were represented by their elder sons, while one served at sea and another nine fought against the Scots.

While exact numbers are impossible to judge for the gentry, anecdotal evidence suggests that they too became less likely to fight and die in the Wars of the Roses in the years after 1461. McFarlane pointed to the degree of choice available to members of the gentry and that even the most powerful lords lacked the means to compel their servants to fight against their will. We have already noted the effective refusal of men like Sir Henry Vernon to answer their master's command to attend him on the battlefield, but others found more subtle ways to remain aloof from conflict. When Henry, Lord Grey of Codnor (who had fought with the Lancastrians at Towton), indented with Edward IV's chamberlain, William, Lord Hastings, in 1464 he agreed to serve him in peace and war excepting his duty to the king, George, Duke of Clarence, and Sir Thomas Burgh. Malcolm Mercer has recently suggested that the majority of the gentry 'hedged their bets' and as the wars progressed became increasingly reluctant to commit themselves to one side or the other.[10] It may be that during the 1460s and 70s more and more put their personal safety ahead of any political principles or allegiance to a great lord or dynasty. Sir William Catesby, for instance, had been a member of Henry VI's household and fought for the Lancastrians at Northampton and Towton. He had been attainted by Edward IV's first parliament and forced into exile. He was soon pardoned, however, and attached himself to the Earl of Warwick (whose mother, the countess of Salisbury, may have had a hand in his rehabilitation). Warwick's lordship may have been effective in gaining possession of the disputed manor of Lapworth and in 1470, during the Readeption, he was appointed sheriff of Northamptonshire. Nevertheless, Catesby's experiences in 1461 may have led to him to choose a more cautious approach on the renewal of war and he failed to turn out for the regime at either Barnet or Tewkesbury, dying in his bed in 1479.

Clearly then the years after 1461 witnessed a gradual disengagement from armed political conflict by the political elite. The reasons for this are complex. Edward IV's promotion of his Woodville relations may have been important in the 1460s, while during the 1470s he manipulated the law to disinherit the heirs of five noble families. Personal circumstances may explain an individual's inactivity. Ralph Neville, 2nd Earl of Westmorland (1425–84) played a negligible role in the Wars of the Roses possibly due to some mental incapacity (although he was at least present alongside Queen Margaret at the second Battle of St Albans). Yet for the most part the decision not to turn out and fight was a measured, personal decision. In 1461 there was clear choice to be made, to fight for the legitimate king regardless of his personal failings or champion the cause of reform for the good of the commonweal. The combination of the horrors of war and a growing cynicism with politics, as the hopes for reform were dashed against the cut-throat reality of late fifteenth-century politics, saw the aristocracy quite simply disengage themselves from the affairs of those who would be king and stay at home while a small group of motivated individuals in effect decided the fate of the kingdom. Perhaps the advice of John Blount, Lord Mountjoy, to his brother, Sir James, in 1484 not to take up the estate of baron if it was offered him nor 'to desire to be grete about princes for it is dangerous' was a sentiment shared by many members of the aristocracy at the end of the Wars of the Roses.[11]

THE IMPACT OF THE WARS: (II) THE COMMONS

If the political elite initially participated en masse in the battles of the Wars of the Roses but increasingly withdrew from direct involvement from the 1460s, did the peculiar nature of the civil war preclude the mass involvement of the common people from the beginning? It was certainly the opinion of Philippe de Commynes that the general populace suffered little as a result of civil war. He stated that 'if any conflict breaks out in England one or other of the rivals is master within ten days' and concluded that 'out of all the countries which I have personally known, England is the one where public affairs are conducted and regulated with least violence to the people. There neither the countryside nor the people are destroyed nor are buildings burnt or demolished'.[12] Commynes had been confirmed in this opinion by no less a source than Edward IV, who had assured him that it was the custom to kill the nobles yet spare the commons. Given all that we have seen, however, this might seem unlikely. The mid-fifteenth century saw a dramatic and well documented rise in the political conscious-ness of the commons and in their direct involvement in politics, particularly in the 1450s. If the aristocracy were willing to fight and die in large numbers for political principles in 1459–61 then it is not inconceivable that a similarly engaged commons would do so too.

Unfortunately, the nature of the evidence precludes any definitive answer to this question. It is impossible to gauge with any certainty the number of combatants in any of the battles of the Wars of the Roses. Certainly none were so large as contemporary chroniclers claimed. More than one observer put the number of those present in the Yorkist army at the Battle of Towton in 1461 as 200,000. Writing shortly after the battle the Milanese ambassador reported that some 28,000 men had lost their lives, while William Paston reported 20,000 killed. As John Gillingham pointed out, if the estimate for the Yorkist army was true (and the Lancastrian army was agreed by most contemporaries to be even larger), then it follows that most English-men of fighting age were actually present on the battlefield of Towton. Clearly, estimates of armies of this size are absurd but the campaign of 1460–61 probably witnessed the mobilisation of unprecedented numbers of men. Without doubt, the Towton campaign was fought by large armies and the battle had a major impact on those who fought there or were touched by its consequences. From the few fragments that survive it is clear that the aristocracy were able to bring consid-erable numbers of their servant, tenants and followers with them in moments of crisis. In 1455 Humphrey, Duke of Buckingham, brought 90 men from his estates in Surrey and Kent to the first Battle of St Albans, while five years earlier 74 mounted men had ridden from his estates in Staffordshire to Blackheath at the time of Cade's Rebellion. Evidence of the effects of civil war on ordinary people is anecdotal but suggests that they suffered like their aristocratic neighbours. In 1461 the master of the Hospital of St Katherine by the Tower of London ordered the admission to their almshouse of Christine, the widow of a Dartford hosier recently killed at Towton. The massive scale of participation at the Battle of Towton may explain the efforts of successive Archbishops of York to maintain a chapel to the memory of the souls of 'the first and greatest in land as well as great multitudes of other men . . . first slain and then buried and interred in the fields around'.[13] Their efforts, which continued into the early sixteenth century apparently met with little success, perhaps suggestive of a communal longing to forget the excesses of civil war.

Further evidence of the scale and impact of the war of 1459 to 1461 comes from the extraordinary discovery in 1996 of a mass grave on the site of the Battle of Towton. The grave contained the remains of at least 37 men who fell during or shortly after the battle. Analysis of their bones showed that their average age was nearly thirty, some five years older than the typical age of soldiers in pre-modern armies, suggesting they were drawn from a cross section of society. The men were equally diverse in their health and stature and 'these individuals . . . come from every walk of medieval life, including a broad age range and average stature, as well as some individuals who stand out today, as indeed they would have in their own day'.[14] All the men had suffered horrific wounds. All but one appears to have died from blows to the head, while only two seem to have been wounded by projectiles. It has been suggested that the bodies, found a mile away from the main scene of fighting, were Lancastrian soldiers, caught in the rout having discarded their arms and armour and brutally killed by the victorious Yorkists. The Towton killings, moreover, may not have been unique. In the aftermath of the Battle of Hexham in 1464 relatively humble supporters of Henry VI were executed alongside their aristocratic comrades. For these men and their families at least Edward IV's boast that it was common practice to 'spare the commons' would have been cold comfort.

The scale of popular involvement in the conflict of 1469 to 1471 is similarly impossible to determine with any accuracy. Nevertheless, in 1471 it is clear that the commissions of array succeeded in putting several thousand men into the field. The author of *The Arrivall of King Edward IV* recounts how the king and his small band of followers, recently landed in Yorkshire, were confronted by a force of local levies, numbering six or seven thousand, assembled by the commissioners of array and led by a local gentleman and a vicar, Edward escaped a fight by claiming he had come back to England merely to claim his birthright of the Duchy of York. At Barnet the following month the Yorkist army probably numbered less than 9,000 (including 3,000 drawn by William, Lord Hastings, from the Duchy of Lancaster's estates in the north Midlands), while Warwick's army was probably slightly larger. According to one chronicler a total of 4,000 men from both sides perished. At Tewkesbury in May the size of the armies involved was probably smaller: no more than 6,000 on the Yorkist side and considerably fewer fighting for Queen Margaret. Regardless of the precise numbers involved, however, the campaigns of 1471 clearly involved a major mobilisation of the realm's military resources albeit one smaller than that of ten years earlier. How many of the ordinary individuals who donned their harness actually committed themselves to fight and die is, however, another matter. Nevertheless, if the testimony of Phillippe de Commynes is to be believed, 1471 saw Edward IV abandon his policy of sparing the commons. In the immediate aftermath of both Barnet and Tewkesbury the Yorkists slaughtered hundreds of ordinary soldiers who had fought on the Lancastrian side as Edward took revenge on 'the great favour the people bore towards the Earl of Warwick'.[15]

By 1485 the number of men from all social classes who were willing to fight and die appears to have dwindled to a mere fraction of those who had been engaged in 1461. At the Battle of Bosworth the total number of combatants numbered less than 10,000 and large contingents, most notably that brought by Henry Percy, Earl of Northumberland, sat idly by while the battle was decided. Richard III's difficulties in mobilising support are well documented: the commis-sioners of array were slow to mobilise men, while the king's greater subjects were equally tardy in assembling their own contingents. Polydore Vergil claimed that Richard's forces deserted in great numbers prior to the battle. Goodman has argued that a campaign in August was unpopular as it interfered with the harvest, but if this was the case it underlines even further the popular disengagement with politics.[16] If the royal forces were meagre, however, Henry Tudor's predicament was even worse. Few men had rushed to join his standard on the march from Milford Haven, while attempts to obtain the loyalty of the Stanleys had brought no firm commitment. In these circum-stances Henry was forced to rely on his small group of men-at-arms that had been with him in exile since 1483 and on perhaps a thousand French mercenaries. Richard, on the other hand, relied principally on the military strength of his household and on the contingent brought by the Duke of Norfolk. The critical intervention of Sir William Stanley demonstrates just how small a battle Bosworth was. At best this most decisive battle of the Wars of the Roses involved less than 10,000 men actively engaged on the field.

While fighting, and possibly dying, for political principles or out of loyalty to the crown or one's lord was for many the most immedi-ate impact of the Wars of the Roses, the political turmoil of the fifteenth century also allowed for an increase in other forms of violence. In other words, civil war provided a cover for personal vendettas to be pursued and for random acts of violence to be perpetrated. The parlia-ment of 1472 recognised the destabilising effect of the Wars. Richard Alcock, Bishop of Rochester, delivering the opening address argued that although Henry VI, 'the grete occasion of trouble and long dis-ease of this londe' was now dead, yet 'many a grete sore, many a perilous wounde' still remained and large numbers of 'riotous people' remained committing robbery and oppressing the commons.[17] MPs also drew attention to various notorious recent incidents, such as the murder of John Glyn in Cornwall, of Richard Williamson in York-shire, and the Talbot/Berkeley dispute in Gloucestershire. While violence was to some extent endemic in late-medieval England, the political turmoil evident from 1450 provided a new context to interpret crime and disorder. High profile murders, such as that of Bishop Moleyns of Chichester in January 1450 or the West Country lawyer Nicholas Radford in 1455, were seen as symptomatic of the failure of royal government and of the 'unnaturalness' of internal political strife.

Civil war also provided a cloak of legitimacy to pursue private quarrels. It is difficult to see how John Stafford could have escaped retribution for the brutal murder of Sir William Lucy in July 1460 were it not for the fact that it took place during the Battle of Northampton. Stafford it seems coveted Lucy's young wife, Margaret. His enjoyment of his new bride was, however, short-lived as Stafford himself was killed at the Battle of Towton the following March. More frequently personal vendettas and violent disputes over property were pursued under the legitimising cover afforded by political disorder. Such was the case in Lincolnshire in 1470 where the Yorkshire rebellions of the previous year had led to a breakdown in local administration. This provided the opportunity for Richard, Lord Welles, to pursue with violence his dispute with Sir Thomas Burgh of Gainsborough. Robin Storey saw the origins of the civil war in the violent disputes between the nobility that were symptomatic of Henry VI's ineffectual rule.[18] While most modern historians have dismissed this casual link between aristocratic violence and civil war, it is certainly the case that some individuals used the civil war to pursue their own ends and the connection between civil war and violent disorder in the localities was one made time and time again in parliament and in contemporary chronicles.

THE IMPACT OF THE WARS: (III) THE TOWNS

By the standards of contemporary Italy or the Low Countries England was not a particularly urbanised country. London, the largest city with a population of some 40,000 in the mid-fifteenth century, was unique both in terms of its wealth and its political importance. Only Norwich, York and Bristol had populations anywhere near 5,000, with the majority of county towns having two to three thousand inhabitants. There were, of course, dozens of market towns, some of which were incorporated by charter although the majority were seignorial boroughs.

Their population ranged from over a thousand in relatively large towns, such as Newark-upon-Trent, to boroughs of just a few hundred inhabitants. Yet few villages were more than a day's ride from an urban centre and towns played a crucial role in the politics, economy and culture of late-medieval England. The fifteenth century was, however, a crisis time for English towns. Changes in the pattern of overseas trade and the domestic economy, environmental factors, frequent outbreaks of plague and other endemic diseases, and the growth of London contributed to a decline in the size and wealth of almost all provincial urban centres. While some, such as Coventry or Sandwich, suffered spectacular decline in the fifteenth century, the sentiment expressed by the citizens of York at the end of the century that 'ther is not half the nombre of good men within your said citie as ther hath been in tymes past' would have been one recognised by most townsmen.[19]

Few urban historians, however, would argue that the Wars of the Roses had any appreciable impact on English towns. The authors of the recent Cambridge Urban History of Britain suggest that the governors of most towns sought to minimise their communities' involvement in the civil war, avoiding commitment to one side or the other and succeeding in remaining aloof from political concerns while seeking to mitigate the effects of urban decline in general. Yet if this were true it would mark a significant departure from the experience of many English towns in the fourteenth century. The demands of war with Scotland and France (for men, money and ships) had been instrumental in shaping the relationship between urban elites and the crown and between the rulers of English towns and their fellow inhabitants. Similarly, in the early Tudor period war had a dynamic effect in consolidating town/crown relations and strengthening oligarchic rule. In many towns the Wars of the Roses also had a similar impact, but perhaps in more complex and subtle ways. Seeking financial help from Henry VII, the citizens of York outlined the effects of the recent civil war on their community. They had always stood ready to serve the king (whoever that might be) and they had 'to ther grete charges and costes not oonely sent unto the battell of Wakefeld CCCC armed and well arrayed men to do hyme [Henry VI] service, conveing afterward the quene grace then being and the famous prince Edward ther sunne unto the batell of Saint Albones with othre CCCC of like men to thassistence of ther said souverian lord' and at 'the lamentable batell of Tolton [Towton], called Palmeston feld, where ther were of your said citie at ther owne costes about a M[l] men defensible araied, of the which many was salyne and put in exile'. Their failure to support Edward IV in 1471 had resulted in his displeasure and the removal of royal patronage, a situation only remedied by the patronage of Richard, Duke of Gloucester. This in turn had led to further costs and charges as they supported his Scottish campaigns and usurpation in 1483. Now on the visit to the city of the new king the citizens pleaded the effects of civil war in seeking royal approval for the levying of new tolls and the pardon of old debts.[20]

Towns frequently faced demands for soldiers throughout the Wars of the Roses. York, as one of the largest cities in the kingdom, was probably called on more often than most, but it is likely that every town in England saw its inhabitants engaged in fighting to some degree. Hull sent thirteen men to the Battle of Northampton and another contingent to St Albans the following year. In September 1470 the townsmen assembled twenty soldiers in response to a signet letter by Edward IV calling on them to gather men 'for the defence of his aune person'. In 1460 Coventry had sent men to support Henry VI but by February the following year the townsmen had switched their allegiance, providing soldiers for the Yorkist cause at St Albans; in March a hundred men from the town fought with Edward IV at Towton. This, however, was not the end of Coventry's involvement and in June forty men marched north to assist in the Earl of Warwick's suppression of Lancastrian rebels. During the 'Second War' of 1469–71 Coventry sent men to attend the earl of Warwick at Grantham in March 1470. Their allegiance to the Earl was short-lived, however, and they sent forty men to accompany Edward IV to the south-west the following month and a further forty to Nottingham in August. In February 1471 the governors of Coventry assembled forty men, ostensibly to accompany the Earl of Warwick to Flanders, but they were used in an attempt to resist Edward IV's landing in York-shire. These may have been the same twenty footmen and twenty horsemen who served with the earl at the Battle of Barnet. Warwick's defeat meant a crisis for the townsmen of Coventry and they quickly assembled a new force to answer Edward IV's summons.[21] Significantly, however, there is no evidence that Coventry sent soldiers to support Richard III at Bosworth. Smaller towns also contributed men to the battles of the Wars of the Roses: the Kentish port of Lydd, for example, sent men to support the Yorkists at Northampton, St Albans and Towton.

The extent to which these urban contingents took active roles in the battles of the Wars of the Roses is not clear, but some townsmen paid the ultimate price for their support of York or Lancaster. Richard Anson, the mayor of Hull, was killed alongside the Duke of York at Wakefield in December 1460, although his fellow townsmen did not share his sympathies and remained loyal to the House of Lancaster. Similarly, the mayor of Canterbury, Nicholas Faunte, paid a high price for his loyalty to the Earl of Warwick. In May 1471 he was executed in the city's Buttermarket, in the presence of Edward IV himself, for his role in Fauconberg's rebellion. Occasionally urban elites found themselves the reluctant victims of the violence associated with the Wars. In May 1454 the mayor of York, Thomas Nelson, was imprisoned and beaten by followers of Thomas Percy, Lord Egremont, and Henry Holland, Duke of Exeter, who had entered the city in the wake of their rebellion against the protectorate government of the Duke of York and his Neville allies. More frequently, however, the battles of the Wars of the Roses led to political confusion and recriminations against individuals who had supported the wrong side. In the aftermath of Richard Anson's death the mayoralty of Hull remained unfilled and in March 1461 the townsmen made frantic efforts to convince the victorious Edward IV of their loyalty, expelling Lancastrian sympathisers and riding to York to submit themselves to the new king. The aftermath of fighting also allowed personal grudges to be exploited. One can only sympathise with the dilemma of the Beverley mercer, John Reddisham, who received a Lancastrian commission of array for the town in late 1460. He was advised by another townsman, John Newport, to show the commission to the Earl of Warwick's brother, Sir Thomas Neville. Newport offered to take the commission to Neville himself, but, anxious to gain property belonging to Reddisham, he instead went straight to the Earl of Northumberland landing the unfortunate Reddisham in jail accused of treason.

More significant than the real dangers of death and imprisonment, however, were the perceived threats of destruction of property and disruption to the urban economy posed by marauding armies, rebellious subjects and foreign invaders. These fears permeated urban society throughout the period. In 1450 the citizens of Canterbury mounted a watch and bought gunpowder to guard their city against Cade's rebels, while for the authors of the London chronicles the devastation wrought on the city by the rebels became synonymous with the failure of Lancastrian government. Throughout the 1450s many towns mounted watches, purchased and made new guns and other weapons, and rebuilt and refurbished their walls amidst a growing sense of national political crisis. These precautions appear to have gained pace following the failure of the Loveday of 1458. The city of London imposed a curfew that summer and assembled 500 men to keep watch over the noble retinues camped just outside the walls. This uneasiness may have been felt nationwide: in May the aldermen of Salisbury ordered all men between the ages of 16 and 60 to assemble defensibly arrayed for the midsummer watches. When open conflict broke out in 1459 many towns increased their defensive measures. Robert Moleyns, Lord Hungerford, visited Canterbury early in 1460 to inspect work on its defences. In October 1459 the townsmen of Hull decided to mount a permanent watch for the time being and in November the following year they placed a large iron chain across the harbour to prevent a landing by the Yorkist lords, further increased the watch, and purchased guns to defend the town walls. Fear of the rampaging Lancastrian army galvanised many midland and southern towns in the winter of 1460–1. It was probably instrumental in persuading the townsmen of Coventry to switch their allegiance to the Yorkist lords, while it was an important factor in persuading the Londoners to refuse entry to the Lancastrian forces in February. Although accounts of the destruction wrought by Queen Margaret's northerners in February 1461 may have been prone to exaggeration, it is certain that towns along the Great North Road experienced pillage and destruction in varying degrees. Similar fears emerged again in 1470–1. In Canterbury payments were made to two captains, 'Quynt' and 'Lovelace', followers of the Bastard Fauconberg, to keep them and their men out of the city. Similarly, the purchases of guns and the flurry of activity of riders sent to seek information and news testify to the concerns of the inhabitants of Coventry in those years.

The most immediate impact of the Wars, however, was probably felt by townsmen in their pockets. While national taxation decreased markedly in the 1450s, and only rose slowly throughout the 1460s and 70s, the Wars of the Roses saw a significant increase in the frequency and cost of local taxation. One of the most important developments in urban political society during the late middle ages had been the development of local systems of taxation, often based upon assessments made for the collection of parliamentary grants. In the late fourteenth century disputes over local taxation had arisen in several major English towns as ordinary townsmen had railed against impositions placed upon them by the ruling oligarchies. These local disputes had mirrored the great national crises of the 1290s and 1340s and revolved around the issue of whether taxation was being levied and spent with the consent of the community and for the common good. During the Wars of the Roses, however, towns faced a clear and present danger. They felt compelled to augment their defences and make provisions to ensure the safety of their communities. Equally, town oligarchies had little choice but to accede to royal (and to a lesser extent noble) demands for soldiers lest they lose their political power in the aftermath of victory and defeat.

Again the well-preserved records of Coventry and Hull probably reflect the wider success of town oligarchs throughout the realm in expanding their power to tax their fellow townsmen during the Wars of the Roses. On 5 July 1460 the mayor, aldermen and commons of Hull met in the town's guildhall and agreed to provide thirteen soldiers for the king. The community agreed to pay their wages and to do so authorised the levy of a tax equivalent to half a parliamentary tenth (about £32) which would have more than met the men's expenses. Later in the year the iron for the chain across the harbour was provided by a town-wide assessment, with 120 of the wealthiest inhabitants contributing in kind. In 1470 the town council imposed another levy for soldiers, again based on the parliamentary subsidy, assessed by six aldermen and six commoners. These grants had a wider significance. In 1440 Hull had been granted county status and the collection of taxes and levying of soldiers allowed the oligarchy to flex its muscle in relation to the neighbouring villages now under the jurisdiction of the county of Kingston-upon-Hull. Indeed, throughout the late fifteenth and early sixteenth centuries the power to raise soldiers and levy taxation was an important weapon in Hull's struggle to assert its control over its rural hinterland. Similarly, the governors of Coventry regularly taxed their inhabitants to meet the demands placed upon them by the Wars. Between February and May 1461 the townsmen paid £190 in taxes for soldiers, some four times the amount of a parliamentary fifteenth and tenth, as well as a gift of £100 for Edward IV's first visit to Coventry. These local levies were assessed and collected in the same way as a parliamentary tax, with collectors appointed for each of the town's ten wards. In 1469–71 the costs of war were even heavier: £33 7s. 11d. in 1469 for soldiers' wages, over £150 in 1470, and almost £300 in 1471. Finally, in July 1471 the town council collected a further £200 for the restitution of their liberties. The Wars of the Roses were a costly affair for many English towns, but they also afforded the opportunity for the growth of urban oligarchies.

Coventry's experience of dealing with the king and powerful nobles, such as the Earl of Warwick, and, finally, having to pay to buy pardon for their role in the Wars illustrates how civil war played an important role in shaping the relationship between English towns and royal government. Urban authorities were forced to make difficult choices and sometimes got it wrong. The decision to back the wrong side, as in the case of the men of the Cinque Ports who had supported the Earl of Warwick in 1470–71, could lead to the suspension of liberties and a costly series of negotiations to win back royal favour. Wise, or fortunate, choices on the other hand could pay dividends. In 1462 Edward IV granted the townsmen of Leicester an annuity of 20 marks for twenty years in consideration of their 'good and faithful and unpaid service ... cheerfully rendered of late in our behalf against our enemies ... as also of the heavy burden of their no small losses incurred touching such business of ours'.[22] The demands of war also provided the opportunity to appeal for royal help. In 1460 the inhabitants of Southampton asked for help in repairing their town walls to withstand attack, while the costs of war remained a constant theme of the dialogue between the city of York and the crown in the later fifteenth century. Other towns appealed for arms to help defend their towns, as did the inhabitants of Gloucester who received thirty guns and other weapons from the royal arsenal in the winter of 1459. While civil war was undoubtedly a factor in determining both internal and external political relationships for most English towns in this period, its significance in relation to other factors is often difficult to gauge accurately. Nevertheless, far from being walled islands immune to the aristocratic struggles of the Wars of the Roses, it is clear that the impact of civil war was felt heavily in most English towns.

The impact of the Wars of the Roses upon all levels of English society has been underestimated by most recent historians. Particularly in the years 1459–61, but also in 1469–71, the wars made huge demands, comparable to those of royal campaigns abroad, in terms of men, money and blood. For various reasons the extent of engagement in the wars and thus the demands made upon the populace and their impact lessened as the fifteenth century progressed. Fewer noblemen, gentry, villagers and townsmen appear to have been involved in 1485 than in 1471 and far fewer than in 1461. Nevertheless, it would be wrong to assume that the impact of the Wars as a whole was negligible. It shaped the attitude of the aristocracy towards its role in government and its relationship with the crown, and it helped shape social and political relations within English towns. This, of course, is to say nothing of the hundreds, if not thousands, of families throughout England who were affected by death and disability resulting from civil war. As we shall in the next chapter, however, the greatest impact of the Wars of the Roses was in the way in which it transformed English political culture in the second half of the fifteenth century.

8

WAR AND POLITICAL CULTURE

In the second half of the fifteenth century English politics and society were dominated by the experience of civil war. Dynastic upheaval, mass participation in the Wars, and a general revulsion at the scale of political violence transformed the ways in which the realm was governed, the modes of political behaviour, and the language of politics itself. The degree to which the various component parts of the polity were involved in the political process also underwent substantial and long-lasting change. This chapter will examine three ways in which the Wars of the Roses transformed the political culture of late-medieval England. This transformation affected the institutions and systems of governance, perceptions of what constituted legitimate political action and, most importantly, precisely who was qualified to take part legitimately in the political process.

THE RISE AND FALL OF THE COMMONS

It is a commonplace among historians that the late middle ages witnessed a broadening participation in politics. 'Popular politics' or 'the public' intruded upon elite discourse and challenged the claims of the aristocracy and the church to be representative of the community of the realm. The public included burgesses, yeoman farmers and even literate peasants, and the mid-fifteenth century witnessed the zenith of their participation in politics. The civil wars, however, ultimately led to a fundamental change in the perception of the legitimacy of the commons' involvement in the political process. Before discussing these changes, however, it would be useful to more clearly define 'the commons'. From around 1300 'the commons' increasingly denoted the community of the realm in its widest sense. That is to say, it represented membership of a national political community, as much imagined as real and regardless of social or economic status. Its formal embodiment was as the parliamentary Commons, but its imagined membership included all those who, by paying taxes, partaking of the king's justice and fighting in his wars, were active members of the national community. The commons spoke with one voice. This was sometimes through their representatives in parliament, but it also occurred through a range of other media; they were 'part of the *communitas regni* whose interests were recognised to be the purpose of all government'.[1] Thus by the mid-fifteenth century the political aspirations of the commons had long been recognised as synonymous with the good government of the realm and, that most evocative and contested of contemporary terms, the 'commonweal'.

The rise of the commons is thus one of the dominant themes in late-medieval English history. There are several reasons for this development: social, economic, political and cultural. There can be little doubt that the pestilences of the mid-fourteenth century had profoundly altered the social and economic stratification of England. In a trend that had been apparent since Edward I's reign, more and more unfree peasant tenants were drawn into the crown's orbit through access to royal justice, by paying royal taxes and, through the mechanism of the commission of array, serving in royal armies. By the late fourteenth century in villages throughout England substantial peasants and farmers were acting as jurors, constables, tax collectors and representatives of their communities in hundred and shire courts. Thus the English peasant, emboldened by the experience of the Black Death to demand better wages and more political freedom, had emerged by 1400 as a full member of the community of the realm. Similarly, from 1327 representatives of English towns had been routinely summoned to meetings of parliament. Within towns tensions existed between various social and economic groups, and struggles between oligarchic and more inclusive forms of urban government dominated the political agenda of most of the larger English towns in the late fourteenth century. Nevertheless, the terms of reference for these struggles remained consistent. Both would-be oligarchs and their political opponents shared a common language of '*communitas*' and perceived of the town as a political body with all its inhabitants forming part of the same commonwealth. In 1381 the peasants who rebelled against the king's traitorous counsellors and unjust taxation had the same concerns (and used the same language) as the MPs who had impeached the king's ministers five years earlier. In other words, to be 'common' in 1381 'was to be part of the *communitas regni*, to speak and act for the community of the realm in a manner parallel to the magnates of 1215, the knights of 1259, and the MPs of the fourteenth century'.[2]

Political and cultural factors also assisted in the rise of the commons. First, a politicised commons needed a common language. By the beginning of the fourteenth century there existed a commonly understood vernacular, based on the written word (so-called Middle English) but intelligible when spoken among people of widely differing dialects. Thus a popular, vernacular 'literature of clamour', based upon older forms of peasant complaint and couched in the legalistic language of petitioning, grew in both scale and importance during the late fourteenth century, once again reaching a crescendo during the Peasants' Revolt of 1381. One of the most important sources of this clamour literature in the early fifteenth century was that associated with Lollardy, the popular, anti-clerical movement which challenged some fundamentals of the church's teaching, advocated a vernacular Bible, and argued for the disendowment of the church. From the 1370s, but reaching a climax in the first and second decades of the fifteenth century, Lollard petitioners appropriated and transformed the language and forms used by the Commons in parliament. Whereas fourteenth-century parliamentary petitions had been in French, later Lollard petitions were in English, bypassing the elite forms of political debate in parliament and engaging directly with the wider public. It was this literature of clamour, a tangible expression of the political voice of the commons, that was one of the dynamic forces behind the changing discourse of Lancastrian politics. Petitions in English representing the commons, such as those who posted anti-clerical bills in Warwickshire in 1407, harked back to 1381 and the idea of the 'true commons'. This form slowly emerged as the legitimate means of expressing political grievances and calling for change. In 1414 the first official parliamentary petition in English was recorded on the Parliament roll, while the early fifteenth century saw the steady growth of petitions written in English for the king's justice recorded in the court of Chancery and before the king's council.

The legitimacy of the Lancastrian regime, moreover, depended in part on this vernacular discourse with the commons. The emergence of Middle English as *the* language of political discourse was confirmed by the fact that Henry IV legitimised his claim to the throne in parliament in English. This discourse was two-way. To some extent early Lancastrian poetry, such as John Lydgate's *Troy Book* (1412–20) and *Siege of Thebes* (*c.*1422), justified royal policy to the public, but it also offered correctives and sought to influence the decisions of kings and their counsellors. Thomas Hoccleve's *Regement of Princes* (1412) is just such a text, and even Lydgate consistently challenged the nature of Lancastrian ambitions in France. The Lancastrian kings engaged with their public, looking for acceptance and to legitimise their policies through proclamations, poetry and debate. This explains the very full justifications for loans made in 1436, amidst the Burgundian siege of Calais, and 1443, or even the sermon preached in 1421, prior to Henry V's final departure to France and delivered in the context of growing popular disquiet over the cost of the king's ambitions in France. But the commons also questioned and debated royal policy. Snapshots of ordinary people's engagement with politics emerge from the growing number of prosecutions for seditious speech in the 1430s and 40s. It is also evident in the discussion and complaints of poverty that met royal commissioners seeking loans. It may be that a perception that the commons' voice was becoming too loud lay behind the decision in 1429 to restrict the franchise at county courts to those receiving more than 40*s.* p.a. income from lands and in 1445 to prevent those below the rank of gentlemen from being elected as MPs.

The 'comyne voyse' was heard at its loudest in 1450. In the mid-fifteenth century '*commune* words were linguistic fireworks, exploding in the crowded streets, setting up a multitude of associations'.[3] Throughout the 1430s and 40s a collection of vernacular poems, bills of complaints and other forms of writing had been circulated throughout the realm, commenting on the war with France, taxation and the king's counsellors among other things. These texts derived their power not from the fact that they were circulated and read in private, but that they were capable of being read aloud and understood by the commons who were fully immersed in a shared lexicon of political terms. Thus the poor tenants of the wealthy Hampshire landowner, William Flete, who protested in person with ploughshares and coulters in the parliament chamber in 1431 shared a language of extortion and oppression with their contemporaries who rose in Abingdon that year under the leadership of 'Jack Sharp', or the rebels who assembled with Jack Cade on Blackheath in June 1450. Their complaints were expressed in both written bill and the spoken word. In 1450 the catalyst was the national feeling of shame evident in the wake of the defeat in Normandy. Poetry and bills directed against the king's counsellors were copied, distributed and amended to suit particular audiences. They complained of treacherous counsel and selfish behaviour leading to defeat in war and the impoverishment of both the crown and the commons. Although their grievances were something of a commonplace in late-medieval political culture, they were given an immediacy and violent focus by the loss of Normandy and the parliamentary proceedings against Suffolk. Cade's first manifestoes were drafted while parliament was in session and contemporaries noted the profusion of bills posted in London and elsewhere during the final session of parliament between April and June. The commons reinterpreted recent events in this context and took their bloody revenge on the men they considered responsible: the Duke of Suffolk, Bishops Moleyns and Aiscough, and Lord Saye. A sophisticated understanding of the polity was also revealed by the shipmen accused of Suffolk's murder who claimed, when the duke showed them his royal safe conduct, that 'they did not know the said king, but they knew well the crown of England, saying that the aforesaid crown was the community of the realm and that the community of the realm was the crown of the realm'.[4]

In 1450 politics were driven by an agenda that was unmistakably set by the commons. Suffolk, facing impeachment by parliament in January, recognised what was happening and railed against 'the odious and horrible langage that renneth thorough your lande, almoost in every commons mouth.'[5] As early as April the government made proclamations in London and Middlesex (albeit on this occasion in Latin) against the posting of bills. Yet, clearly, the crown and political elites were powerless to stop the profusion of rumours and the commons' direct intervention in the political and judicial process. Later in the year the crown began to issue proclamations in English in an attempt to regain control over the discourse of politics. Cade's rebellion may have been ignited in the first instance by the rumour that the commons of Kent were to be punished for the murder of the Duke of Suffolk, but its origins lay in the popular reaction to the defeat in France and the perception of misgovernment at home. Its more long-term roots, however, could be found in the rise in the commons as a political force in late-medieval England and the way in which the Lancastrian polity was built upon an uneasy discourse between elite and popular politics.

Throughout the following two decades the form and language of political dissent and the agenda for reform that had originated with the commons was appropriated and employed by the political elites. Most importantly, the platform of reform on which Richard, Duke of York, sought to challenge the crown in the 1450s was essentially that of the commons. The judicial proceedings against royal officials in Kent during the summer of 1450 and the petitions against household servants of the king in the parliament of November that year echoed the demands of Cade's rebels, demands which were now central to the critique of royal government offered by York. Rather than Cade's rebellion being a plot orchestrated by York to attack his enemies at court (as his Lancastrian opponents would later claim), the duke had, to all intents and purposes, become an opportunistic 'Cadist', jumping on a popular bandwagon to end his self-imposed political exile. York's supporters, such as Sir William Oldhall in 1453, appropriated the forms of popular political action, the writing and distribution of bills, to attack their political opponents and by 1456 this 'Yorkist literature of clamour was answered with Lancastrian counter claim'.[6]

More important than the forms of political debate, however, was the language. As David Starkey pointed out, the period from 1450 saw the emergence of the term 'commonweal' as the key phrase in political debate. Before 1450 it had been more usual for official sources to employ the term 'common profit', but from the later years of the decade both Lancaster and York claimed to represent the 'good publique' or common 'wele' ('good', 'welfare' or 'happiness'). The first official usage of the term 'commonweal' was in 1446, but the rebels of 1381 had claimed to have acted for the 'wele' of the realm, a sentiment embraced, quite consciously, by Cade and his followers in 1450 (even if they did not employ the exact phrase 'commonweal'). During the 1450s the elite in effect lost control over the language and forms of political discourse. This was starkly apparent in the fact that when the Yorkist lords landed in Kent in June 1460 their manifesto was nothing more than a reissuing of Cade's petition of ten years earlier. The Yorkist platform was essentially populist, a notion apparent in Edward IV's claim to have ordered the killing of Lancastrian noblemen while sparing the commons. Moreover, this appeal to populism was accepted as the right and proper way of doing politics by the commons. The West Country peasants, who believed in 1462 that they had brought Edward IV to the throne and claimed the right to depose him 'if he will not be ruled after us as we will have them', were merely expressing a widely held belief in the normative pattern of late-medieval English politics.[7]

We do not have to accept the notion of class struggle to realise that a political agenda driven by the common people was anathema to the political elite. From 1470–71 there is evidence that the political elites attempted to wrest the dynamic force in politics from the commons' control. Colin Richmond has drawn attention to the fact that the officially sponsored *Chronicle of Rebellion in Lincolnshire* and, more importantly, *The History of the Arrivall in England of 1471* represented the Yorkist regime's attempt to determine the contours of political discourse and provide an irrefutable, official history of recent events.[8] Indeed, the Yorkist and early Tudor period as a whole saw a steady rise in the number of proclamations, tracts, histories and genealogical tables that can rightly be described as royal propaganda. Moreover, the crown sought to delegitimise and extinguish other forms of news, rumour and political discussion. Bill-casters were increasingly demonised from the late 1470s and between 1483 and 1485 Richard III mounted a concerted and violent campaign against popular rumours and bills. William Collingbourne may have been hanged, drawn and quartered partly for his rhyming couplet ('The Cat, the Rat and Lovell our Dog / Rule all England under the Hog') lampooning the king's counsellors, but a proclamation in 1485 underlined the duty of every subject to counter seditious rumours by removing bills 'without reding or shewing the same to any othre persone' and taking them to the king's council.[9]

The extinguishing of the commons' legitimate role in the political process during the last decades of the fifteenth century was one of the most important consequences of the Wars of the Roses. The ensuing redefinition of the term 'commons' itself was of paramount importance to the development of a distinctly Tudor political culture. By the beginning of the sixteenth century the term had gained a socio-economic context. To Tudor writers, such as Sir Thomas More, Sir Thomas Elyot or Thomas Starkey, the commons were the lower orders, the 'vulgar' sort or the plebs, and were not part of the legitimate political nation. Rebellion and calls for reform originating with the commons were now unacceptable and treasonable. The Tudors' response was, on the one hand, repression, but on the other an increasingly sophisticated discourse of obligation and obedience. Of course, the monastic chroniclers who had decried the plebeian origins of the rebels in 1381 were of a broadly similar opinion to later Tudor writers, but the fifteenth century had witnessed the incorporation of the commons as a legitimate partner with the king, lords and parliamentary Commons in the process of politics and government. Indeed, the legitimacy of the Lancastrian regime from 1399 in part depended on the approbation of the commons. In 1450 the commons had removed their support, revealing a crisis of legitimacy that lay at the heart of the Lancastrian polity; the initial Yorkist response, the platform of reform and 'commonweal', was one essentially driven by the commons as the dynamic force in English politics. However from the 1470s, partly in response to the civil wars, the Yorkists and early Tudors begin to redefine the English polity from above.

THE WARS OF THE ROSES AND THE FISCAL CULTURE OF MEDIEVAL ENGLAND

To Sir John Fortescue, the aged former chief justice of king's bench, writing in the early 1470s, England was a *dominium politicum et regale*. This happy fact differentiated England from France, which was a *dominium regale*. In France the tyrannical king could impose taxes at will. As a result the French had 'gon crokyd, and ben feble, not able to fight, nor to defende þe realme nor thai have wepen, nor money to bie thaime wepen with all. But verily thai liven in the most extreme pouertie and miserie, and yet dwellyn thai in on of them most fertile reaume of the worlde.' In England, by contrast, the liberties of the subject were protected by the law and by parliament. The king was bound to obey the laws which were made by the community of the realm in parliament. Similarly, he was bound to ask parliament for supply and was unable to tax arbitrarily. Therefore, the English 'ben mighty, and able to resiste the adversaries of this reaume, and to better oþer reaumes that do, or wolde do them wronge. Lo this is the fruyt of *Jus Polliticum et regale*, undre wich we live.'[10] The problem for Fortescue and his contemporaries, however, was that the poverty of the crown, its reliance on just and constitutional methods of raising money, had led to extreme poverty, and this in turn had been one of the principal causes of the recent troubles. From the 1470s therefore, England experienced a profound shift in its fiscal culture, one which attempted to reverse the crown's poverty and which ultimately threatened to undermine those freedoms celebrated by Fortescue.

The fiscal culture of late-medieval England had been developed during the reigns of the three Edwards. In a series of crises the crown's freedom to demand a portion of its subjects' wealth to fund royal policy was questioned by the baronial opposition and by parliament. In 1297 and 1340, for instance, the crown had granted political concessions in return for supply. During the same period the exchequer was established and confirmed as the principal guardian of the fiscal system. The Ordinances of 1311 made it responsible for all revenues and gave it primacy over the financial offices of the king's household, while the Walton Ordinances of 1338 included a requirement of the Treasurer of England to present an annual account of the realm's finances. Thus by the middle of the fourteenth century, 'Royal finance had become truly public: revenue from both the fisc [the crown lands and sources of regular revenue] and taxation had a public function, to maintain the crown and to defend the realm. Monarch and people each contributed their goods for the common profit, and if it remained the monarch's right to spend revenue for this purpose . . . it fell to the Commons, representing the community of the realm, to criticise the king and call him to account in the same terms'.[11]

In the late fourteenth and early fifteenth centuries the collection and spending of revenue was a transparent process, open to the scrutiny of the political classes, in which the political nation was intimately involved at a number of levels. First, and most symbolically, public finance was the concern of parliament. Parliament controlled the granting of indirect and direct taxation and frequently placed conditions on its collection and spending. Although the customs were, in effect, a permanent levy by the middle of the fourteenth century, the subsidy on wool was not and was subject to parliamentary control. Although it was collected almost continuously from 1342, the restraints that parliament imposed on its collection during the 1380s were important reminders of its nature as an extraordinary tax. Even after the parliaments of 1398 and 1415 established the principle of life grants, the idea that it remained subject to parliamentary approbation remained an important feature of the consensus over public finance. The situation with direct taxation was even more explicit. In November 1404 the grant of two fifteenths and tenths to Henry IV was made conditional on the appointment of war treasurers whose receipts and expenditure were recorded on separate rolls. This is not to say, however, that the process of public finance was characterised by conflict between the crown and a political community unwilling to support royal policy. Much has been made of the generosity of parliament in making grants of taxation in the late fourteenth and first decade of the fifteenth century: in 1401 taxation was granted for the vague purpose of 'good governance', while on three occasions between 1404 and 1407 parliamentary taxation was explicitly made available to meet the costs of the king's household. Indeed, the period from the mid-1380s to the mid-1420s witnessed the high water mark of parliamentary taxation in late-medieval England. Nevertheless, the parliamentary debates over taxation were a means by which the political community could challenge the crown in a formalised and mutually understood way. The calls for the resumption of crown lands made in 1404, for instance, were a manifestation of a wider disquiet over royal spending. Indeed, linking redress of grievances with grants of taxation was a fundamental component of the dialogue between the crown and its subjects.

Second, royal finance was public finance because of the involvement of the political nation as royal creditors, taxpayers and officials. The burgeoning 'tax state' of the late thirteenth and early fourteenth century had involved more and more of the king's subjects in the daily business of state finance. The growth of the customs system relied on the cooperation of merchants as collectors, searchers and controllers. More important, however, was the shift, from $c.1340$, towards seeking loans from the king's subjects rather than from overseas merchants and bankers. Clearly, the crown's English creditors could not be treated in the same cavalier fashion as foreign ones and the repayment of loans became intimately linked to the granting of direct taxation in parliament. Nevertheless, the crown consistently borrowed more than it could repay and the crown's creditworthiness among its own subjects was a barometer of its political standing. The public nature of royal finance also ensured that comment on the crown's fiscal policies was not restricted to the parliament and council chambers. Several political poems of the late fourteenth and early fifteenth century commented explicitly and offered advice on the crown's policies. One of the most interesting is *Crowned King*, written on the eve of Henry V's departure for the Agincourt campaign. In this work the reciprocity which was central to the system of public finance was underlined: the king asks for supply in parliament, but in return is reminded of the virtues of good kingship and given instructions on the proper conduct of the forthcoming campaign.[12]

However, for both the crown and its subjects this system was wrought with problems. These were both structural and political. One of the most obvious was the need to get cash quickly to where it was needed. By the second half of the fourteenth century, although the exchequer was nominally responsible for controlling revenue and expenditure, much of the day-to-day business of public finance was conducted locally. Revenue was increasingly collected and spent locally by the crown's agents and only the 'book-keeping' entries of assignments and reassignment of revenue recorded at the exchequer. This invariably led to a loss of control by the exchequer which routinely 'spent' more money than actually existed. Second, the crown's activities were constrained by the political community's unwillingness to adapt and expand its revenues. While, for example, the Commons were willing to be generous in granting the established form of parliamentary lay taxation, the fifteenth and tenth, they were less willing to grant innovative taxation that would raise more revenue. Similarly, although the wool subsidy became a regular feature of indirect taxation from the middle of the fourteenth century, the crown was unable to effectively tax the growing cloth export trade. The revenue from the wool customs and subsidy thus declined as the export of raw wool gave way to that of woollen cloth. An effective king with the support of the political nation could make the system still appear sound and profitable, but this should not hide the fact that there were underlying structural, procedural and political problems with English public finance at the beginning of the fifteenth century.

Evidence of this weakness is the use that successive kings made of their household as a financial institution outside the constraints of the 'public' exchequer. At times of financial crisis kings were forced back on their truly private resources, the cash, jewels and plate they kept in their chamber. By the late 1390s Richard II had acquired a sizeable personal treasure: in his will he left £20,000 for the payment of his household debts and it was claimed he had amassed a fortune of £300,000 in jewels and plate. The opportunities this afforded a tyrannical king are obvious. More interesting, however, is the importance of the king's chamber during the reign of Henry V. In some ways Henry V's Normandy campaigns offer an exemplar of English public finance in action: backed by the political nation, which through parliament had granted generous taxation, a dynamic king was able to wage war with spectacular success. Nevertheless, equally important to Henry V's wars were the private resources of his chamber, into which the revenues of the royal duchies and his own profits of war were paid. The size of this personal fortune is not known, but Henry had with him at Harfleur £30,000 in gold and £2,000 in silver. Significantly, the king also used his chamber to bypass the public finances both literally and metaphorically. On the eve of the Agincourt campaign, the Bishop of Norwich, treasurer of the king's chamber, made indentures with several lords, knights and esquires, pledging the king's jewels in security for their wages of war. Rather than choosing to offer security on future taxation, the king made a symbolic reminder that war was private and seignorial, as well as public and national. It is in this context that the king's personal tour of the realm to appeal for financial assistance in 1421 must be seen. Having failed to gain adequate supply in the public forum of parliament, Henry V used the private power of kingship in asking individual subjects for loans.

The premature death of Henry V was a disaster for a system of public finance already at breaking point. The accession of a minor, coupled with the stresses of the Hundred Years War, further undermined the basis of public finance. This was apparent throughout the 1420s. In 1425 parliament agreed to the crown borrowing £20,000 on the security of the customs, and in the following year twice that amount. Still this would not suffice: in 1429 Treasurer Hungerford informed the council that the crown's projected expenditure exceeded its revenue by at least 20,000 marks (£13,666 6s. 8d.) There were two main reasons for this. First, during the first years of the reign parliament did not grant extraordinary taxation. While the wool subsidy and tonnage and poundage were extended, it was not until 1428 that a lay subsidy was granted, while the first fifteenth and tenth was not paid until January 1430. Second, there was the financial legacy of Henry V. The late king's debts, and those of Henry IV, were such that in 1423 parliament had set aside 40,000 marks (£26,666 13s. 4d.) of the king's own jewels to meet them. A part of the income of the Duchy of Lancaster had also been set aside to meet the terms of Henry V's will. Yet without the intervention of an adult king it proved impossible to ensure that English resources were made available for the needs of his French realm. The trend for the crown to borrow from its own subjects, introduced more blatant calculations of self-interest into the financial relationship between crown and subject. As the number of royal creditors grew so did the pressure on resources and the scramble to avoid or recoup losses. At its worst this could directly threaten the conduct of the crown's affairs, as in February 1424 when John, Lord Talbot threatened not to relieve the siege of Le Crotoy unless satisfied of his arrears for the custody of Montgomery Castle. Generally, this constant pressure from its creditors further weakened the crown's financial position. The sale of wardships, the alienation of and preferential leases granted on crown lands, and customs licenses were all necessary to maintain the creditworthiness of the Lancastrian regime, but they ultimately undermined the public finances. All these problems, which had existed before 1422, were magnified by the accession of a minor and the crisis of royal authority which this inevitably caused.

The Commons' lack of confidence in the king's government is exemplified by their attitude to granting taxation during Henry VI's majority. Although parliamentary subsidies were granted in every parliament between 1433 and 1453 (with the exception of 1447 and November 1449), their yield and the frequency with which they were paid declined. No significant innovations in taxation were made during this period: the receipts for the alien subsidy introduced in 1440 were negligible, while the income taxes of 1431, 1435, 1450 and 1453 failed to raise any more than the traditional fifteenth and tenth. Moreover, trade taxes were not increased and the rate of tonnage and poundage was actually cut in 1442. Each grant of taxation was accompanied by pleas of poverty from the Commons. The fiscal crisis is highlighted by the frequency with which the records of the exchequer were presented to the Commons. A declaration was made to the Reading parliament of 1439 and the Commons again inspected the financial records in 1447, 1450, 1453 and 1455. The last years of Henry VI's rule witnessed the final collapse of public finance in Lancastrian England. The civil war was fought outside the national and public framework of king, lords and commons. Like its noble opponents, the crown was forced to rely on its private wealth in the form of the cash, plate and jewels in the chamber, but also, and more significantly on, its private landed estates to fund its military campaigns. Little evidence survives of precisely how this was done, but it seems that the king's chamber and the crown lands played a pivotal role. From the beginning of 1457 large portions of the cash received at the exchequer was transported from Westminster to Chester, Coventry and Kenilworth. Following the attainder of the Duke of York and his allies in 1459, most of their forfeited estates were placed under the control of special receivers who also probably paid their receipts directly to the chamber. Payments made directly to the king's chamber were nothing new of course, but their scale and frequency from 1456 suggests it enjoyed a new importance. By 1461 the 'public' fiscal culture of late-medieval England had clearly failed both the king and his subjects.

Edward IV continued to use his chamber as an instrument of national finance and from the mid-1460s the exchequer was supplanted as the leading institution of royal finance. The king's chamber administered revenues based principally on the expanded crown estates and this appears to have restored the crown to solvency by the late 1470s at the latest. Mark Ormrod has recently suggested that this was achieved by a return from the 'tax-state' of the later-Plantagenet and Lancastrian kings to the 'domain-state' of earlier kings. In effect, the ambitions of kings waned as they reached the limit of the political community's willingness to support them.[13] This, however, is to oversimplify and misunderstand the nature of Yorkist finance. Their 'land revenue experiment' in many ways satisfied Fortescue's call for the re-endowment of the crown, but it also utilised the normal methods that magnates used to manage their own income. This had important and far-reaching consequences. First, the fact that Edward IV's chamber income was private meant it was not recorded at the exchequer. Second, Edward IV did not abandon efforts to seek extraordinary taxation, but showed himself an innovative monarch who, at times, directly challenged the authority of parliament to grant supply and to oversee its expenditure, particularly in the 1460s. While the parliamentary commons still conducted their protests using the rhetoric of public finance, having their disquiet at Edward's actions formally enrolled on the parliament roll, the king essentially chose to disregard them. Similarly, in 1472–74 the Commons attempted to impose conditions over the collection and spending of the subsidy but, while the king agreed in principle, there is no evidence that the administration of the tax proceeded according to the conditions of its grant. Edward's benevolences of 1474 and 1481 should also be seen in this context. Rather than being extensions of earlier general loans, they were forms of taxation outside the existing constitutional framework and as such were vilified by Richard III. Yet, as these debates over taxation show, much of the theory and practice of royal finance under the Yorkist kings was still constrained by the rhetoric of 'public' finance. Significantly, however, after the first parliament of the reign there was no attempt to offer a detailed picture of royal income and expenditure to parliament.

Henry VII, on the other hand, does not appear to have been so constrained by the rhetoric of public finance. Although from 1487 he revived the institutions of Yorkist chamber finance, the importance of his financial policies lay not so much in their administrative innovation but in the theories and assumptions that underpinned them. As in other aspects of his rule, Henry may have looked to France for inspiration. The security of the French crown was guaranteed by its wealth for which it was accountable neither to its noble subjects nor to a parliament. Thus the private financial apparatus of the chamber offered Henry a means of political security. Although the king's chamber may have surpassed the exchequer in terms of the amount of cash passing through its coffers by the end of the Edward IV's reign, for most of the 1460s and 70s the principal function of the crown lands and royal prerogative rights remained political, rather than offering an alternative means of funding royal government. By the 1490s this had changed. Henry VII succeeded in altering three fundamental features of the system of medieval public finance. First, most of the crown's revenues were 'private', in that they were under the control of the treasurer of the king's chamber. They were not recorded in the exchequer, nor were their accounts audited there. Trade taxes were also appropriated and made 'private': the account books of the chamber show that tonnage and poundage, granted to Henry for life in

Towards the end of the fifteenth century the printing press began to revolutionise the distribution and consumption of history and other works that shaped English political culture. Here we have the first page of William Caxton's 1480 edition of *The cronicles of England* (STC 9991).

1486, was treated in this way. Once within the 'private' sphere of the chamber, Henry was free to spend this money however he wished, free from conciliar or parliamentary interference. The massive sums spent on jewels given as gifts to Emperor Maximilian and Archduke Philip (the equivalent of almost one year's income alone in April 1505) to buy support against erstwhile Yorkist pretenders later in the reign represent the foreign policy of a king freed from the fiscal constraints of earlier kings. Edward IV and Henry VII had constructed alternative means of financing their royal ambitions that were not wholly dependent on the generosity of the Commons and support of the political community. This was a response to the poverty of the crown and the perception that this had undermined royal authority. Royal finance under the early Tudors was essentially different from its late-medieval predecessor. It was based upon the crown's private, landed resources and channelled through the king's chamber, rather than the 'public' resources granted by parliament and controlled by the excheq-uer. In part the changes that occurred from the 1470s satisfied Fortescue's blueprint for 'a newe ffundacion of is crowne', but they did so at the cost of undermining England's status as '*dominium politicum et regale*'.[14]

HUMANISM, THE RENAISSANCE AND THE WARS OF THE ROSES

In general terms, the fifteenth century has long been recognised as a period of cultural transformation in Europe. The nineteenth-century German scholar, Jakob Burckhardt, characterised the 250 or so years before 1600, but especially the fifteenth century, as a period of momen-tous change in every aspect of culture, society and art. This 'Renaissance' (a concept 'invented' by the French scholar, Jules Michelet, in the 1850s) first flowered in Italy and had two main aspects. First, a rediscovery or revival of the Classical learning meant a jettisoning of the irrational, religious world of the Middle Ages. Second, this led to a new spirit of individualism that ushered in the modern era. More recent scholars have dismissed the more over-arch-ing, philosophical aspects of Burckhardt's thesis. Instead the Renaissance was primarily a cultural and literary movement, one centred upon a revival of Antiquity and the *studia humanitatis* or Humanism. The leading scholar of Renaissance Humanism, Paul Oskar Kristeller, has dismissed any notion of Humanism relating to the condition of man or a concern for the humane; instead it was 'that broad concern with the study and imitation of classical antiq-uity which was characteristic of the period and found its expression in scholarship and education and in many other areas, including the arts and sciences.'[15] By the 1430s the *studia humanitatis* was defined as the study of grammar, rhetoric, poetry and moral philosophy which had its origins, in part, in the rediscovery by the Italian poet and scholar Petrarch, of the letters of Marcus Tullius Cicero, a first-century B.C. Roman author, a century before. Throughout the fifteenth century Humanism spread from Italy into the universities, royal courts, and schoolrooms of Western Europe. Its impact was rapid and devastat-ing: before the end of the century the Humanist revolution was complete and its proponents had convinced 'European society that without its lessons no one was fit to rule or lead'.[16]

Recent research has demonstrated how England was involved in this cultural revolution. The early influence of Humanism in England was through one particular aspect of the larger Humanist project: the translation and adaptation of Classical authorities into the vernacular. The English interest in Humanism can be traced to the opening decades of the fifteenth century, but the most influential early patron of Humanism was Humphrey, Duke of Gloucester, the youngest son of Henry IV. Gloucester's friendship with Italian Humanists led to translations of Aristotle and other classical authors and the amassing of a large collection of Humanist books. He also employed an Italian secretary, Tito Livio Frulovisi, who around 1438 wrote the *Vita Henrici Quinti*, ostensibly to celebrate Henry's achievements but also to advance Duke Humphrey as defender of the late king's legacy. Gloucester himself knew no Greek and preferred his Latin classics in the words of French translators, and it has recently been argued that his patronage of Humanism little affected his own politics or had any great impact on the politics of Lancastrian England. Yet if Gloucester's literary patronage had any lasting significance it was to popularise a Humanist approach to the Classics within the elite political circles of mid-fifteenth-century England. In 1445 the Augustinian friar, Osbern Bokenham, presented Richard, Duke of York, with a translation of Claudian's *De Consulate Stilichonis*. To present Duke Richard with a text about Flavius Stilicho, the fourth-century Roman general who had been trusted by Emperor Theodosius with the safety of the Empire, at a time when English fortunes with France were at a crisis was 'an act of careful deliberation.'[17] Indeed, Daniel Wakelin had recently argued that the style and composition of those Humanist manuscripts commissioned by Duke Humphrey in the 1430s and 40s directly influenced the composition of other manuscripts and texts in the 1450s and 60s that more explicitly engaged with the political events of the day. As Wakelin observes: 'English writers during the upheavals and battles of the Wars of the Roses use allusions and classical similes to glorify people, events and ideas, or just to fatten their own style. It is as if they wrote in togas.'[18]

Humanism offered fresh perspectives on the familiar problems of war, government, finance, counsel and politics. Above all, from the 1460s, these involved the application of Ciceronian models and principles to the issues affecting the English polity. Cicero, of course, had been well known to medieval authors and his importance to men like John of Salisbury and Peter of Blois (writing in the twelfth century) is well established. Yet early fifteenth-century English writers (such as the author of the 1439 *Tractatus de Regimine Principum*) had largely obtained their knowledge of Cicero second-hand, from authorities such as Augustine of Hippo (354–430). Later fifteenth-century authors, however, used their own first-hand readings of Cicero to formulate new ideas about the English polity and to offer solutions to the problems that had caused and been aggravated by the Wars of the Roses. John Watts has identified three fifteenth-century writers in particular, Sir John Fortescue, William Worcester and Bishop John Russell, whose ideas were influenced by Ciceronian principles. The first and most obvious impact was the translation into English of Cicero's concept of the *res publica*. By the second half of the fifteenth century the English term 'commonweal' was increasingly being identified with Ciceronian and republican ideals. The term's meaning moved from merely denoting a common interest to representing the just and proper government of a polity. In *The Boke of Noblesse*, presented to Edward IV on the eve of his French campaign in 1475 but first penned during the 1450s, Worcester recognised the Ciceronian influences on this change of meaning: 'the terme of Res publica whiche is in englisshe tong clepid a comyn profit it ought aswelle be referred to the prouision and wise gouuernaunce of a mesuage or a householde as to the conduit and wise gouernaunce of a village Towne. Citee. Countree. or Region.'[19] Worcester and Sir John Fortescue, in his *Governance of England*, took the Ciceronian republican logic one step further. To Fortescue Cicero's *gubernatores*, the leading citizens of the Roman Republic, exercised a corporate responsibility for the *res publica* (or 'commonweal'). He found an English parallel in the 'wysest and best disposed men' in the realm who were to 'comune and delibre uppon the materis of defeculte that ffallen to the kynge; and then upon þe materes off þe pollycye of the reaume.'[20] Fortescue advocated a formal council of 24, headed by a *Capitalis consiliarius*, to advise the king and, although similar arguments about how Rome had flourished under conciliar rule had been made in the Middle Ages, he would have been aware that Cicero in *De Re Publica* had stated that every 'common-wealth . . . needs to be ruled by some sort of deliberation in order to be long lived.'[21] This stress on conciliar government, to combat the weaknesses of kings and the ambitions of great magnates, was evident in the address to parliament written by Bishop Russell in 1483–4. Russell saw the lords not as great regional magnates but as senators, whose proper role was to advise the king in council and in parliament. The executives of government, in Russell's view, were not local lords, but 'the kynges juges and commisses, carrying out the instructions of 'hys hyghenes and hys nobylle counselle' for 'the politik establysshynge of the Reme'.[22] Indeed, the diminishing of the independent, territorial power of the nobility was a theme also apparent in Fortescue's work. This was again perhaps inspired by his reading of Cicero and other Roman authors, such as Sallust. While in chapter IX of *The Governance of England* Fortescue deployed examples from Capetian France and thirteenth-century England, he might equally have been informed by tales of Julius Caesar, Mark Antony and other destroyers of the Republic in illustrating the dangers of over-mighty subjects.

Moreover, by the end of the fifteenth century such ideas were not restricted to a few intellectuals. Bishop Russell was one of the very first Englishmen to own a printed copy of Cicero's *De Officiis* (which he purchased in Bruges in 1467), but by 1500 numerous editions of Cicero's writings, printed in both England and abroad, filled English classrooms and homes. Moreover, popular Humanist works designed for use in the new Humanist schools (such as Magdalen College School, Oxford) spread Ciceronian ideals widely throughout the emerging class of Yorkist and early Tudor administrators. Lorenzo Traversagni's *Nova rhetorica*, printed by Caxton in 1479 and entering a second edition only a year later, extolled the virtues of grammar and rhetoric to a generation of would-be Humanists and plundered Cicero shamelessly. In 1481 Caxton printed Worcester's translation of Cicero's *De Senectute,* in which the second-century B.C. republican, Cato the Elder, pronounces with the wisdom of old age. This text offered further Classical models for renegotiating the English commonweal in the wake of the civil wars, suggesting, for example, that good citizens offer their goods and bodies to serve the 'comyn wele' and not their 'singuler proufytte.'[23] As Wakelin has suggested, fifteenth-century English readers read their Cicero and other Humanist authors not only with an eye to Latin grammar and elegant prose, but also to inform their own changing view of the world around them and seek ways to ensure a peaceful and prosperous commonweal. They sought not only to 'reproduce Cicero's style, but to imitate his ideas.'[24]

As well as its positive, cultural and philosophical aspects Burckhardt identified a darker side to the fifteenth-century Renaissance. Writing of the Italian character in particular, he argued that 'the fundamental vice of this character was at the same time a condition of its greatness, namely, excessive individualism . . . in each single instance [the Renaissance Italian] forms his decision independently, according as honour or interest, passion or calculation, revenge or renunciation, gain the upper hand in his own mind.'[25] Thus the poisoning and adulterous Borgias were just as much a product of the Renaissance as was the art and brilliance of da Vinci. The epitome of this ruthless, individualistic, even amoral, form of politics is, of course, to be found in the writings of the early sixteenth-century Florentine, Niccolò Machiavelli. Machiavelli found his inspiration not only in the actions of contemporary Italian politicians (most notably Cesare Borgia, Duke of Romagna), but also in those of Louis XI, Ferdinand of Aragon, Emperor Maximilian and their successors. Indeed, Machiavelli's pragmatic approach to politics, his belief that the effects of Fortune could be ameliorated and that men could shape their own destiny through their actions, had been prefigured in part in the work of Philippe Commynes, the Flemish writer who served both Charles the Bold and Louis XI and who observed the Wars of the Roses at first hand. The second half of the fifteenth century witnessed a changing approach to politics, both imaginatively and in practice. It was an approach to politics in which deception, plots, and a belief that great (or virtuous) men could shape their own destiny found new significance. Paul Strohm has argued that from the 1450s England

experienced its own 'pre-Machiavellian moment'. 'Politique' behaviour, it is suggested, no longer referred solely to 'those who make
generous arrangements for the good of all but also to those who make
the best possible arrangements for themselves. Stretched far from its
earlier, optimistic shape, *politique* behaviour now extends to those
who employ lies, deceptions and even falsely sworn oaths as possible
elements of good political practice.'[26] In this respect at least, the Wars
of the Roses amounted to a revolution in the English politics.

Several political texts of the mid-fifteenth century, already encoun-
tered in this book, reveal an appreciation of this new form of politics.
It is not to say that such dissimilation and the like had not previously
featured in English politics; rather it is to make the point that during
the Wars of the Roses these ideas were first openly discussed and then
embraced (and even celebrated) by the protagonists. The *Somnium Vigilantis*, the Lancastrian defence of the attainder of the Yorkist lords in
1459, claimed that York and his allies had used such the language of
reform to fool the commons and as a cloak to their own ambition.
'Thoghe thay dyd many glorius and bostynge dedes with a colorable
semblant and pretens of the commen welth and sayd that they entended
but goode . . . how so be it that þe peple in many places was desayved
and blyndede by þe subtile and coverte malice and colorable frauds
that they used in all thinges.' The author recognised how the Yorkists
had exploited the prevailing political culture of Lancastrian England
and its self-conscious need for the approbation of the commons: 'The
peple favoureth hem, *ergo* thay be good.'[27] Fears over widespread deception and the malicious intent of the protagonists were also reflected in
a widely articulated concern over forsworn oaths. The Yorkists claimed
in 1461 that the Lancastrian dynasty itself was based upon perjury and
that Henry IV had disregarded the oath made in 1399 that he had
returned to England merely to reclaim his Duchy of Lancaster. Yet,
forsworn oaths emerged as a defining feature of Richard, Duke of York's
political career in the 1450s. From 1452 Duke Richard made several
solemn oaths to obey Henry VI and eschew the 'wey of feyt'. These
were broken with alarming regularity, so much so that York 'must be
considered one of the leading perjurers of all time.'[28] Indeed, in 1461
Margaret of Anjou reminded the city of London that he had acted

'contrary to his liegeaunce and divers solempne othes of his owne offre made uncompelled or constraigned.'[29] In 1471 Edward IV used the same tactic as Bolingbroke in 1399 of returning from exile to ostensibly claim his rightful inheritance. Yet Edward was far more subtle, more 'Machiavellian' if you will, and was careful not to perjure himself. *The Arrivall* tells us that he instructed his companions to say that he came 'only to claime to be Duke of York' and as he approached the city of York 'he and all his felowshipe pretendyd by any manar langage none other qwarell but for the right that was his fathers, the Duke of Yorke.' This expression of his 'right' was sufficient to gain his admission to the city, but as the author of *The Arrival* explains with some relish the citizens had forgotten one important detail: 'not discovering, ne remembringe, that his sayd fathar, bisydes that he was rightfully Duke of Yorke, he was also verrey trew and rightwise enheritoure to the roylme and corone of England &c. and so he was declared by [the] iij astates of the land . . . unto this day never repelled, ne revoked.'[30]

Indeed, *The Arrivall* marks a watershed in the political culture of fifteenth-century England. As we have seen, it was one example of a new form of propagandist writing circulated by the Yorkists in 1471, both at home and abroad, to provide an official and irrefutable account of recent events. *The Arrivall* celebrates Edward's 'deliberate attempt to deceive.' Perjury, it seems, had 'now become a perverse badge of honour.'[31] Edward was not alone in his 'politique' behaviour. Elsewhere, the author of *The Arrivall* notes how the Earl of Northumberland dissembled, refusing to commit himself openly one way or the other, and thus did the king good service. New rules of political behaviour among the English are also apparent in the writing of Phillippe de Commynes. He delights in describing how in 1470, despite being in receipt of a royal office and a pension from the Duke of Burgundy, John, Lord Wenlock secretly aided and abetted the Earl of Warwick in securing the Readeption of Henry VI. However, Wenlock himself was deceived by an unnamed English lady, a servant of the duchess of Clarence, whom he had hoped would mediate between the French king and the Earl of Warwick. In fact she was on a secret mission to persuade the Duke of Clarence to renounce his support of Warwick and reconcile himself to his brother. She was, of course, successful and Commynes recalls 'however cunning Lord Wenlock was this woman deceived him and carried out this secret assignment which led to the death and defeat of the Earl of Warwick and his followers.'[32]

To some extent, in so far as it was a form of politics associated with the Italian principalities, the Wars of the Roses witnessed the emergence of a 'Renaissance style' of politics in England. Indeed, it was probably no coincidence that one of the most celebrated English aristocratic patrons of Humanism, John Tiptoft, Earl of Worcester, was also associated with the cruelty and barbarism that the English considered typical of Italian (or 'Renaissance') politics. In 1458 Tiptoft had left England to visit Italy and make a pilgrimage to the Holy Land. He remained abroad until September 1461, studying civil law at the University of Padua and emerging as a patron of Humanist scholarship. Unlike his predecessor, Humphrey, Duke of Gloucester (to whom he was compared as a patron by the University of Oxford), Tiptoft was a scholar himself: he translated Cicero's *De Amicitia* (printed by Caxton in 1481) and Buonaccorso de Montemagno's *De Vera Nobilitate*, and in 1460 he made an oration before Pope Pius II that allegedly moved the Pontiff to tears for the elegance of its Latinity. In February 1462 he was appointed Constable of England and proceeded to hear cases of treason according to civil law instead of common law. The constable's court had long employed civil law, but it was the savagery of Tiptoft's punishments that caused alarm. In 1467, as Clarence's deputy in Ireland, he tortured and executed the two young sons of the rebel, Thomas Fitzgerald, Earl of Desmond. To the usual horrors of hanging, drawing and quartering, he introduced the novelty of impalement when executing 20 of the Earl of Warwick's men in 1470. In October of that year he was himself executed for treason by the Readeption regime. To contemporary English chroniclers Tiptoft's cruelty stemmed from his Italianate sympathies. He had, they claimed quite wrongly, introduced the 'lawe padowe' into England, while the practice of impalement made him 'behatede emonge the peple, for ther dysordinate dethe that he used, contrarye to the lawe of the londe.'[33] The chroniclers' dislike of Tiptoft reflected a wider unease that the civil wars had somehow ushered new and foreign modes of political behaviour into England. These fears continued to grow up to the end of the fifteenth century and were given renewed vigour by the policies and actions of Henry VII. Henry, of course, had received his political apprenticeship in France and his style of rule was certainly very different from his Lancastrian, and even Yorkist, predecessors. In 1498 the Spanish ambassador, reporting the rumours he had heard at the Henrician court, observed that the king 'would like to govern in the French fashion, but he cannot.' Indeed, it was this perceived foreignness and novelty of Henrician political culture that would lie behind many of the internal political crises of the reign.[34]

The second half of the fifteenth century saw profound and far-reaching changes in English political culture. While it is true that many of the institutions of government, both at a national and local level, remained the same, the ideas and principles that underpinned them were transformed. The language of politics changed, both in response to the pressures of the civil wars themselves and as part of wider cultural changes experienced throughout Europe, and fundamental tenets of late-medieval English constitution were renegotiated. The role of the commons in politics and notions about precisely who was legitimately entitled to participate in the political process changed. The broad, inclusive political community of the late Middle Ages gave way to a more restricted, exclusive political class comprised of both landowners and, significantly, those educated in the law or the new Humanist learning. The impact of Humanism on the political culture of late-medieval England is only beginning to be recognised. It gave rise to new, almost Republican, ways of imagining the state, redefining key terms in the political lexicon (especially notions of the 'common profit' or 'commonweal'). It also placed England firmly within the intellectual and cultural mainstream of Europe, encouraging kings like Edward IV and more especially Henry VII (and their ministers) to imagine ways of governing that owed as much to emerging Renaissance ideals of kingship and government as they did to any older English traditions. The Wars of the Roses, and the fiscal and political crises that caused them, did not transform England in themselves, but they provide the opportunity for Englishmen to think about and apply fresh ideas about government and the state.

Epilogue

EARLY TUDOR ENGLAND

On 24 February 1525 a Spanish-Imperial army attacked and defeated a French army, led in person by King Francis I, just outside the walls of the Italian city of Pavia. For the French it was a disaster: their king spent the next year or so as a prisoner in Madrid, while the victory assured Habsburg domination of the Italian peninsula. Killed fighting alongside Francis was Richard de la Pole, 'the White Rose', grandson of Richard, Duke of York and the last member of the Yorkist dynasty to actively claim the English throne. By the 1520s, however, the Wars of the Roses were a distant memory and Yorkist plots and pretenders existed only in the suspicious imagination of Henry VIII. Nevertheless, early Tudor England had continued to be shaken by rebellion, political struggles at court, and, from the late 1520s, the events that led to the English Reformation. Yet the nature of and solutions found to these crises reveal the extent to which the civil wars of the fifteenth century had transformed the realm.

Henry VIII's relationship with his Yorkist relations reveals just how much the practice of politics had changed. During the second half of the 1530s Henry ordered the executions of the Duke of Clarence's daughter, the ancient Margaret, countess of Salisbury, and Henry, Marquess of Exeter, great-grandson of Edward IV. He also arrested for treason Arthur Plantagenet, Viscount Lisle, the elderly illegitimate son of Edward IV. These arrests and executions, however, were not part of any struggle against Yorkist pretenders in the localities; rather they were part and parcel of a campaign designed to eliminate opponents of the king's religious and diplomatic policies at court. They demonstrate how by the 1530s the court itself, rather than any interplay between the king and his household and his noble opponents in the localities, was at the centre of politics. There were several reasons for this. First, the tendency of the Yorkist and early Tudors to inflate the size of their households and retain large numbers of gentry as members of an expanded royal affinity exerted a 'centripetal' force on the polity, drawing the political classes towards the centre.[1] Second, this was reinforced by the emergence of the crown in the late fifteenth century, as a result of attainders and changes in dynasty, as the largest lay landowner in the realm. Magnates could no longer sit and sulk on their estates but were either drawn to the king's court or risked being excluded from political life altogether. Those magnates who chafed against this new reality, like Edward Stafford, Duke of Buckingham, in 1521, risked accusations of treason and execution.

Changes to the balance of power were also reflected in parliament and in the fiscal relationship between the crown and its subjects. Since 1334 the parliamentary Commons had successively resisted the crown's attempts to develop a form of extraordinary taxation that realistically reflected the wealth of its subjects. In 1523 parliament granted a subsidy that for the first time in nearly two hundred years accurately assessed real wealth. Whereas the usual fifteenth and tenth (which continued to be granted alongside these innovative subsidies) brought in £31,000, the 1523 subsidy collected over £155,000. This came on top of loans in 1522 and 1523 totalling some £200,000. These loans were written off as retrospective grants of taxation in 1529 by parliament. During the 1540s the state's ability to tax its subjects grew even more and between 1543 and 1552 almost £1,000,000 was collected in lay taxation.[2] Again, the reasons for this were various. On the simplest level, the growth of the royal affinity meant that the parliamentary commons was more pliant with more elected MPs personally bound to the king by ties of service. Far more subtle and important, however, were the developing notions of obedience to an increasingly powerful crown. Service to the commonweal, the dominant theme of political culture in the fifteenth century, had given way to obedience to the king and his magistrates. The king had a duty to defend and uphold the commonweal, but it was not for ordinary subjects to advise, let alone question, the king. From the 1480s a growing crescendo of official proclamations, the preambles to parliamentary statutes, sermons and the work of official propagandists declaimed the duty of obedience owed to the prince by his subjects. This was the inevitable consequence of the transformation of political culture described in chapter eight. As Richard Morison, one of the most outspoken proponent of royal supremacy during Henry VIII's reign, wrote in 1536: 'it far passeth cobblers' craft to discuss what lords, what bishops, what counsellors, what acts, statutes and laws are most meet for a commonwealth.'[3]

These new notions of royal supremacy, proscribing rebellion and political dissent as treason, were also fuelled by Humanism and the growing influence of common lawyers in royal government. Morison, as well as being a royal propagandist, was one of the most accomplished Humanists of his age. Others who developed and articulated this new definition of the reciprocal obligations of king and subject had a background in the English common law. Like Fortescue in the 1470s, they sought to re-equip the crown with the institutional, political and intellectual tools to assert its authority against threats from both within and outside the realm. Common lawyers, such as Edmund Dudley, Sir Richard Empson and Sir Thomas Lovell, were among the most prominent councillors of Henry VII and helped forged a distinctly Tudor political culture. In the 1520s and 30s common lawyers, such as Christopher St German, Thomas Cromwell and Simon Fish, developed new theories of royal supremacy, asserting the imperial jurisdiction of the English crown and arguing that the kings of England recognised no superior, either lay or spiritual, within the realm of England. Coupling legal arguments for royal supremacy with their sympathy for emerging Evangelical doctrine, these men paved the way for the English Reformation.

Scholars outside the discipline of history have increasingly seen the fifteenth and early sixteenth centuries as a time of 'reform and cultural revolution.'[4] The second half of the fifteenth century was not the end of the moribund Middle Ages but a time of intense political and cultural upheaval and innovation that was refracted through the prism of the civil wars. The Wars broke out not merely because of the inadequacy of Henry VI or the ambition of Richard, Duke of York and his sons, but because the decades after 1450 afforded the right circumstances in which the fundamental, structural problems of the English polity could be tackled and solved. Thus the Wars of the Roses should be restored to their rightful place as a pivotal period of 'Our Island Story.'

Notes

Preface

1 H.E. Marshall, *Our Island Story: A History of England for Boys and Girls* (London: T.C. and E.C. Jack, 1905).
2 Gerald Harriss, *Shaping the Nation: England 1360–1461* (Oxford: Oxford University Press, 2005).

Introduction

1 C. Behan McCullagh, *The Logic of History: Putting Postmodernism in Perspective* (London: Routledge, 2003), pp. 125–7.
2 J.R. Lander, *Crown and Nobility 1450–1509* (London: Hodder and Stoughton, 1976), p. 57.
3 *The Crowland Chronicle Continuations: 1459–1486*, ed. N. Pronay and J. Cox (Stroud: Sutton Publishing, 1986), p. 185.
4 *An English Chronicle 1377–1461*, ed. W. Marx (Woodbridge: Boydell and Brewer, 2003), p. 79.
5 *Hall's Chronicle*, ed. Henry Ellis (London: J. Johnson, 1809), p. 13.
6 A.J. Pollard, *The Wars of the Roses* (Basingstoke: MacMillan, 1988), pp. 9–10.
7 W. Stubbs, *Select Charters and Other Illustrations of English Constitutional History* (Oxford: Clarendon Press, 1870) p. xv.
8 W. Stubbs, *The Constitutional History of England* (3 vols., Oxford: Clarendon Press, 1897), Vol. 3, p. 294.
9 Pollard, *Wars of the Roses*, pp. 12–13.
10 J.R. Green, *A Short History of the English People* (London: Harper and Brothers, 1878), p. 301

11 C.L. Kingsford, *Prejudice and Promise in Fifteenth Century England* (Oxford: Clarendon Press, 1925).

12 The best introduction to McFarlane is G.L. Harriss, '(Kenneth) Bruce McFarlane (1903–1966)', in *Oxford Dictionary of National Biography.*

13 K.B. McFarlane, 'The Wars of the Roses', in *England in the Fifteenth Century*, ed. G.L. Harriss (London: Hambledon Press, 1981), pp. 238–9.

14 Harriss, *Shaping the Nation*, p. 653

15 Michael Hicks, *The Wars of the Roses* (New Haven, CT: Yale University Press, 2009), pp. 262–4.

16 Dale Hoak, *Tudor Political Culture* (Cambridge: Cambridge University Press, 1995), p. 1.

17 This is discussed at further length in Christine Carpenter, 'Introduction: Political Culture, Politics and Cultural History', in *The Fifteenth Century IV*, ed. Christine Carpenter and Linda Clark (Woodbridge: Boydell and Brewer, 2004), pp. 1–19.

Chapter One

1 Rosemary Horrox (ed.), 'Edward IV: Parliament of 1461, Text and Translation', in *PROME: The Parliament Rolls of Medieval England*, ed. Chris Given-Wilson *et al* (Leicester: Scholarly Digital Editions, 2005), item 9.

2 *PROME*, Chris Given-Wilson (ed.), 'Henry IV: Parliament of 1399 October Text and Translation', item 17.

3 *Eulogium Historiarum sive Temporis*, ed. F.S. Haydon (3 vols., London: Rolls Series, 1863), Vol. 3, p. 409

4 Michael Bennett, *Richard II and the Revolution of 1399* (Stroud: Alan Sutton, 1999), p. 204.

5 *Calendar of Patent Rolls, 1401–1405*, p. 126.

6 A.J. Pollard, *Late Medieval England 1399–1509* (Harlow: Longman, 2000), p. 63.

7 K.B. McFarlane, *Lancastrian Kings and Lollard Knights* (Oxford: Oxford University Press, 1972), p. 133.

8 *PROME*, Anne Curry (ed.), 'Henry V: Parliament of 1420 December Text and Translation', item 25.

9 Stubbs, Vol. 3, pp. 134–5.

10 B.P. Wolffe, 'The Personal Rule of Henry VI', in *Fifteenth Century England*, ed. S.B. Chrimes, C.D. Ross and R.A. Griffiths (Manchester: Manchester University Press, 1972), pp. 37, 42, 44.

11 *PROME*, Anne Curry (ed.), 'Henry VI: Parliament of 1445, Text and Translation', item 23.

12 Edward Powell, 'Lancastrian England', in *The New Cambridge Medieval History VII c.1415–c.1500*, ed. Christopher Allmand (Cambridge: Cambridge University Press, 1998), p. 466.

Chapter Two

1 *PROME*, Anne Curry (ed.), 'Parliament of 1449 November, Text and Translation', item 52.
2 I.W.M Harvey, *Jack Cade's Rebellion of 1450* (Oxford: Oxford University Press, 1991), p. 186.
3 *Thomas Gascoigne: Loci e Libro Veritatum*, ed. J.E.T. Rogers (Oxford: Clarendon Press, 1881), p. 189.
4 Harvey, *Cade's Rebellion*, p. 191.
5 John L. Watts, 'Polemic and Politics in the 1450s' in *The Politics of Fifteenth Century England: John Vale's Book*, ed. Margaret Lucille Kekewich *et al* (Stroud: Alan Sutton, 1995), p. 8.
6 Harvey, *Cade's Rebellion*, p. 191.
7 R.A. Griffiths, 'Duke Richard of York's Intentions in 1450 and the Origins of the Wars of the Roses', in *King and Country: England and Wales in the Fifteenth Century* (London: Hambledon, 1991), pp. 281–2.
8 Michael Hicks, 'From Megaphone to Microscope: the Correspondence of Richard Duke of York with Henry VI in 1450 Revisited', *Journal of Medieval History* 25 (1999), pp. 249–50.
9 *Paston Letters and Papers of the Fifteenth Century*, ed. Norman Davies, Richard Beadle and Colin Richmond (3 vols., Oxford: Oxford University Press, 1971–2005), vol. 2, p. 47.
10 Griffiths, 'Duke Richard's Intentions', pp. 299–301.
11 Ibid., pp. 301–2.
12 *The Politics of Fifteenth Century England*, ed. Kekewich *et al*, pp. 187–9.
13 B.P. Wolffe, *Henry VI* (London: Methuen, 1983), p. 272.
14 *Calendar of Patent Rolls, 1452–61*, p. 143.
15 R.A. Griffiths, *The Reign of Henry VI* (London: Earnest Benn, 1981), p. 725.
16 'John Benet's Chronicle', ed. G.L. and M.A. Harriss, *Camden Miscellany XXIV* , (London: Camden Society, 1972), p. 212.

Chapter Three

1 *PROME*, Rosemary Horrox (ed.), 'Parliament of 1455, Text and Translation', item 19.
2 Ibid., item 20.

3   *An English Chronicle* ed. Marx, p. 73.

4   *The Politics of Fifteenth Century England*, ed. Kekewich *et al*, p. 173.

5   *Paston Letters*, ed. Beadle and Richmond, vol. 3, p. 158.

6   Christine Carpenter, *The Wars of the Roses: Politics and the Constitu-tion in England* (Cambridge: Cambridge University Press, 1997), p. 137.

7   *PROME*, 'Parliament of 1455, Text and Translation', item 32.

8   Ibid., item 41.

9   *Paston Letters*, ed. Beadle and Richmond, vol. 3, p. 161.

10 Ibid.

11 Wolffe, *Henry VI*, p. 302.

12 John Watts, *Henry VI and the Politics of Kingship* (Cambridge: Cambridge University Press, 1996), pp. 342–5.

13 *Paston Letters*, ed. Davies, vol. 2, p. 168.

14 *PROME*, Rosemary Horrox (ed.), 'Parliament of 1459, Text and Translation', item 12.

15 *Historical Poems of the XIVth and XVth Centuries*, ed. R.H. Robbins (New York: Columbia University Press, 1959), pp. 189–90.

16 A.J. Pollard, 'The Northern Retainers of Richard Nevill, Earl of Salisbury', *Northern History* 11 (1975–6), p. 52.

17 *Letters and Papers Illustrative of the Wars of the English in France During the Reign of Henry the Sixth, King of England*, ed. J. Stevenson (2 vols in 3, London: Rolls Series, 1861–4), vol. 2, part 2, p. 511.

18 Griffiths, *Reign of King Henry VI*, p. 818.

19 'Gregory's Chronicle', in *The Historical Collections of a Citizen of London in the Fifteenth Century*, ed. James Gairdner (London: Camden Society, 1876), p. 205.

Chapter Four

1   J. P. Gilson, 'A Defence of the Proscription of the Yorkists in 1459', *English Historical Review*, 26 (1911), pp. 512–25.

2   Michael Hicks, *Warwick the Kingmaker* (Oxford: Blackwell Publishing, 1998), p. 184.

3   P.A. Johnson, *Duke Richard of York 1411–1460* (Oxford: Oxford University Press, 1988), p. 214.

4   *PROME*, Rosemary Horrox (ed.), 'Parliament of 1460, Text and Translation', item 12.

5   'Gregory's Chronicle', ed. Gairdner, p. 215.

6   Hannes Kleineke, *Edward IV* (Abingdon: Routledge, 2009), pp. 49–50.

7   Michael Hicks, 'Bastard Feudalism, Overmighty Subjects and Idols of the Multitude during the Wars of the Roses', *History*, 85 (2000), pp. 386–403.

8 Jean de Waurin, *Recueil des Croniques et Anchiennes Istories de la Grant Bretagne*, ed. W. and E.C.L.P. Hardy (5 vols., London: Rolls Series, 1864–91), vol. 5, p. 325.

9 *The Politics of Fifteenth Century England*, ed. Kekewich *et al*, pp. 208–12.

10 C.M. Barron, 'London and the Crown 1451–61', in *The Crown and Local Communities in England and France in the Fifteenth Century*, ed. J.R.L. Highfield and R.I. Jeffs (Gloucester: Alan Sutton, 1981), pp. 88–109.

11 *PROME*, Rosemary Horrox (ed.), 'Edward IV: Parliament of 1461, Text and Translation', item 10.

Chapter Five

1 K.B. McFarlane, 'The Wars of the Roses', in *England in the Fifteenth Century*, ed. G.L. Harriss (London: Hambledon, 1981), p. 238.

2 Pollard, *Late Medieval England*, p. 274.

3 Hicks, *Warwick the Kingmaker*, p. 222.

4 *The Great Chronicle of London*, ed. A.H. Thomas and I.D. Thornley (London, 1938), p. 207.

5 Hicks, 'Bastard Feudalism, Overmighty Subjects and Idols of the Multitude', pp. 386–403.

6 Kleineke, *Edward IV*, pp. 81–82.

7 *The Paston Letters*, ed. Davies, vol. 1, p. 410.

8 John Warkworth, *Chronicle of the First Thirteen Years of the Reign of King Edward IV*, ed. J.O. Halliwell (London: Camden Society, 1839), p. 47.

9 *Paston Letters*, ed. Davies, vol. 1, p. 245.

10 'Chronicle of the Rebellion in Lincolnshire, 1470', ed. J.G. Nichols, in *Camden Miscellany I* (London: Camden Society, 1847), p. 10.

11 *The Politics of Fifteenth Century England*, ed. Kekewich *et al*, pp. 215–18.

12 Carpenter, *Wars of the Roses*, p. 180.

13 *The Historie of the Arrivall of King Edward IV, A.D 1471*, ed. J. Bruce, (London: Camden Society, 1838), p. 10

14 Ibid., pp. 6–9.

15 Ibid., p. 20.

16 Ibid., p. 38.

17 *An English Chronicle* ed. Marx, p. 88.

Chapter Six

1   *The Crowland Chronicle Continuations*, ed. Pronay and Cox, p. 133.
2   *Literae Cantuarienses: The Letter Books of the Monastery of Christ Church, Canterbury*, ed. J.B. Sheppard (3 vols., London: Rolls Series, 1889), vol. 3, pp. 274–85.
3   D.A.L. Morgan, 'The Political After-Life of Edward III: the Apotheosis of a Warmonger', *English Historical Review* 112 (1997), p. 873.
4   *Paston Letters*, ed. Davies, vol. 1, pp. 486–7.
5   Charles Ross, *Edward IV* (London: Methuen, 1974), p. 235.
6   Philippe de Commynes, *Memoirs: the Reign of Louis XI 1461–83*, trans.. Michael Jones (Harmondsworth: Penguin Classics, 1972), p. 362.
7   *Paston Letters*, ed. Davies, vol. 1, pp. 498–9.
8   Michael K. Jones, '1477– the Expedition that Never Was: Chivalric Expectation in Late Yorkist England', *The Ricardian* 12 (2001), pp. 275–92.
9   *Calendar of State Papers, Milan*, vol. 1, p. 227.
10 The National Archives, E315/486, f. 12.
11 Charles Ross, *Richard III* (London: Methuen, 1981), p. 83.
12 Dominic Mancini, *The Usurpation of Richard III*, ed. C.A.J. Armstrong (Oxford: Oxford University Press, 1969), p. 95.
13 *British Library Harleian Manuscript 433*, ed. R. Horrox and P.W. Hammond (4 vols., Gloucester: Alan Sutton, 1979–83), vol. 3, p. 29.
14 Commynes, *Memoirs*, ed. Jones, p. 397.
15 *The Crowland Chronicle Continuations*, ed. Pronay and Cox, p. 163.
16 Ibid., p. 171.
17 *PROME*, Rosemary Horrox (ed.), 'Richard III: Parliament of 1484, Text and Translation', item 19.
18 Ibid., item 1.
19 *Three Books of Polydore Vergil's English History*, ed. Henry Ellis (London: Camden Society, 1844), p. 244
20 David Hipshon, *Richard III* (Abingdon: Routledge, 2011), p. 244.
21 *PROME*, Rosemary Horrox (ed.), 'Henry VII: Parliament of 1485, Text and Translation', item 5.
22 Carpenter, *Wars of the Roses*, p. 205.

Chapter Seven

1   Colin Richmond, 'Identity and Morality: Power and Politics during the Wars of the Roses', in *Power and Identity in the Middle Ages*, ed. Huw Pryce and John Watts (Oxford: Oxford University Press, 2007), pp. 226–41.

2   Gillingham, *Wars of the Roses*, p. 15.

3   Ibid., pp. 15–16

4   William Worcestre, *The Boke of Noblesse*, ed. J.G. Nichols (London: The Roxburgh Club, 1860), pp. 76–78.

5   Lander, *Crown and Nobility*, p. 13.

6   Catherine Nall, 'The Production and Reception of Military Texts in the Aftermath of the Hundred Years War' (University of York, D. Phil. thesis, 2004).

7   Simon Payling, 'War and Peace: Military and Administrative Service amongst the English Gentry in the Reign of Henry VI', in *Soldiers, Nobles and Gentlemen: Essays in Honour of Maurice Keen*, ed. Peter Coss and Christopher Tyerman (Woodbridge: Boydell and Brewer, 2009), pp. 240–60.

8   Colin Richmond, 'The Nobility and the Wars of the Roses, 1459–61', *Nottingham Medieval Studies* 21 (1977), pp. 71–85. I am grateful to Hannes Kleineke for discussing, and correcting, Richmond's figures with me.

9   Lander, *Crown and Nobility*, p. 24.

10 Malcolm Mercer, *The Medieval Gentry: Power, Leadership and Choice during the Wars of the Roses* (London: Continuum, 2010), pp. 25–33.

11 The National Archives, PROB11/7, f. 212.

12 Gillingham, *Wars of the Roses*, p. 28.

13 Anthony Goodman, *The Wars of the Roses: The Soldiers' Experience* (Stroud: Alan Sutton, 2005), p. 220.

14 *Blood Red Roses: the Archaeology of a Mass Grave from the Battle of Towton*, ed. Veronica Fiorato *et al* (Oxford: Oxbow Books, 2007), p. 172.

15 Commynes, *Memoirs*, ed. Jones, p. 195.

16 Goodman, *Wars of the Roses*, p. 196.

17 *Literae Cantuarienses*, ed. Sheppard, vol. 3, pp. 274–85.

18 R.L. Storey, *The End of the House of Lancaster* (2nd edn., Stroud: Alan Sutton, 1999), pp. 1–28.

19 *The York House Books 1461–1490*, ed. L. C. Attreed, 2 vols. (Stroud: Alan Sutton, 1991), vol. 2, pp. 9–10.

20 Ibid., vol. 1, pp. 390–1.

21 *The Coventry Leet Book, 1420–1555*, ed. M. D. Harris, 4 vols., Early English Text Society 134–5, 138, 146 (1907–13), vol. 1, pp. 304–19, 353–8, 362–71.

22 *Records of Borough of Leicester*, ed. M. Bateson (London: C.J. Clay and Sons, 1901), vol. 2, p. 279.

Chapter Eight

1   John Watts, 'Public or Plebs: the Changing Meaning of 'The Commons', 1381–1549', in *Power and Identity in the Middle Ages*, ed. Pryce and Watts, p. 250.

2   Ibid., p. 250.

3   David Rollison, *A Commonwealth of the People: Popular Politics and England's Long Social Revolution, 1066–1649* (Cambridge: Cambridge University Press, 2010), p. 139.

4   Roger Virgoe 'The Death of William de la Pole, Duke of Suffolk', in *East Anglian Political Society and the Political Community of Late Medieval England*, ed. Caroline Barron, Carole Rawcliffe and Joel Rosenthal (Norwich: Centre for East Anglian Studies, 1997), p. 253.

5   *PROME*, Anne Curry (ed.), 'Henry VI: Parliament of 1449 November, Text and Translation', item 15.

6   Wendy Scase, *Literature and Complaint in England 1272–1553* (Oxford: Oxford University Press, 2007), p. 135.

7   Storey, *End of the House of Lancaster*, p. 197.

8   Colin Richmond, 'Propaganda in the Wars of the Roses', *History Today* 42 (1992), pp. 12–18.

9   Ross, *Richard III*, p. xxxiii; York *House Books*, ed. Attreed, vol. 1, p. 350.

10 Sir John Fortescue, *The Governance of England*, ed. Charles Plummer (Oxford: Oxford University Press, 1926), pp. 114–15.

11 G.L. Harriss, *Crown, Parliament and Public Finance in Medieval England to 1369* (Oxford: Oxford University Press, 1975), p. 517.

12 Derek Pearsall, '*Crowned King*': War and Peace in 1415' in *The Lancastrian Court*, ed. Jenny Stratford (Stamford: Shaun Tyas, 2003), pp. 163–72.

13 W.M. Ormrod, 'The Western European Monarchies in the Later Middle Ages', in *Economic Systems and State Finance*, ed. Richard Bonney (Oxford: Oxford University Press, 1995), pp. 147–51.

14 Fortescue, *Governance of England*, ed. Plummer, p. 154.

15 Paul Oskar Kristeller, 'Humanism', in *The Cambridge History of Renaissance Philosophy*, ed. Charles B. Schmitt and Quentin Skinner (Cambridge: Cambridge University Press, 1988), p. 113.

16 Robert Black, 'Humanism', in *The New Cambridge Medieval History VII*, p. 276.

17 A.S.G. Edwards, 'The Middle English Translation of Claudian's *De Consulatu Stilichonis*', in *Middle English Poetry: Text and Traditions*, ed. A.J. Minnis (Woodbridge: Boydell and Brewer, 2001), p. 274

18 Daniel Wakelin, *Humanism, Reading and English Literature 1430–1530* (Oxford: Oxford University Press, 2007), p. 63.
19 *Boke of Noblesse*, ed. Nichols, p. 48.
20 Fortescue, *Governance of England*, ed. Plummer, pp. 146–8.
21 *Cicero: On the Commonwealth and the Laws*, ed. J.E.G. Zetzel (Cambridge: Cambridge University Press, 1999), p. 18.
22 John Watts, '*The Policie in Christen Remes*: Bishop Russell's Parliamentary Sermons of 1483–84', in *Authority and Consent in Tudor England*, ed. G.W. Bernard and S.J. Gunn (Aldershot: Ashgate Publishing, 2002), pp. 49–50.
23 Wakelin, *Humanism, Reading and English Literature*, p. 152.
24 Ibid., p. 159.
25 Jakob Burckhard, *The Civilization of the Renaissance in Italy*, trans. S.C.G. MMiddlemore (London: Penguin Classics, 2004), p. 279.
26 Paul Strohm, *Politique: Languages of Statecraft between Chaucer and Shakespeare* (Notre Dame, ID: University of Notre Dame Press, 2005), p. 5.
27 Gilson, 'Defence of the Proscription of the Yorkists', pp. 520, 521.
28 Strohm, *Politique*, p. 184
29 *Fifteenth Century England*, ed. Kekewich *et al*, p. 142.
30 *The Arrivall*, ed. Bruce, p. 4.
31 Strohm, *Politique*, p. 31.
32 Commynes, *Memoirs*, ed. Jones, p. 185.
33 Warkworth, *Chronicle*, ed. Halliwell, pp. 5, 9.
34 David Grummitt, 'Household, Politics and Political Morality in the Reign of Henry VII', *Historical Research* 81 (2009), p. 395.

Epilogue

1 D.A.L. Morgan, 'The King's Affinity in the Polity of Yorkist England', *Transactions of the Royal Historical Society* 5th series 23 (1973), pp. 1–25.
2 Richard Hoyle, 'War and Public Finance', in *The Reign of Henry VIII*, ed. Diarmaid MacCulloch (Basingstoke: Macmillan, 1995), PP. 89–93.
3 Berkowitz, *Humanist Scholarship and Public Order: Two Tracts against 'The Pilgrimage of Grace' and Related Contemporary Documents* (London: Folger Books, 1984), p. 88.
4 James Simpson, *The Oxford English Literary History, volume 2 1350–1547: Reform and Cultural Revolution* (Oxford: Oxford University Press, 2002).

Bibliography

INTRODUCTION

Several works introduce the main themes of academic debate. A.J. Pollard, *The Wars of the Roses* (Basingstoke: Macmillan, 3rd edn. 2012) remains a good starting point, as does the collection of essays, *The Wars of the Roses*, ed. A.J. Pollard (Basingstoke: Macmillan, 1995). A useful introduction to the historiography and an outline of English political society in the fifteenth century can be found in Christine Carpenter, *The Wars of the Roses: politics and the constitution in England, c.1437–1509* (Cambridge: Cambridge University Press, 1997). The best textbooks for late-medieval England are (in order of publication) Gerald Harriss, *Shaping the Nation: England 1360–1461* (Oxford: Oxford University Press, 2005), A.J. Pollard, *Late Medieval England 1399–1509* (Harlow: Longman, 2000), A. Tuck, *Crown and Nobility* (Oxford: Wiley-Blackwell, 1985), J.A.F. Thomson, *The Transformation of Medieval England 1370–1529* (London: Longman, 1983) and Maurice Keen, *England in the Later Middle Ages* (London: Routledge, 1973). Another useful survey, but narrower in focus, is Richard Britnell, *The Closing of the Middle Ages? England, 1471–1529* (Oxford: Blackwell Publishers, 1997).

For Shakespeare and the Tudor historians of the Wars see *The Cambridge Companion to Shakespeare's History Plays*, ed. Michael Hattaway (Cambridge: Cambridge University Press: 2002) and

Annabel Patterson, *Reading Holinshed's Chronicles* (Chicago, IL: University of Chicago Press, 1994). A stimulating reassessment of the 'Tudor myth' can be found in Keith Dockray, *William Shakespeare, the Wars of the Roses and the Historians* (Stroud: Alan Sutton, 2002). For the London chronicles of the fifteenth century see M.-R. McLaren, *The London Chronicles of the Fifteenth Century: a Revolution in English Writing* (Woodbridge: Boydell and Brewer, 2002). The nineteenth-century historians of the Wars are discussed in Carpenter, *The Wars of the Roses*, ch. 1.

K.B. McFarlane's most important published work is collected in *England in the Fifteenth Century*, ed. G.L. Harriss (London: Hambledon, 1981) and *The Nobility of Later Medieval England* (Oxford: Oxford University Press, 1973). His influence is discussed in *The McFarlane Legacy*, ed. R.H. Britnell and A.J. Pollard (Stroud: Alan Sutton, 1995). See also C. Richmond, 'After McFarlane', *History* 68 (1983), 46–60 and the introduction to J.R. Lander, *Crown and Nobility 1450–1509* (London: Hodder and Stoughton, 1976). For important recent developments in the study of political culture see Christine Carpenter, 'Introduction: Political Culture, Politics and Cultural History', in *The Fifteenth Century IV*, ed. Christine Carpenter and Linda Clark (Woodbridge: Boydell and Brewer, 2004), pp. 1–19.

THE LANCASTRIAN LEGACY

There is, as yet, no satisfactory, modern scholarly biography of Henry IV, but on the deposition itself see Michael Bennett, *Richard II and the Revolution of 1399* (Stroud: Alan Sutton, 1999). Two recent collections of essays are also important: *Henry IV: the Establishment of the Regime, 1399–1406*, ed. Gwilym Dodd and Douglas Biggs (Woodbridge: Boydell and Brewer, 2003) and *The Reign of Henry IV: Rebellion and Survival 1403–13*, ed. Dodd and Biggs (Woodbridge: Boydell and Brewer, 2008). See also Gwilym Dodd, 'Conflict and Consensus: Henry IV and Parliament', in *Social Attitudes and Political Structures in the Fifteenth Century*, ed. Tim Thornton (Stroud: Alan Sutton, 2000), pp. 118–49. The importance of Lancastrian literature in reflecting and shaping the political culture of the early fifteenth century is explored in Paul Strohm, *England's Empty Throne: Usurpation and the Language of Legitimation 1399–1422* (New Haven, CT: Yale University Press, 1998), Jenni Nuttall, *The Creation of Lancastrian Kingship* (Cambridge: Cambridge University Press, 2007), and Cath Nall, *Reading and War in Fifteenth-Century England: From Lydgate to Malory* (Rochester, NY: D.S. Brewer, 2012).

The standard biography of Henry V remains Christopher Allmand, *Henry V* (London: Metheun, 1992). The essays in *Henry V: the Practice of Kingship*, ed. G.L. Harriss (Oxford: Oxford University Press, 1985) provide a glowing endorsement of the king's character and policies, but see T.B. Pugh, *Henry V and the Southampton Plot of 1415* (Gloucester: Alan Sutton, 1988) for a more measured consideration of Henry's place in history. For Henry's contribution to local law and order see E. Powell, *Kingship, Law and Society: Criminal Justice in the Reign of Henry V* (Oxford: Oxford University Press, 1989). For the war in France, and Agincourt in particular, see the contrasting views of M.K. Jones, *Agincourt 1415* (Barnsley: Pen and Sword, 2005) and Anne Curry, *Agincourt: A New History* (Stroud: Alan Sutton, 2005).

The essential starting point for studying Henry VI's reign are R.A. Griffiths, *The Reign of Henry VI* (London: Earnest & Benn, 1981) and B.P. Wolffe, *Henry VI* (London: Eyre Metheun, 1981). John Watts, *Henry VI and the Politics of Kingship* (Cambridge: Cambridge University Press, 1996) offers a radical re-interpretation of the reign, taking McFarlane's idea of a king incapable of ruling as its starting point. Many of the major figures of Henry's reign up to 1450 lack modern scholarly biographies, but see the articles in *Oxford Dictionary of National Biography* and G.L. Harriss, *Cardinal Beaufort* (Oxford: Oxford University Press, 1988). For Bedford and the war in France see M.K. Jones's important article 'The Battle of Verneuil (17 August 1424): Towards a History of Courage', *War in History*, 9 (2002), 375–411.

THE PRELUDE TO WAR

For the events of these years the work of Griffiths, Watts and Wolffe mentioned in the previous chapter remain essential. For the events of

1450 Isabel Harvey's *Jack Cade's Rebellion of 1450* (Oxford: Oxford University Press, 1991) is still the standard account, but see also David Grummitt, 'Deconstructing Cade's Rebellion: Discourse and Politics in the Mid-Fifteenth Century', *Fifteenth Century VI*, ed. Linda Clark (Woodbridge: Boydell & Brewer, 2006), pp. 107–22 and, for Kent in the Lancastrian period, Grummitt, 'Kent and National Politics, 1399–1461', in *Later Medieval Kent 1220–1540*, ed. Sheila Sweetinburgh (Woodbridge: Boydell & Brewer, 2010), pp. 235–50.

The standard biography of the Duke of York remains P.A. Johnson, *Duke Richard of York 1411–60* (Oxford: Oxford University Press, 1988). His intentions in the early 1450s are discussed in R.A. Griffiths, 'Duke Richard of York's Intentions in 1450 and the Origins of the Wars of the Roses', in his *King and Country: England and Wales in the Fifteenth Century* (London: Hambledon, 1991), pp. 277–304 and in Michael Hicks, 'From Megaphone to Microscope: the Correspondence of Richard Duke of York with Henry VI in 1450 Revisited', *Journal of Medieval History* 25 (1999); see also John Watts, 'Polemic and Politics in the 1450s', in *The Politics of Fifteenth Century England: John Vale's Book*, ed. Margaret Kekewich *et al* (Stroud: Alan Sutton, 1995), pp. 3–42. For the origins of York's dispute with Somerset see M.K. Jones, 'Somerset, York and the Wars of the Roses', *English Historical Review* 104 (1989), 285–307.

The classic account of the breakdown of local law and order in the 1450s remains R.L. Storey's *The End of the House of Lancaster* (2nd edn., Stroud: Alan Suttin, 1986). The Neville/Percy dispute is explored in R.A. Griffiths, 'Local Rivalries and National Politics: the Percies, the Nevilles and the Duke of Exeter, 1452–1454', in his *King and Country*, pp. 321–64; see also Peter Booth, 'Men Behaving Badly: the West March towards Scotland and the Percy-Neville Feud', in *The Fifteenth Century III*, ed. Linda Clark (Woodbridge: Boydell & Brewer, 2003), pp. 95–116.

THE BATTLE OF ST ALBANS 1455 AND ITS AFTERMATH

As ever, the basic narrative outline, albeit from very different perspectives, can be found in the works of Griffiths, Watts and Wolffe listed in chapter one. The standard account of the first Battle of St Albans remains C.A.J. Armstrong, 'Politics and the Battle of St Albans', *Bulletin of the Institute of Historical Research* 33 (1960), 1–72. Some useful comments can be found in Michael Hicks, 'Propaganda and the First Battle of St Albans, 1455', *Nottingham Medieval Studies* 44 (2000), 167–83. The question of the king's illness and York's second Protectorate is convincingly tackled by J.R. Lander, 'Henry VI and the Duke of York's Second Protectorate, 1455–6', in his *Crown and Nobility*, pp. 74–93.

The question of the role played by Margaret of Anjou has attracted a fair amount of scholarly attention in recent times. An account sensitive to questions of gendered expectations and behavioural norms is Helen E. Maurer, *Margaret of Anjou: Queenship and Power in Late Medieval England* (Woodbridge: Boydell and Brewer, 2003), and see also Joanna Laynesmith, *The Last Medieval Queens: English Queenship 1445–1503* (Oxford: Oxford University Press, 2004) and Diana Dunn, 'The Queen at War: the Role of Margaret of Anjou in the Wars of the Roses', in *War and Society in Medieval and Early Modern Britain*, ed. Diana Dunn (Liverpool: Liverpool University Press, 2000), pp. 141–61.

There is still no large scale study of the Neville family, but see Michael Hicks, *Warwick the Kingmaker* (Oxford: Blackwell Publishing, 1988) and A.J. Pollard, *Warwick the Kingmaker: Politics, Power and Fame* (London: Continuum, 2007). Pollard's *North-Eastern England during the Wars of the Roses: Lay Society, War and Politics, 1450–1500* (Oxford: Oxford University Press, 1990) is essential on the northern background. *The Oxford Dictionary of National Biography* is the starting point for studying the careers of the leading nobles and other political figures of the 1450s.

THE FIRST WAR 1459–1464

A good account of the period from Ludford Bridge to Wakefield can be found in Griffiths, *The Reign of King Henry VI*. The military history of the period remains problematic, not least because of the lack of official records and the nature of the chronicle sources, but see also

John Gillingham, *The Wars of the Roses* (London: Wiedenfield and Nicolson, 1981). For the Duke of York's actions in 1460 see Johnson, *Duke Richard of York*, ch. 9.

The standard modern biography of Edward IV remains Charles Ross, *Edward IV* (London: Metheun, 1974), while Hannes Kleineke, *Edward IV* (Abingdon: Routledge, 2009) is a readable and up-to-date account. Edward's credentials as a military leader have most recently been considered by David Saintiuste, *Edward IV and the Wars of the Roses* (Barnsley: Pen and Sword, 2010). C.A.J. Armstrong, 'The Inauguration Ceremonies of the Yorkist Kings and their Title to the Throne', *Transactions of the Royal Historical Society*, 4th series 30 (1948), 51–73 remains important. For Edward's policy towards former Lancastrians in the early 1460s see Michael Hicks, 'Edward IV, the Duke of Somerset and Lancastrian Loyalism in the North', in *Richard III and his Rivals: Magnates and their Motives in the Wars of the Roses* (London: Hambledon 1991), pp. 149–84. The concept of the 'Overmighty Subject' has most recently been explored in Michael Hicks, 'Bastard Feudalism, Overmighty Subjects and Idols of the Multitude during the Wars of the Roses', *History*, 85 (2000), 386–403.

THE SECOND WAR 1469–1471

The importance of Elizabeth Woodville and her family in the politics of the 1460s are considered by Michael Hicks, 'The Changing Role of the Wydevilles in Yorkist Politics to 1483', in *Patronage, Pedigree and Power in Later Medieval England*, ed. C.D. Ross (Gloucester: Alan Sutton, 1979), pp. 60–86 and Laynesmith, *The Last Medieval Queens*. An interesting approach to the influence at court on the various parties in the 1460s can be found in Theron Westervelt, 'Royal Charter Lists and the Politics of the Reign of Edward IV', *Historical Research* 81 (2008), 211–33. Other important biographical works include James Ross, *John de Vere, Thirteenth Earl of Oxford* (Woodbridge: Boydell and Brewer, 2011) and Michael Hicks, *False, Fleeting Perjur'd Clarence* (Stroud: Alan Sutton, 1980). The military history of the 'Second War' is as badly served as that of the 'First War', but see Gillingham, *Wars of the Roses* and Saintiuste, *Edward IV*, as well as Malcolm Mercer, 'The Strength of Lancastrian Loyalism during the Readeption: Gentry Participation at the Battle of Tewkesbury', in *The Journal of Medieval History V*, ed. Clifford Rogers (Woodbridge: Boydell and Brewer, 2007), pp. 84–98.

The most important chronicle sources for the period 1464–1471 (*Warkworth's Chronicle*, *The Chronicle of the Rebellion in Lincolnshire*, and *The Historie of the Arrivall of Edward IV*) were all published by the Camden Society in the nineteenth century but are helpfully collected together and reprinted with an introduction by Keith Dockray in *Three Chronicles of the Reign of Edward IV* (Stroud: Alan Sutton, 1988). For their importance as 'propaganda' see Colin Richmond, 'Propaganda in the Wars of the Roses', *History Today* 42 (1992), 12–18, and also Richmond and Margaret Kekewich, 'The Search for Stability, 1461–1483', in *The Politics of Fifteenth-Century England*, ed. Kekewich *et al*, pp. 43–72.

THE THIRD WAR 1483–1487

For Richard, Duke of Gloucester (as both king and duke) the standard scholarly account remains Charles Ross, *Richard III* (London: Metheun, 1981). See also Rosemary Horrox, *Richard III: A Study in Service* (Cambridge: Cambridge University Press, 1989) and David Hipshon, *Richard III* (Abingdon: Routledge, 2011). For Henry Tudor we have S.B. Chrimes, *Henry VII* (London: Metheun, 1972) and Sean Cunningham, *Henry VII* (Abingdon: Routledge, 2007). See also David Grummitt, 'The Establishment of the Tudor Dynasty', in *A Companion to Tudor Britain*, ed. Norman Jones and Bob Tittler (Oxford: Blackwell Publishing, 2004), pp. 13–28 and R.A. Griffiths and Roger S. Thomas, *The Making of the Tudor Dynasty* (Stroud: Alan Sutton, 1985).

The events of 1483–5 are among the most written on in English history. These vary greatly in quality but see C.S.L. Davies, 'Richard III, Brittany and Henry Tudor, 1483–85', *Nottingham Medieval Studies* 38 (1993), 110–26 and C.F. Richmond, '1485 and All That, or what was going on at the Battle of Bosworth', in *Richard III: Lordship, Loyalty and Law*, ed. P.W. Hammond (Gloucester: Alan Sutton,

1986), pp. 199–236 for two particularly penetrating comments. The accounts of Dominic Mancini and the Crowland Chronicler are our most important sources for these years and are published as Dominic Mancini, *The Usurpation of Richard III*, ed. C.A.J. Armstrong (Oxford: Oxford University Press, 1969) and *The Crowland Chronicle Continuations: 1459–1486*, ed. J. Cox and N. Pronay (Gloucester: Alan Sutton, 1986). For Henry Tudor's exile in France see Michael K. Jones, 'The Myth of 1485: did France really put Henry Tudor on the throne?', in *The English Experience in France c.1450–1558: war, diplomacy and cultural exchange*, ed. David Grummitt (Aldershot: Ashgate Publishing, 2002), pp. 85–105 and his controversial reappraisal of the Battle of Bosworth, *Bosworth 1485: Pyschology of a Battle* (Stroud: Alan Sutton, 2002).

For Henry VII's policies early in his reign, especially towards the north, see Sean Cunningham, 'Henry VII and North-East England: bonds of allegiance and the establishment of Tudor authority', *Northern History* 32 (1996), 42–74 and for his first parliament, Paul Cavill, *The English Parliaments of Henry VII* (Oxford: Oxford University Press, 2009). For an illuminating discussion of parliamentary justifications in general, see Lucy Brown, 'Continuity and Change in the Parliamentary Justifications of the Fifteenth-Century Usurpations', in *The Fifteenth Century VII*, ed. Linda Clark (Woodbridge: Boydell and Brewer, 2007), pp. 157–74.

WAR AND SOCIETY

The best starting point for the military impact of the Wars is Anthony Goodman, *The Wars of the Roses: The Soldiers' Experience* (Stroud: Alan Sutton, 2005). J.R. Lander, more than any other historian, has championed the argument that the Wars had little impact, see *Conflict and Stability in Fifteenth-Century England* (London: Hutchinson, 1969) and 'The Wars of the Roses', in his *Crown and Nobility*, pp. 57–73. For the military organisation of medieval England see Michael Prestwich, *Armies and Warfare in the Middle Ages: the English Experience* (New Haven, CT: Yale University Press, 1996), while for the early Tudor period see Steven Gunn, David Grummitt and Hans Cools, *War, State and Society in England and the Nether-lands, 1477–1559* (Oxford: Oxford University Press, 2007).

The debate over the impact of the wars is masterfully summarised by A.J. Pollard in his 'Society, Politics and the Wars of the Roses', in *The Wars of the Roses*, ed. A.J. Pollard (Basingstoke: Macmillan 1995), pp. 1–19. The work of Christine Carpenter, Ralph Griffiths, Michael Hicks, J.R. Lander K.B. McFarlane, A.J. Pollard, Colin Richmond and others are vital when considering the role of the nobility in the Wars, but for a recent important study of gentry motivation see Malcolm Mercer, *The Medieval Gentry: Power, Leadership and Choice during the Wars of the Roses* (London: Continuum, 2010). There are plenty of books on individual battles, some better than others, but an inter-esting angle is provided in *Blood Red Roses: the Archaeology of a Mass Grave from the Battle of Towton*, ed. Veronica Fiorato *et al* (Oxford: Oxbow Books, 2007). For the economic impact of the Wars in general see Richard Britnell, 'The Economic Context', in *Wars of the Roses*, ed. Pollard, pp. 41–64.

There is no satisfactory general account of the urban experience of war and much of the evidence for this chapter is taken from the relevant printed and manuscript primary sources. See, however, Lorraine Attreed, *The King's Towns: Identity and Survival in Late Medieval English Boroughs* (New York: Peter Lang, 2001), while for individual towns we have J.L. Bolton, 'The City and the Crown, 1456–61', *London Journal*, 12 (1986), 11–24, Peter Fleming, 'Politics and the Provincial Town: Bristol, 1451–1471', in *People, Places and Perspectives*, ed. Keith Dockray and Peter Fleming (Stroud: Alan Sutton, 2005), pp. 79–114, Hannes Kleineke, "The Kynges Cite': Exeter in the Wars of the Roses', in *The Fifteenth Century VII*, ed. Linda Clark (Woodbridge: Boydell and Brewer, 2007), pp. 137–56 and Alan Rogers, 'Stamford and the Wars of the Roses', *Nottingham Medieval Studies* 53 (2009), 73–108.

WAR AND POLITICAL CULTURE

Our understanding of the role of the commons in fifteenth-century England has been transformed in recent years by the work of John

Watts. Three essays in particular stand out: 'Polemic and Politics in the 1450s', in *The Politics of Fifteenth Century England*, ed. Kekewich *et al*, pp. 3–42; 'The Pressure of the Public on Late Medieval Politics', in *The Fifteenth Century IV: Political Culture in Late Medieval Britain*, ed. Linda Clark and Christine Carpenter (Woodbridge: Boydell and Brewer, 2004), pp. 159–80; and 'Public or Plebs: the Changing Meaning of 'The Commons', 1381–1549', in *Power and Identity in the Middle Ages*, ed. Pryce and Watts, pp. 243–60. See also I.W.M. Harvey, 'Was There Popular Politics in Fifteenth-Century England?', in *The McFarlane Legacy: Studies in Late Medieval Politics and Society*, ed. R.H. Britnell and A.J. Pollard (Stroud: Alan Sutton, 1995), pp. 155–74, Michael Bush, 'The Rising of the Commons, 1381–1549', in *Orders and Hierarchies in Late Medieval and Renaissance Europe*, ed. J.H. Denton (Basingstoke: Macmillan, 1999), pp. 109–89, and most recently David Rollison, *A Commonwealth of the People: Popular Politics and England's Long Social Revolution, 1066–1649* (Cambridge: Cambridge University Press, 2010). The literature generated by the commons in this period is contextualised in Wendy Scase, *Literature and Complaint in England 1272–1553* (Oxford: Oxford University Press, 2007).

For Sir John Fortescue see the modern edition of his major works, *On the Laws and Governance of England*, ed. Shelley Lockwood (Cambridge: Cambridge University Press, 1997). See also Anthony Gross, *The Dissolution of Lancastrian England: Sir John Fortescue and the Crisis of Monarchy in Fifteenth-Century England* (Stamford: Paul Watkins, 1996). For crown finances and the Yorkist 'Land Revenue Experiment' see B.P. Wolffe, *The Royal Demesne in English History: The Crown Estate in the Governance of the Realm from the Conquest to 1509* (London: Allen and Unwin, 1974). For changes under Henry VII see David Grummitt, 'Henry VII, Chamber Finance and the New Monarchy', *Historical Research* 72 (1999), 229–43.

The question of the impact of Humanism on English political culture has only begun to be explored recently, but Daniel Wakelin, *Humanism, Reading and English Literature 1430–1530* (Oxford: Oxford University Press, 2007) is the essential starting point. See also the classic Roberto Weiss, *Humanism in England during the Fifteenth*

Century (Oxford: Blackwell Publishing, 1941). For the question of the impact of the Renaissance on English politics see David Rundle, 'Was there a Renaissance Style of politics in Fifteenth-Century England', in *Authority and Consent in Tudor England*, ed. G.W. Bernard and S.J. Gunn (Aldershot: Ashgate Publishing, 2002), pp. 15–32 and David Grummitt, 'Household, Politics and Political Morality in the Reign of Henry VII', *Historical Research* 81 (2009), 393–411. For the European context and the idea of 'Renaissance Monarchy' at the end of the fifteenth century see Steven Gunn, 'Politic History, New Monarchy and State Formation: Henry VII in European Conext', *Historical Research* 82 (2009), 380–92. John Watts's forthcoming volume in the *New Oxford History of England* series promises to fully explore the influence of the Renaissance and Humanism on English political culture.

Index

206